DEATH, WITCHCRAFT
AND THE SPIRIT WORLD
IN THE HIGHLANDS OF
PAPUA NEW GUINEA

Developing a Contextual Theology
in Melanesia

Neville Bartle

Melanesian Institute

General Editor: Nick de Groot

Special Editors: Priscilla Winfrey and Dr Robyn Tucker

Graphic Design and Layout: Mrs Issabella Dick Kapinias

Editorial Board: Philip Gibbs, Hermann Spingler, Mary Tankulu, Franco Zocca

Typesetting: Priscilla Winfrey

ISSN 0253-2913
ISBN 9980-65-003-6
National Library of Papua New Guinea

Published by The Melanesian Institute
PO Box 571, Goroka 441, EHP
PAPUA NEW GUINEA

Telephone: (675) 732 1777
Fax: (675) 732 1214
Email: emmai@online.net.pg
Web site: http://www.mi.org.pg

Printed by Sat Prachar Press, Indore, India

Cover photo by Philip Gibbs
Cover design by Priscilla Winfrey

CONTENTS

LIST OF MAPS

LIST OF TABLES

LIST OF FIGURES

ABSTRACT

One hundred years ago, Christianity was practically unknown in Papua New Guinea, but today ninety-six percent of the population identifies itself as Christian (Zocca 2004:41). Christianity was brought to Papua New Guinea primarily by Western missionaries whose world-view was very different from the world-view of Melanesians. Consequently, many questions that are raised by the Melanesian world-view are not answered adequately by Western theology. The aim of this work was to develop a biblical theology that addresses the issues of death and the spirits of the dead. In the process of doing ethnographic research, the issue of witchcraft emerged as a dominant concern for Melanesian Christians.

A model for constructing a Melanesian Christian theology was developed and applied to these problems. The model has seven essential elements: Scripture, cultural context, church tradition, reason/dialogue, life experience, Christ centred, and directed by the Holy Spirit. These are arranged diagrammatically to resemble a house.

By testing the model in three conferences attended by pastors, Melanesians were able to see its usefulness and effectiveness. With it they developed a theology of death and the spirits of the dead. They also discussed the churches' response to the problem of witchcraft.

The biblical drama of Jesus' death, his descent to the world of the dead, his resurrection and ascension to the highest place as Lord of creation, is connected with the reality of the Melanesian spirit world. The resulting theology is true to Scripture and related to the fears, questions, hopes, and myths of Melanesian culture. It shows how Melanesian Christians can negotiate the fear of death, the problems of witchcraft, and the fear of evil spirits, while remaining vitally connected to their own culture. In this way, the Christian gospel becomes a transforming power within the culture.

ACKNOWLEDGMENTS

I wish to express my appreciation to the pastors of the Church of the Nazarene in Papua New Guinea for accepting me as their brother, sharing their stories with me, probing me with questions and pushing me to learn more. They also gave generously and sacrificially to help me do this study. I will always be deeply grateful to them.

I sincerely thank Dr Darrell Whiteman for encouraging me to pursue studies at Asbury. I appreciate his love for Melanesia and for helping me to understand the Melanesian world-view in a deeper way and for his constant encouragement and help. Thanks also to Dr Terry Muck and Dr Stephen Seamands, for their valuable suggestions and guidance.

I thank Asbury Theological Seminary, the Soutar Foundation of Perth, Scotland, and the H.F. Reynolds scholarship fund of the Church of the Nazarene, for financial assistance to help me in pursuing this study. I thank the leaders of the Church of the Nazarene for the support they have given as I have pursued these studies.

I am grateful for the many people who have supported me in prayer as I have done this study. Without their prayers this work would not have been accomplished. I want to particularly express my appreciation for two faithful prayer warriors, my father Oliver Bartle, who went to be with the Lord during the final stages of writing, and Sarah Siune of Papua New Guinea.

I thank Joyce, my wife and fellow missionary in Papua New Guinea for 32 years, for her love, support and encouragement in this research. Her diligent and careful proof-reading is appreciated more than words can say. I am also very grateful to our children Kathryn and Russell, Susie and David for their encouragement, love and support. Finally, I thank God for his faithfulness, and for giving me cultural and spiritual insights, wisdom and strength throughout this period of study.

INTRODUCTION

THE PROBLEM AND ITS SETTING

There was a knock at the door and I was surprised to see Mol standing there without his usual bright smile. Mol was a recent Christian convert. I invited him in, gave him a cold drink, and he quickly came to the reason for his visit. "Neville," he said, "My grandfather came back last night!"

"Which grandfather?" I replied. As a new missionary, I was struggling to keep track of the complex social organisation of the highlanders of Papua New Guinea. "You know," he replied, "the one we buried last Saturday." That was not the answer I expected. And so he began to tell the story.

About ten o'clock at night, Mol and his family had heard noises of someone outside the house. They called out: "Who is there?" but there was no definite response. The noises continued but no one responded to their challenge. One of the older women said: "It's your grandfather. I recognise his voice." Everyone got very quiet, hoping the spirit would go away, but the noises continued. Others agreed it must be the grandfather, but they were too worried to move. Suddenly the door of the house burst open, a vague black object burst into the room, flew around above people's heads with a flapping sound like a big bat, and then disappeared out the door. The people were terrified. Early the next morning, one woman went down to the little stream to wash, and she was sure she saw the grandfather in his coffee garden. She called out and he mysteriously disappeared. Mol said the men would

7

kill another pig tomorrow. Maybe that would keep grandfather happy and his spirit would go away.

Mol then asked me: "Neville, why did he come back? What should we do? Do you think he will come back again?" I had never faced such questions before and had no ready answers. I saw that these were theological questions, and so quite naively I went to the bookcase and opened a big fat theology book, but it had no answers either.

Lesson number one: there are theological questions that the books do not answer. This event took place in 1970. Appointed by the Church of the Nazarene, I was a new missionary living at Kudjip Nazarene Mission Station in the Western Highlands of Papua New Guinea (PNG).[1] Some years later (after I had started several churches and was supervising national pastors), I was informed by mission executives that I needed to get ordained. Consequently, when we were on furlough, I embarked on a crash course in the Bible and theology to meet the requirements for ordination. I was at the Nazarene Theological College in Manchester, England, and my instructor gave me several books to read on theories of the atonement. The further I read, the more discouraged I became, because I kept seeing the faces of Papua New Guineans in front of me. All of my preaching was done either in Pidgin or in *tok ples*, the local language.[2] I thought to myself: "If I can barely understand these ideas in English, my mother tongue, how will I ever be able to express these same concepts in a foreign language to people from a different culture?"

I went to my instructor with the textbooks and said: "Do you have anything else? I struggle to follow the authors' detailed reasonings, and there is no way that I could explain these to my congregation. If Jesus died for everyone then surely the atonement must make sense to everyone. But these explanations don't." Lesson number two: Theology that is meaningful in one context may not be meaningful in another context. The instructor thought for a moment and then came back with another book. I glanced at the title, *Christus Victor*. The next day I was back with a smile on my face. "At last, theology that makes sense. We know about tribal fighting and we understand the difference between defeat and victory. I will have no problem explaining the death of Christ from this perspective."

"Theology that makes sense to listeners" has become my abiding concern and is the driving force behind this book. The two men in the next two scenarios are representative of many pastors and Bible school teachers. These are the people this book is aimed at.

A Village Pastor

Martin sits in his house and thinks about his church. It is a church he started himself just over two years ago. He had been away from his village, living down at one of the coastal towns, and attended an evangelistic rally where he heard preaching unlike anything he had ever heard before. It was certainly not like anything he had heard in the little church in his village which had been there for forty years. As he listened, he was convicted of his sinful lifestyle, and there at the evangelistic rally he confessed his sins, and Christ transformed his life. He found a joy and a peace that he had never experienced before. His life was turned around and he had a real hunger to read the Bible. His cousin introduced him to an evangelical church which he really enjoyed. He attended home Bible study groups during the week, and after six months he decided that he must give up his job in the town, go back to his village, and share what he had experienced with his family and the community.

His family responded eagerly, although some of the people in the old church were not very happy, for they were sceptical of new ideas. Too many things were changing too quickly and they preferred the simplicity of the old familiar ways. But together, he and his extended family built a little church building. About fifty people attended each week. Some found the same joy and peace that he had discovered and were enthusiastic about the personal relationship they had with Jesus Christ. Others were happy to attend, but did not make any formal commitment.

Eighteen months went by, and Martin had preached himself dry. There were questions that were raised for which he had no answers. Some parts of the Bible were really hard to understand. There were a lot of people in his village who were afraid of spirits, and especially sorcery and witchcraft. He himself had once been afraid, but now Jesus had taken away that fear. He found it hard, however, to explain it to others. "I really need some help," he thought to himself, "I cannot take this congregation any further than I have come myself. How can I teach them what I do not know?" He thought of the Christian bookshop he had seen in the city. There were thousands of books in it, but they were all in English. His English was limited and they were no help. He needed something in his own language that would speak to the needs of the village people. He needed a book that would help him grow in his understanding of the Bible, and which could help him teach others.

A Bible College Teacher

Joseph sat in his office at the Bible college and looked at his teaching schedule. He was a teacher of theology to first year students. He picked up the theology textbook and flipped its pages. He knew what was in it, for he had taught this course before — and that was what bothered him. The last time he taught it, the students were bored, and seemed unmotivated. He tried to make the class exciting, but it was difficult: even he didn't see the relevance of all that he was teaching. He encouraged them to persevere, saying: "This is the theology of our church. Very learned men in America wrote this book, and this is the theology that our church uses all around the world. If you want to be a pastor in our church, it is very important that you know this, or else you cannot be ordained. Anyway it is good to learn, and even if you do not understand it all now, one of these days you may come across a problem and this information may just be what you need."

But secretly Joseph questioned: "If God is alive and dynamic and all powerful, then why does theology seem so dry and boring? Will these studies really help students to answer the questions that the people in the village are asking? Is God greater than sorcery? How do we go about breaking a curse or a spell? How do we relate to the spirits of the dead? If God is all powerful, then why do we see so few miracles? Can Christians still consult the traditional practitioners in times of illness? After all, the aid post has not had any medicine for the last two months. Is clan loyalty good or evil?" He pondered all these questions. Unfortunately, he knew that the book didn't even try to address many of them.

He thought of the social issues of tribal fighting, payback killing, the break down of law and order, and the rampant spread of sexually transmitted diseases. He thought of the frustration of the school leavers who felt they had been cheated by the system. They had done all that work at school for nothing, for there were so few jobs available. Educational standards were dropping, health care was failing. It was now 2005, thirty years since Papua New Guinea had gained independence, and most changes seemed to be negative rather than positive. The

11

government services were less efficient. The rich had become richer, whereas the numbers of the poor had grown - and they'd become poorer. What do we do about these things? "But, I guess that I don't really need to worry about such things," he thought to himself. "Even though the people in the village talk about these issues, theology is not concerned about them. My job is to teach theology, not to deal with life issues."

But in his heart, there was still the question, "Is God only interested in what we do in church on Sunday, and taking us to heaven at the end of life, or does God care about how we live?"

In this book, these are the two people I want to keep in mind. How can pastors and other church leaders present the gospel to the people in the towns and villages of Melanesia so that it makes sense to them and answers the questions that arise in their daily lives?

Ralph Winter writes: "There are already about 2 million pastors/ evangelists in Africa, Asia, and Latin America. Ninety five percent of them have never had any formal theological training — and never will under the present circumstances. Yet the future of the Christian movement is largely in their hands" (1994:51). These people need help. Traditional Western theology books will not answer many of their questions.

Background

Melanesian people live in the southwest Pacific, namely the island nations of Fiji, Vanuatu, New Caledonia, Solomon Islands, Papua New Guinea and the province of Irian Jaya in Indonesia. They are physically distinguished by their dark skin and tight curly hair. Melanesia has been described as the "most complicated anthropological jigsaw puzzle on the earth's face" (Trompf 1994:xiii), and so this study will limit itself primarily to just a small section of

12

that jigsaw puzzle, namely four cultural groups all located in the Highlands of Papua New Guinea. They are: the Kuman speakers of Simbu Province, the people of the Enga Province, the Imbongo people of the Southern Highlands, and the Kobon people, a small language group on the border of the Western Highlands and the Madang Province.

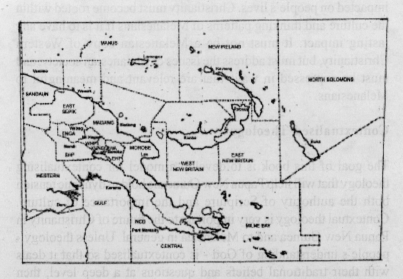

Map 1. Provincial Boundaries of Papua New Guinea

Although there are hundreds of languages in Melanesia (over 800 in Papua New Guinea alone) and therefore a great number of diverse cultures, it is possible to speak generally of a Melanesian world-view.[3] Although there are differences in culture between highlanders and coastal people, and between one group of highlanders and another, there are still basic similarities of world-view assumptions that are common to Melanesians in general.

In 2000, 96 percent of the 5,171,548 million Papua New Guineans described themselves as being Christians (National Statistical Office: 25). Churches are found throughout all islands, in or near most villages.

13

The church, however, suffers from a high degree of nominalism.

Papua New Guinea is experiencing a variety of social and cultural challenges. Bribery and corruption are common, and law and order are seen as ineffective. HIV/AIDS is spreading rapidly, and gender and economic inequalities are great. Many people live in fear of sorcery and evil spirits. It appears that Christianity has not seriously impacted on people's lives. Christianity must become rooted within the culture and thinking patterns of Melanesians if it is to have any lasting impact. It must not be a Melanesian copy of Western Christianity, but must address the issues of Melanesian society, and must be expressed in ways that are relevant and meaningful to Melanesians.

Contextualised Theology

The goal of this book is to develop a model for contextualising theology that will help Papua New Guineans hold in dynamic tension both the authority of Scripture and the importance of culture. Contextual theology is very important to the future of Christianity in Papua New Guinea and to Melanesia in general. Unless theology - people's understanding of God - is contextualised so that it deals with their traditional beliefs and questions at a deep level, then Christianity will remain superficial, and merely an imitation of the "white man's religion".

It is essential that Melanesian church leaders understand both the importance of contextualisation, and the process of contextualising the gospel, for contextualisation must be done by Melanesians themselves. Melanesian church leaders need to give clear leadership and direction to the church as it works to make its theology both truly Christian and truly Melanesian. In this way it should be able to avoid both syncretism and nominalism, and develop a strong healthy church with a positive cultural self-esteem, and a dynamic vibrant faith in Christ that is lived out in daily communal life. Missionaries can have a role to play as resource persons and outside catalysts to

14

the process, but the indigenising of theology in Melanesian cultures must be done by Melanesian people. For this can happen effectively, the church leaders need to know that this is part of their responsibility as Christian leaders, and also understand what is involved, and how to go about doing it.

This book seeks to provide a model for contextualising that can be easily understood. Much of what is written about contextualisation is written in abstract and technical language to which most people have no access. Even if they were to read it, they might have a struggle understanding or applying it (e.g. Schreiter 1985, 1997). In this book a model for contextualising theology is developed and its validity tested by indigenous pastors. It is a synthetic model for theologising, founded upon Scripture, centred in Christ, appreciative of church tradition, related directly to the experience of indigenous Christians, constructed by Melanesians dialogically, and open to the direction of the Holy Spirit. The model I have used is distinctive because it is in a visual diagrammatic form and uses a minimum of abstract language. I have found that it can be readily understood by people who have an education of grade six or less.

The theoretical background for this model is described in detail in Chapter Four. The working model that I am suggesting is summarised in diagrammatic form (Figure 13). It has the following essential elements that must be in place for true theologising to take place. Those elements, though not necessarily in sequential order, are as follows:

1. Scripture is the foundation. The whole Bible is available in Pidgin and the people I worked with were all literate in Pidgin.
2. Theology must be Christ centred, with a strong focus on the incarnation, death, and resurrection of Jesus as being God's decisive actions in human history.
3. Theology is influenced by Culture. The questions that we seek to answer come out of the cultural/social situation.

15

4. Church tradition, doctrines, and creeds can give helpful insight and guidance.
5. Theology must relate directly to people's experience.
6. Theology grows out of dialogue as people reason together.
7. Theological reflection must be guided by the Holy Spirit.

Comments on Approach

There are many issues related to theology and the people of Melanesia that could and should be addressed, but this study concentrates on developing a contextualised theology of death and the spirits of the dead. In traditional Melanesian religions, it is generally believed that the spirits of the dead have a greater influence on the living than any other type of spirit (Swain and Trompf 1995:209). As I progressed with my research, I discovered that the most common motivation for contacting the spirits of the dead was to find out who had caused the death of the person being contacted. This then prompted me to investigate the practice of *sanguma* (witchcraft or sorcery).

Throughout this book, I assume that the Bible is the written record of God's revelation of himself and is our primary religious authority; and that the sixty-six books of the Old and New Testaments are divinely inspired, revealing the will of God in all things necessary for our salvation.

Culture is one of God's gifts to humanity. It is a part of human creativity which in turn is a reflection of us being created in the image of God. There is much in culture however, that is evil and ugly, for although originally made in the image of God, humanity has rebelled against God and sinned. Consequently, all human cultures are tainted and tarnished by sin. It therefore needs to be transformed so that it can reflect more of God's glory.

God, in his grace reaches out to people and seeks to draw them to himself. God is not silent, for God speaks through nature (Psalm

16

19:1-2), and within each culture, for "he has not left himself without testimony" (Acts 14:17 NIV).[4] It is God's desire that people "would seek him and perhaps reach out for him and find him" for "he is not far from each one of us" (Acts 17:27). In each culture God finds ways to reveal himself to people. "What may be known about God is plain to them, because God has made it plain to them. For since the creation of the world God's invisible qualities — his eternal power and divine nature — have been clearly seen, being understood from what has been made" (Romans 1:19-20). Although God speaks and reaches out to people, not all hear, and not all respond to God's revelation in nature. Self-centredness and sin have ways of blinding people to God's revelation in the world around them.

Within each culture and language there are stories, rituals, and beliefs which can be used to help people come to an understanding of God and the way of salvation. These do not replace the work accomplished by Christ, but rather they are cultural expressions that can be used to help people understand the work of God in Christ.

I also assume that all Christians should be able to explain their faith in terms that are meaningful to them and to their people. "Always be prepared to give an answer to everyone who asks you to give the reason for the hope that you have. But do this with gentleness and respect" (1 Peter 3:15). People need to understand their faith in Christ, their experience of the grace of God, and be able to share it with others. In order to do this their theology must be contextualised, and related to their life situation; otherwise their faith appears irrelevant. Paul also emphasised the need for the gospel to be handed on from person to person. "The things you have heard me say in the presence of many witnesses entrust to reliable men who will also be qualified to teach others" (2 Timothy 2:2).

There are many Christian denominations in Papua New Guinea, but my study is focused upon the pastors and key lay people in the

17

Church of the Nazarene because of the relationships I have established with them through thirty years of missionary service.

18

CHAPTER ONE

THE MELANESIAN CONTEXT - RELIGIOUS AND SOCIAL ORGANISATION

In 1968, a Papua New Guinean leader published his autobiography and called it *Ten Thousand Years in a Life Time* (Kiki 1968). As Albert Kiki's book title suggests, although contact with the Western world has been brief, people have been in Papua New Guinea for a very long time: it is the written history that is brief, going back only a few hundred years at the most, and in many places only a life time. Kiki's title also indicates that after many years with little change occurring, huge changes are now taking place, especially in the areas of technology and material culture.

Bipo-Tru

The many languages and cultures in Melanesia suggest a long, complex and varied past. There are no ancient written records, but archaeology and language groupings give clues. It is assumed that people came to Melanesia from Asia via the islands of Indonesia about 50,000 years ago, and that they came by sea, for there was no land bridge between Papua New Guinea and the Asian mainland (Whiteman 1984:90). The first group of people are known as non-Austronesian speakers, and it is thought that they settled in the lowlands near the coast where they remained for the next ten to twenty thousand years. These people are now found mainly in the centre of New Guinea, and in the interior of some of the other large islands. Stone tools have been found on a few sites in the Highlands that reportedly go back as far as 26,000 years before the present (Bellwood 1978:63). Settlement in most of the main valleys of the Central Highlands began nearly 10,000 years ago. Archaeological evidence also indicates that Papua New Guineans were some of

19

the world's first gardeners. Sea shells found in archaeological deposits in the Highlands indicate trade links with the coast have existed for at least 10,000 years. It is not known when pigs, Asian yams, taros, and bananas were introduced, but it was at least 5,000 years ago (Swadling 1981:31).

About this time, other migrations took place of people who spoke Austronesian languages. Austronesian languages are found in many coastal areas of Papua New Guinea and the New Guinea islands, as well as most other Pacific islands, including those of Polynesia and Micronesia (Bellwood 1978:120).

More recently – only 300 years ago – the sweet potato was introduced to Papua New Guinea. Originating in South America, it was taken by the Portuguese to Europe, from there to places in Africa, to islands in Indonesia such as Ambon and Timor, and from there to Irian Jaya. Sweet potatoes tolerate poor and cold soils and therefore allowed people to settle in areas of higher altitude. Ideally suited to the Highlands valleys, it is believed that the introduction of the sweet potato 300 years ago made possible a population explosion in the Highlands. The luxuriant growth of sweet potato also enabled the pigs to flourish. This no doubt had an impact on, or probably helped give birth to, the elaborate pig exchanges which are such a prominent feature of Highlands society (Golson 1982, Wiessner and Tumu 1998:3).

Recent History

Compared to other areas of the world, Melanesia has had a very brief contact with outside civilisations. In the Highlands of PNG that contact, though brief, has been very intense. The first recorded contact by Europeans with the coastal people of Papua New Guinea was by the Portuguese in 1511. In 1567, Alvara de Mendana from Spain landed in the Solomon Islands looking for gold; although the Spanish spent six months in the area visiting a number of islands, the visits were not very positive or friendly, and they did not find the gold they dreamed of (Sherry 1994:107-109). Almost thirty years later, Mendana returned to the Solomon Islands and tried to set up a colony in Santa Cruz, but he died and the colony also died out (Snow and Waine 1979:31).

The islands of Melanesia were largely left alone for a couple of centuries until the Dutch laid claim to the western half of the island of New Guinea in 1824. The Germans claimed the northern coast in 1884, and the British promptly claimed the south coast (Snow and Waine 1979:175). In 1906, British New Guinea was handed over to Australian control, and when World War I began, the Australians quickly took the German headquarters in Rabaul (in 1914). Following the war, in 1920 the League of Nations officially handed the northern half of the island to Australia as a mandated territory (Tudor 1974:15).

The rugged interior of the island was considered inhospitable and largely uninhabited until the 1930s, when aided by aircraft and driven by the search for gold, the Leahy brothers trekked into the wide fertile valleys of the central Highlands.[5]

During World War II, the Japanese took control of the northern coastline and the northern islands. After four years of fighting they were forced by American and Australian forces to withdraw leaving the eastern half to Australian colonial governance. After the war, the Highlands areas were opened up by Australian patrol officers, and tea and coffee plantations were established. Many airstrips had been built during the war and aircraft now sped up the rate of exploration and development. Government and mission presence increased, with schools and clinics being built in many places (Sinclair 1981).

In 1973, the country became self-governing, and in 1975 it made a peaceful transition from colonial rule to become an independent nation under the leadership of Prime Minister Michael Somare (Campbell 1989:204). This quick overview of political developments does not do justice to the dramatic social changes that have taken place, and continue to take place in the countless villages of Papua New Guinea.[6]

Overview of Melanesian Religions

The purpose of this study is to identify the best ways to contextualise the gospel message so that it relates to the culture and world-view of Melanesians. The first thing that must be done is to understand the religious beliefs and practices of Melanesians. As Don McGregor, a pioneer missionary to Papua New Guinea, writes:

> Real problems arise when the speaker and the hearer belong to different cultures, where assumptions, beliefs, values and customs are not the same. In such a situation, statements based on the speaker's cultural background are understood in terms of the hearer's different cultural background and this frequently results in a twisted message ... If the missionary does not know the people's assumptions and beliefs, he will neither be able to help Melanesians correctly relate biblical teaching to their lives, nor adequately suggest how the message may be interpreted. (1976:176, 206)

There are hundreds of different religions in Melanesia. There are over 800 languages in Papua New Guinea alone and hundreds more in Irian Jaya, Solomon Islands, Vanuatu, New Caledonia, and Fiji. As the languages differ, so too do the various beliefs, rituals, and deities. G.W. Trompf in his book, *Melanesian Religion*, writes: "Melanesia has been revealed to be the home of about one-third of mankind's languages, and that means — considering how languages are so crucial in defining discrete cultures — just as many religions" (1991:10). Although it is closer to one fifth, Trompf's point is clear. Melanesia is very complex both linguistically and in the area of traditional religions. In the midst of this diversity, there are "recurrent motifs and themes begging for analysis", even though names, terms, and rituals differ greatly from place to place (Trompf 1991:12).

Melanesians do not have a term for "religion" as such, for they do not have a compartmentalised world-view that divides life into categories (of agriculture, education, economics, etc.). Instead, life is an integrated whole, where all is influenced and controlled by spiritual beings and religious rituals. We will look first at the Melanesian world-view and then at some of the dominant features and prominent themes of Melanesian religions.

Melanesian World-View

The world-view of Melanesians can be thought of as being in two parts: the visible material world which includes the "natural environment, its economic resources (including animals), and its human inhabitants; and the non-empirical which includes spirit beings, non-personalised occult forces and sometimes totems" (Lawrence and Meggitt 1965:7). The diagram (Figure 1) shows this as an integrated world-view. It is significant that there is no clear dividing line between the spiritual world and the physical world, or between the visible world and the unseen world of the spirits: they are in constant interaction. People, or more specifically the clan, is at the centre. The clan consists of the living the dead, and those who are not yet born. The activity of the spirit world is evidenced by changes in the physical material world. The spirits, especially the spirits of the dead, are never far away. They live nearby and are concerned about the welfare of the clan; as one old man said: "When they are happy, life goes well, but when they are unhappy, we feel it."

The integrated Melanesian world-view can be contrasted with the compartmentalised world-view that is typical of modern scientific thinking and is shown in Figure 2. In modern thought there is a strict division between the world of God and spirit, and the physical world. The socioeconomic and political order is primarily secularised. This oversimplified diagram (Figure 2) demonstrates the compartment-alisation of such thinking, which divides religion from aspects of daily life like agriculture, health and economics.

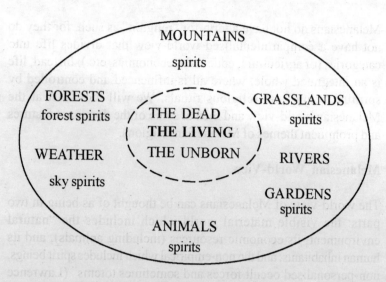

Figure 1. Melanesian World-View

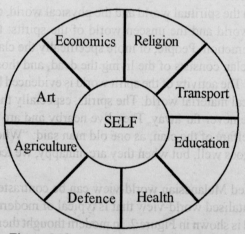

Figure 2. Compartmentalised World-View

In contrast to a Melanesian world-view that is clan-centred, this modern style of thinking is individualised, with the focus on self. The religion sector can be replaced by any one of a variety of religious beliefs without having a dramatic impact on the other parts of one's life. In modern society religion is expected to be private, so that one's religious convictions do not impinge on anyone or anything else. Most of life is outside of the religious sector and is influenced more by economics and technology.

Whiteman writes:

> Melanesians do not live in a compartmentalised world of secular and sacred domains. Rather, they have an integrated world-view in which physical and spiritual realities dovetail. They are not segregated and fragmented as they often are for Western Christians. The physical and spiritual, secular and sacred, function together in a Melanesian's world-view. (1984:88)

Underlying this world-view are certain themes that pervade and influence all of life. These world-view assumptions or themes are not reasoned out, but are assumed to be true without prior proof. People usually do not think about or question them, they just know them to be true. Basic assumptions are challenged when the people face experiences that they cannot interpret, such as when they come into a culture or behaviour which is greatly different to their own.

Life is Clan-Centred

One of the striking features of Melanesian societies is the lack of large tribal groups. Even in those areas where one language may be spoken by 80,000 people, such as the Kuman speakers in Simbu, there is no Kuman tribe: instead there are many clans and sub-clans that exist as individual units. They will sometimes cooperate with each other, but just as often, they will fight with each other. Gardening, house-building, fighting, *singsings*, economics and politics are all centred on the clan.[7] We have seen that for Melanesians religion is part of all of life. Rather than being a segment of their world-view, it is in many ways the glue that holds their world together. Religion is concerned with obtaining and maintaining life that is full and worthy

25

of celebration. Closely tied to this is the fact that traditional religion is clan centred, for there is no life outside of the clan. Defense, security and well-being are all dependent upon the clan members supporting each other. Marriages are contracts between two clans, not just between two individuals. Tribal dances and ceremonies are owned by clans, and the daily activities of gardening, hunting, and house building are all clan activities. The spirits of the dead are the spirits of the clan. Since the main source of supernatural help is the spirits of the dead, the religious aspects of life are centred in the clan and focus chiefly on the spirits of the clan. This leads to the following values or beliefs:

1. Good and Bad are Relative. "Good" is whatever is perceived to strengthen or benefit the family, clan, or tribe. Conversely, "bad" is whatever is perceived to weaken or hurt the family, clan, or tribe. The well-being of the tribe or clan is of greatest importance. Papua New Guineans come from a background of tribal fighting Whether it be a country like Britain in World War II or a tribal fight in the Highlands, there are certain basic assumptions that are derived from the state of war. These are:

- People must stick together. Solidarity is essential.
- Orders must be obeyed.
- Personal desires must be denied for the sake of the common good.
- Activities that would be considered bad if done towards the members of one's group are praised if done towards the enemy group.

Fighting, stealing, murder, and arson, which, in a peaceful society, are antisocial crimes, are considered to be deeds of bravery and daring when undertaken during fighting time, and are commendable if done against the enemy. (This type of mentality is not restricted to Melanesia. One only has to look at "civilised" Europe during World War II and see the same type of thinking. It is common to all societies who are at war.) Because of endemic tribal fighting for centuries,

26

many Melanesians have developed a world-view that presupposes a warfare situation as the norm. No one is neutral; they are either friends or enemies (Hovey 1986:104).

2. One's Most Important Obligation is to Build Up One's Own Clan (Hovey 1986:107).

It is not merely the "good" thing to do to help one's *wantok*.[8] It is an obligation that takes precedence over other obligations. For this reason, graft and corruption flourish in government offices. Stores expect to lose a considerable percentage of their sales in theft. If a shop worker sees a *wantok* stealing, he just turns a blind eye. If a relative asks a government worker to get something for him from government supplies, he takes it. The obligation to help a fellow group member comes before obligations to the business or government.

3. Security is Belonging to a Clan.

To most Melanesians, the concept of independence from a group means isolation and insecurity. In contrast, modern cultures have valued independence as something to be prized. In PNG, people who belong to a clan have other clan members to protect them in time of war, or to help in time of need. This is the Melanesian insurance and social security system that contributes to bride price payments, house-building, settling of land disputes, gardening, payment of school fees, and helps to look after people in old age. The clan gives security.

Religion is a social activity and involves the whole clan. Decisions that concern the religion of the people should not be made on the individual level, but on the clan level. Where people have deliberately geared the gospel presentation to the family or clan unit they have had much greater success (Hovey 1986:188).

Life is Governed by the Theme of Reciprocity

The purpose of reciprocity or payback is to provide equality and harmony in life. This is demonstrated in the development of an

27

exchange partnership between two people, clans, or groups. In an exchange partnership, goods are given and received.

> The purpose of the exchange partnership is not simply the free flow of goods but rather the achievement of a friendly and trusting relationship between the partners. Every time an exchange is made it builds up a greater sense of friendship, a greater sense of trust, a greater sense of brotherhood ... It is the relationship rather than the exchange of goods that is the more important achievement. (Whiteman 1984:109)

Payback is the above example in reverse. Traditionally, the law of payback functioned as a means of social control. It was understood by all that if they kill one of us, we will kill one of them as payback. There was the certainty of punishment; someone in the clan would suffer for suffering inflicted. It also had an equalising factor, for it tended to prevent one tribe from overwhelming another. But with the present court system and the influence of the *wantok* system, there is now no certainty of punishment. The *wantok* system, which gives priority to a relative, conflicts with the modern concept of impartial justice. The European court system seeks to prove which *individual* caused the death. In Melanesian thinking, it is sufficient to assert that *one of them* caused the death. This conflict between clan thinking and individual blame and responsibility, results in a breakdown of law and order. The greatly increased mobility of people between provinces and the increase of accidental deaths (i.e. in car accidents), means that the payback system now causes more fights than it settles.

Compensation follows the same law as reciprocity. Unfortunately, there are now frequent situations where it seems to have gone beyond the idea of equality, and has become a money-making racket in order to gain more wealth.

Bride price is another example of the law of reciprocity. It is not the buying of a bride, but an exchange or compensation that is paid to the girl's family to compensate for her loss from the clan. In the same way, head payments for children that are born to the marriage follow the law of reciprocity. The payments to the wife's clan are to balance the children that the wife has provided for the husband's clan.

Economics in Melanesian society are based on this same principle of reciprocity. A gift is not a gift, but a form of trade. I give to you when I have excess and you have need, but you will return it to me when I have need. In a culture where there are few ways of preserving food, the best thing to do with it is to give it away, then, when the recipient has a surplus he or she returns your gift. In this way, not only is a supply of fresh pig meat assured, but also friendships are cemented. This leads to two values:

- A friend is someone you can trust with a loan, and conversely, a friend is someone who will give you a loan. A friend is someone who will help you in time of need.
- Security is having someone in debt to you (money in the bank).

Sickness is also related to the law of reciprocity. Sickness fits into the "eye for an eye and a tooth for a tooth" pattern. Sickness and death always have spiritual, not just physical, causes. Either the sick person has done something wrong to displease the spirits, or someone has performed sorcery against him.

This model of reciprocity is not a one-way street of reliance where human beings are dependent on ancestral spirits for their welfare. It is a two-way street of reciprocity and interdependence. This means, for example, that ancestral spirits are equally dependent on human beings for their welfare ... It is a relationship of mutual help and interdependence, a relationship of reciprocity, a giving and a taking between human beings and the spirit world. (Whiteman 1984:110)

29

Sickness indicates that harmony in society has been broken. Sickness will only be cured when that harmony is restored.

The Goal of Life is to be Known as a "Big Man"

In the Highlands, there is no tribal hierarchy as is found in Polynesian societies. Rather, each clan and sub-clan is led by a "big man". Social status, authority and prestige are greatly valued and to a large extent secured through money and material possessions. This position is not acquired by birth, but achieved by a person's own effort and skill: "The Big Man is neither an elected head man nor a hereditary chief, but is a man who has utilised his kin and non-kin ties to build up wealth and a following of supporters" (Bellwood 1978:94).

The big man concept plays a larger role in the Highlands than it does in other parts of Papua New Guinea. It is one of the major themes underlying tribal fighting, oratory, politics and the complex pig exchanges that are so prominent in the Highlands. Every man wants to be known as a "big man".

> An aspiring Big Man is typically an ambitious and energetic individual who is able to accumulate wealth and organise large scale activities. He usually builds up his wealth by hard work in gardening, pig-raising and through successful exchanges. He tries to attract followers from among his kinsmen and from neighbouring groups by distributing wealth generously and thus placing people in his debt. For instance, he may assist young men with their bride price or with other forms of exchange and these young men thus become his dependants and supporters. (Chao 1984:134)

This is also one of the underlying reasons for polygamy. Marriages sometimes originate as political alliances. By marrying into a number of different clans, a person has more resources upon which he can draw in times of fighting, pig kills, elections, etc. He is known over a wider area and his prestige and influence increase.

30

This desire to be known as a "big man" is partly behind the tremendous appeal that politics has in the Highlands, where up to a hundred people have been known to contest one seat in Parliament. Elected, they have access to government money which they can give away so as to further enhance their power. Even if they are not elected, they have established relationships with lots of people and so have become known as a "big man".

The "big man" concept explains the many political groups in PNG. The groups are not centred on political ideology, but on an individual. Each party leader is a "big man". He attracts followers from the various political candidates by helping them with their campaign expenses. They in turn support him as he seeks to gain a ministerial position in Parliament. Once in, he distributes positions of power to his supporters, who in turn pass on whatever funds, jobs and privileges they can to their supporters.

Life is Event- Not Time-Oriented

Kevin Hovey writes about the Melanesian view of time as follows:

> Time as we know it has been an unknown concept to Papua New Guineans. Events rather than minutes and seconds were the things in focus and so the passage of time was remembered by favoured events. This results in a lack of time depth and consequently a telescoping together of past events.
> (Hovey 1986:100)

In contrast to linear time, which stretches back into the distant past and reaches forward into the distant future, Melanesian time is of very short duration. In tribal legends, it appears that the original ancestors lived only five or six generations ago. At the same time, there is no concept of a distant future, but only a foreseeable future. The different concepts of time are outlined in the following description: a Westerner sits in a truck gripping the steering wheel. He is tense, staring straight ahead, trying to anticipate the future. Melanesians,

31

however, are on the back of the truck; they are relaxed and talking together. They look back to where they have come from. The mountains in the distance are clear and unmovable. The present flashes past them and only as it moves a little into the distance does it become clear. The future is unknown and uncontrollable. Little attempt is made to guess what may be around the next corner or five kilometres down the road.

As modern and traditional Melanesian cultures become more entangled, these differences tend to blur and become less pronounced.

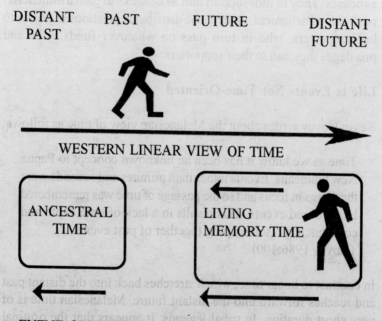

EVENT ORIENTED VIEW OF TIME LOOKS TO THE
PAST AS FUTURE IS UNPREDICTABLE

Figure 3.Differing Concepts of Time

The Pidgin word for the past is *bipo* (before) and the word for the future is *bihain* (behind). Since the Melanesians are looking towards the past, then all that has happened in the past is *before* them, and whatever might happen in the future is *behind* their backs: out of sight and therefore unknown.[9]

Bruce Blowers found that in working with national informants in Bible translation, there was no clear concept of a distant future (personal correspondence). Since life is event-oriented, time consists only of remembered events. The future, which has no remembered events, obviously has no time, except for the immediate foreseeable future. This understanding of time is important, especially when we think about the Christian message which is future-oriented: it looks forward to the "day of the Lord". We will look more at this when we consider the Melanesian responses to the missionary message.

Main Themes of Melanesian Religions

A number of general themes run through Melanesian religions. They help us to gain a general understanding of Melanesian religions.

Life is to be Abundant

Mantovani refers to the Melanesian world-view as being *biocosmic*. He suggests that Melanesian religions can be defined as: "An ultimate concern with 'life'" (1984b:29). This "life" is a "biological life or material existence" – and something more:

> The biocosmic religious experience is not characterised by
> an Ultimate called God, *theos*, but by an Ultimate experience
> as *bios* — the Greek word for life. It is characterised by the
> experience of "something" which is absolutely necessary for
> existence, of "something", in which everything participates. I
> call this "something", "life". The more a reality participates
> in that "life", the stronger, healthier, richer and more important
> that reality becomes. (Mantovani 1984b:31-32)

33

This "life" is a pervasive spiritual quality that has a cosmic dimension. All of creation participates in this cosmic life to varying degrees, and through this cosmic life, all of nature and the unseen world are bound together. Mantovani summarises by saying:

> Animals and plants are different from humans, but are still linked together into a cosmos, an ordered whole, by that "life" without which nothing could exist. Everything that exists shares in that same "life". I call this experience "biocosmic". (1984b:32)

Mantovani has captured the essence of Melanesian religion. This view of the cosmos as being alive has carried over into people's approach to Christianity. I recall, for example, hearing a village pastor as he greeted the congregation one Sunday morning: "What a beautiful day to worship the Lord. I woke this morning to hear the shrill whistling of the insects and the chirping of the birds as they had their early morning choir practice giving praise to Almighty God their creator. Now it is our turn to join with creation in praising our God." I also heard a well educated pastor at a baptismal service declare to the baptismal candidates as they stood on the riverbank: "This is a very important declaration that you are making today. The river, the trees, the rocks and the sky are witnesses to this event, as are also the members of your family and this congregation. Today, God the Father, our enemy Satan, the demons, and the angels in heaven also witness this declaration of faith in Jesus Christ as your Lord and Saviour."

Melanesian Christianity thus sees the whole cosmos as involved, active and witnessing. This view is also apparent in the words of Jesus, when requested by Pharisees to restrain the people's praises and jubilation at the time of the triumphal entry: "If they keep quiet, the stones will cry out" (Luke 19:40). Likewise in the story of Jonah: although the prophet is disobedient at first and only reluctantly obeys at the end of the story, the sea, the great fish, the vine, the worm and the scorching east wind all obey God's instructions. In this story, it is not only the people who repent: the cattle have to fast, and both men and beast are clothed with sackcloth. In the final verse, God proclaims his concern not only for the 120,000 people but also for the cattle (Jonah 3:7-8; 4:11). Revelation 7:13 says that: "every creature in heaven and on earth and under the earth and on the sea" is praising their creator and redeemer. Perhaps the Melanesian cosmic world-view is closer to the biblical world-view than is the compartmentalised world-view of modern societies, including Western Christianity.

The focus of the Melanesian world-view is the pursuit of life. Whiteman writes:

> The most fundamental value, central to Melanesian cultures and religions, is the continuation, protection, maintenance and celebration of Life. Life with a capital "L" ... Make certain that it is abundant, that it is protected, that it continues, that it is more than just biological existence and that it is worthy of celebration. Time, energy, and attention are given to pursuing this value. (1984:92-93)

Religion therefore is focused not on the "hereafter", but on the "here and now". People are concerned with threats from enemies and of shortages of food. Religion is the source of life and is concerned with health, fertility of women, pigs and gardens, the ongoing strength of the clan, and defence from attacks. The spirits of the dead are very involved in this pursuit of "Life": if there is harmony between the living and the dead then there will be harmony in the natural environment, and the gardens and pigs will demonstrate fertility. Conversely, if the spirits are displeased they will withhold their blessing; sickness, infertility and death will result.

This abundant "Life" is demonstrated primarily through feasting and celebration, as is seen graphically in the huge pig kills of the Highlands (Whiteman 1984:96). Tribal dancing that symbolises the strength and wealth of the tribe sometimes goes on for months in preparation

35

for the event. The spectacular headdresses made with bird of paradise plumes are obvious displays of wealth, for the feathers have been traded from other tribal groups, collected and preserved for this event. On the final day of the festival that I attended in the Wahgi Valley in 1976, between 1500 and 2000 pigs were killed by four different sub-clans, each in their own clan area. They were butchered, cooked and distributed that afternoon and the next day. These pigs were not eaten by the owners, but were given away to repay past debts and further cement and develop trading partners with other clans and families. If twenty people helped to consume each pig (and they were huge pigs), then about 40,000 people must have participated in the eating of the 2,000 pigs. (This is not much short of the entire population of the Wahgi Valley.) When pig meat is such a delicacy, it is not hard to see how this event enhanced the prestige and status of those clans who hosted the pig festival.

Mantovani relates the pig kill to the celebration of life. He writes:

> "Life" is expressed through the long rows of pigs, the heaps of foods, and the abundance of shells etc. That wealth is the proof of the abundance of "life" for everyone to see. Relationships are at the centre of the celebration, with the exchange aiming to strengthen old relationships, create new ones, and restore the broken. The community emerges strengthened in its identity, cemented by the experience of the cooperation, and with a new sense of meaning. (1984d:149)

This celebration of life through feasting is also seen at events like the giving of a bride price. The plumes with which the bride is adorned demonstrate the bride's family's wealth. The wealth and prestige of the groom's family is demonstrated by the "bride wealth" of pigs, cassowary birds and cash (in the Highlands) that are given in the exchange. This theme of celebration through feasting is also apparent in the feasts for a baptism or the opening of a new church.

36

The large pig kills of forty years ago are not as common as they used to be, for other events are taking precedence. At the time of national government elections, each candidate tries to out do the other candidates by demonstrating his "life force" by the number of supporters he can gather, and by the amount of food and cash he is able to give away to potential supporters. Although its context may change, celebration continues to be a very important theme in Melanesian culture.

Spiritual Power Should Have Observable Results
Power is not power unless it does something. It must have the ability to change things.[10] Jesus likened the power of the Spirit to the wind that blows. One does not see the wind, but rather the effect of the wind. Melanesians similarly like to see the power of God in observable ways.

European Christianity is very concerned with "correct" doctrine. Every church has its Articles of Faith, and one of the first items translated by missionaries is some form of catechism. However, these make little impact upon many people. The Melanesian question is not, "What must I believe?" but: "What must we do?"

The people of PNG have grown up in a society where the sources of power are many. There is the power of tribal spirits; the ancestral spirits, including the remembered dead; and the bush spirits. There is magic and also the evil power of sorcery. Life involves keeping these powers working for the benefit of one's clan or family, rather than working against them. "The main religious question in Melanesia is how to gain access to power and how to control it in order to make life successful" (Ahrens 1977:143). These powers affect all of life: health, wealth, hunting, gardening, fertility, death, sickness, childbirth and weather. Natural and supernatural forces are interrelated. Abundant life can only come from abundant power. The more power people have working for them, the greater are their chances of success.

37

There is a very strong correlation between life and power. A religion without power is a religion without life. Melanesians are concerned about "life", rather than an ultimate truth. The big questions in Melanesia are, "Does it work? Is it effective? Does it bring abundant life?" The main criticisms of churches is not so much that they do not have the truth, but that they are dead or lifeless. Whiteman says, "To a Melanesian a lying god, a false god, a god who cannot be trusted is one who claims to be a god but in fact is impotent and is unable to keep his promise. A lying god is not so much one who does not tell the truth as one who cannot do what he claims" (1984:97). Western missionaries have come with an emphasis on propositional truth and correct doctrine that is spelled out in catechisms and concise statements of faith. Melanesians, however, are interested in power that results in abundant life here and now, rather than at some distant time in the future. Melanesian religion is primarily experiential, it is felt rather than reasoned, and is experienced through one's feelings more than perceived through the mind.

The Goal of Religion is Well-Being or Harmony
Well-being results from harmony among all members of the tribal group, including those presently living and those who have died. It is not individualistic but clan-centred; well-being will enhance the prestige and strength of the clan.[11]

If social, physical and economic well-being comes from harmony, then the reverse also applies. Disease, poverty and social unrest come from disharmony. It is not enough, however, to have harmony among the living members of a group: this harmony must also be between the living and the "living-dead", those who have died but are still alive in the spirit realm and are actively participating in the ongoing life of the clan.

Lawrence and Meggitt argue that: "The prevailing attitude towards religion is essentially pragmatic and materialistic. Religion is technology rather than a spiritual force for human salvation." They also state, "Everywhere religion is regarded as a means to, or

38

guarantee of, material welfare " (1965:18, 22). The search is for "life" - not life in some distant land after we die but life here and now. This is often expressed by the Pidgin term *"gutpela sindaun"*. *Gutpela sindaun* (literally: good - sitting) conveys the concept of peace: people are not standing on guard, watching for enemies, but are sitting down in peace. It also conveys the concept of plenty: people have a chance to relax from the day to day labor of producing food, have time to sit down to enjoy it. And it conveys the concept of social harmony: people sitting down, relaxing and talking together.

Gernot Fugmann defines *gutpela sindaun* as follows: "It means fulfilment in every aspect of life, be it health, success, fertility, respect, honour and influence over others. Ultimately it is the absence of ... sickness, death, defeat, infertility, contempt or poverty" (1984:282). *Gutpela sindaun* is communal. It is interwoven with all the members of the community to which the individual belongs. "Such a cosmic community embraces the living and the dead, all things visible and invisible, beings, deities, and various powers in the cosmos" (Fugmann 1984:282).

Gutpela sindaun is the same as the concept of abundant life. It is the norm or goal that is sought after. "Health is the expected norm for all humans, young and old; it results from a harmony of spiritual powers with the physical and social order" (Habel 1979:6). But how does one experience this life?

Whiteman links this search for the abundant life with the concept of *"mana"*. *Mana* is a Polynesian word and a concept that was first introduced to the Western world by Robert Codrington, an Anglican missionary of a hundred years ago. Codrington describes *mana* as:

A power or an influence, not physical, and in a way supernatural: but it shows itself in physical force, or in any kind of power or excellence which a man possesses. This *mana* is not fixed in anything, and can be conveyed in almost anything; but spirits, whether disembodied souls or

39

supernatural beings, have it and can impart it ... All Melanesian religion consists, in fact, in getting it used for one's benefit. (1891:119)

Mana is not something that can be seen or measured except in results. It is the difference between success or defeat in war, and the difference between being a leader in society or a man of no special significance. *Mana* is revealed in having many children, healthy pigs and fertile gardens. Its meaning is covered by the Pidgin words, *strong* (strength) or *pawa* (power). Wayne Dye writes that:

> Family health and success are the surest proof that he has *mana* ... This life force is somehow quantitative. Success in daily affairs requires an adequate amount; the presence of life force is confirmed by success. (1984:59)

Melanesians see the spiritual and the material aspects of life as interrelated (in contrast, modern scientific thought teaches that the material and spiritual are unrelated). There cannot be success in one without success in the other. The good life, the abundant life, comes to the person who has power, *mana*. This results in *gutpela sindaun*: people living in harmonious relationships, not only with each other, but also with the departed members of the clan, the supernatural spirit beings, and the natural world in which they live.

The Spirit World is Very Important
Melanesians live in a world that is populated with spirits. In order to understand Melanesian thinking and beliefs, it is necessary to understand the spirit world in which they live (Rowsome 1993:36). In thinking about Melanesian religions, we are not dealing with theology, but rather, with cosmology, the total cosmic order that a people believes to exist. Looking at these beliefs, we see that "[t]here is no uniform pattern of belief about 'spirit-beings' in Melanesia. The number of such powers in the host of traditional cosmoi vary from the many to the one" (Trompf 1991:12).

40

It is possible, however, to divide the spirit world into several main groups; each group has greater or lesser importance, depending upon the cosmology of each particular language group. These groups are:

1. Gods and cultural heroes;
2. Ghosts of ancestors and spirits of the dead;
3. Bush spirits or nature spirits; and
4. Evil occult forces connected with sorcery and witchcraft - *sanguma.*

Gods and cultural heroes. Mary MacDonald defines "gods and heroes of the past" as "somewhat like people, the ghosts are more like people, and the spirits of nature are least like people" (1984:125). The fourth group - *sanguma* - is almost always evil.

There is enormous variety in the group of gods and heroes. These are the spirit beings who were involved in creating or fashioning the world as we now know it. They shaped various geographic features and were the progenitors of various tribes. Habel subdivides this group into four (1979:2):

1. Creator gods or heroes, who are attributed to creating or shaping the world, but who now generally have little to do with daily life.
2. "Divine Rulers": These are similar to the above, but are more active in ruling, regulating and directing the life of a society. This is done from a distance (i.e. the sky or a distant lofty mountain). For the Enga, for example, sky people control the weather, are the source of good and bad luck, but who overall are basically indifferent to the needs of humans. They are seldom mentioned except by the older people and are not really part of the immediate social and physical environment (Meggitt 1965:109).
3. Dema deities: These are cultural heroes who figure in important myths. In the myth they die a violent death, and

41

from their grave or dismembered body come crops or animals that are essential to people's life, e.g. coconuts, taro or pigs. These myths portray the theme that out of the violent death of one, comes abundant life for many. Such stories are not found in all cultures.

4. Cultural heroes: they are more than tribal ancestors; they are heroes from the primordial past to whom is attributed clan identity, sacred skills, special rituals etc.

Ancestral spirits. The spirits of the remembered dead, also sometimes referred to as the living dead, "are ever present among the living, and ... are part of the clan" (Habel 1979:6). The spirits of the dead are felt primarily in the social realm (MacDonald 1984:132). They are never far away and are always aware of all that takes place in the village. Usually there is a distinction made between the spirits of the remembered dead and the spirits of the ancestors, who died in the distant past and who are often addressed or treated as a collective whole. The recent dead are part of daily conversation and almost all injuries or mishaps are attributed to them. When a man, dies his spirit leaves his body and becomes a ghost. It stays near the corpse until burial, after which it wanders freely around the clan territory. Rituals are employed to find out a spirit's intentions, to satisfy its desires and to drive it away (Meggitt 1965:110).

In contrast to the recent dead, distant ancestors are generally beneficent and are powerful as a group (Lawrence and Meggitt 1965:22). It is the collective ancestors of the tribe who are the focus of the *kong gar* ceremonies of the Wahgi people, when a tribe will kill two to three thousand pigs in their honour. It is believed that this offering will please the ancestors so that they will bless the tribe with prosperity, fertility and good health.

Nature spirits. These beings are not deities, nor are they cultural heroes or of human origin. They are believed to be spirits that inhabit trees, streams, rivers, mountains, caves and swamps. The stories surrounding these spirits vary greatly from one area to another.

Generally they are regarded as evil, or as capricious and easily offended. People normally observe taboos in order to avoid the risk of offending them. The Kobon people used to offer a portion of any animal that was killed in the forest to the bush spirit who was regarded as the guardian of the forest. It is common in many places of Papua New Guinea to make some sort of offering to secure the approval of the guardian of the bush before people commence to slash down the bush to make a new garden. People in the Wahgi Valley will kill one of a litter of piglets to the spirit who watches over the pigs near the Wahgi River. People in the Wahgi and many other places also give an offering of first fruits to the spirits who live near the gardens so as to appease them. If this is not done, sickness could occur.

Sanguma - **occult powers**. *Sanguma* is one of the most feared forces by people in many parts of PNG, though as with other beliefs, there is great variation from one part of Papua New Guinea to another. My information comes primarily from the Simbu and Western Highlands Provinces. *Sanguma* refers to an evil power or spirit that reveals itself in animal form and urges individuals to bring sickness or death on other people. This death is often brought about by the "evil eye", where the practitioner stares strongly at a person, or by willing the person to die; the victim will suddenly fall sick and die. It is believed that the *sanguma* person then goes disguised as a rat, dog, snake or possum, exhumes the body either physically or supernaturally, and together with other *sanguma* people, eats the body. *Sanguma* is always evil, and people who are accused of being *sanguma* are seen as a threat to society; they are frequently hunted down and burnt alive or killed.

Most unexplained illnesses are attributed to witchcraft, and people with *sanguma* power are greatly feared. Some people no doubt use this reputation as a means of gaining control over others.[12] While it is wrong to regard Melanesian religion as being satanic and evil, it is also wrong to fail to acknowledge the presence of the occult and evil in traditional religion.

43

We have looked briefly at four main classes of spiritual beings. Of these four groups, it is the spirits of the dead who are the most involved in people's everyday life. Whiteman summarises these relationships:

> There are many Melanesian religions that do not have a "Great Spirit" at all. It seems however that where they do exist, creator spirits have become the object of legend and myth, but not the object of worship. They are inactive and often unapproachable by people. It is ghosts and spirits that are active in the affairs of human communities and so it is to them that Melanesian people turn in veneration and propitiation. (1984:108)

For most Melanesians, the Christian God does not replace this traditional hierarchy of spirits, but rather is added to them. Often God has been seen as the same as the high god of the ancestors. Bulmer believes that Christianity has not replaced belief in spirits: "Christians still believe in these, but they think that Jesus Christ has greater power ... they think that the ghosts may be more immediately influential in their everyday life" (1965:159). Many Christians have divided loyalties and choose whichever source of power they think will be most appropriate at any particular time. Any theology that ignores the traditional cosmology will result in a truncated gospel. Such a truncated gospel gives the impression that although Jesus can help with the ultimate issues (such as eternal salvation), he is powerless to deal with the daily fear of sorcery and witchcraft. The teaching of an imported Western gospel that ignores the spirit world does not prevent syncretism, but actually helps to cause syncretism, thus forming an unhealthy mix of the old and the new which is neither one nor the other.

CHAPTER TWO

MISSIONARY MESSAGES AND MELANESIAN RESPONSES

I flew to Negabo, in the southern part of Simbu Province, in a little plane operated by the Missionary Aviation Fellowship. Then I walked for two hours to one of the village churches. This was an area that had had very little contact with the outside world; the Church of the Nazarene had only recently established churches in the area.

It was Sunday. After a good church service, a group of us were having a dinner of sweet potatoes. The old leader of the village began to tell a story.

Back when we used to eat people, an Australian government officer came through here on a patrol.[13] We ambushed their patrol with a shower of arrows. The carriers dropped their goods and fled, and the white man went with them. We picked up the stuff that was dropped and were puzzled by all these foreign objects. Among the things that were dropped was a black box with knobs on it. One of the men turned a knob and it started to talk.[14] We were surprised, for obviously there was a little man inside who was talking. We told him to come out, but he just kept talking. Someone suggested that he was shy and so we hid behind the bushes and watched, but still no one came out. Obviously someone was hiding in the box and talking to us. Another person suggested that perhaps some food would tempt him to come out. Very soon a sweet potato on a banana leaf was placed carefully before the little radio. We withdrew and watched from the bushes. But again no response; the little man did not come out of the black box.

Once again the men got together for a consultation. The little man was hiding in the box, would not come out, and had rejected our offering of food. This rejection of food was a clear indication that whoever was hiding inside had rejected our friendship. He had not responded to kindness and so we decided that stronger tactics were needed. One of the men took his stone axe and crept around behind the black box. Then raising it high above his head, he brought it down hard on the box. Crash!

Silence! There were no more words from the little man. We looked inside and there was no one there.

The old man laughed until tears ran down his face. "Oh, back then there was so much we did not understand. Everything from the outside world was so strange." That world "back then" was the world into which the Western missionaries entered with the gospel, and also with their cargo.

A Brief History of Missions in Papua New Guinea

Christian missions arrived in Papua New Guinea around the same time as colonial governments. For many Melanesians they were two aspects of the one event. "B.C." is often understood as "Before Contact", which was a turning point in recent history. Since contact with Westerners, life has never been the same.

The first missionaries to Papua New Guinea arrived in 1847. Between 1871 and 1877, the missionaries Samuel McFarlane from Samoa, William and Fanny Lawes from Niue, and Mr and Mrs James Chalmers from Rarotonga, arrived; all were of the London Missionary Society. Each came with Pacific Islander missionaries from the places where they had previously served (Garrett 1982:206-218).

46

In 1875, George Brown and a number of Fijian pastors and teachers arrived in the Duke of York Islands and began the Methodist work in the New Guinea Islands. They continued the pattern set throughout the rest of the Pacific: the Pacific Islanders led the way in evangelisation (Crocombe 1982). Many of these island missionaries came as single men and married into the local tribes and villages, and so became part of the local culture. Today people from the coastal areas of Papua New Guinea mention with pride that some of their ancestors came from the Cook Islands, Fiji, Samoa or some other island group.

In 1885 Catholic missionaries began work at Yule Island (104km from Port Moresby), and in 1890 the Anglican missionaries began work in the Dogura area. On the northern part of the island, which was under German control, the Lutheran Mission began work near Finschhafen in 1886. This was led by Johannes Flierl. In 1895, the Catholic Society of the Divine Word (SVD) missionaries began work further west along the northern coast line (Forman 1982:8).

The growth of the church in Melanesia was very different to that in Polynesia, and this was largely due to Melanesian culture. In Polynesia, there were many people movements where large segments of the population - and at times entire tribes - turned to Christianity (Tippett 1971). These movements often came as the result of a "power encounter" between the traditional gods of the people and the Christian God. After a demonstration of the power of the Christian God, the chief might decide to become a Christian and the whole tribe would follow. Although the missionaries who came to Melanesia were experienced and familiar with the Polynesian people movements, they did not find the same widespread response in Melanesia.

Melanesian social units were small and so the conversion of one village did not necessarily spread to other villages. In fact, because of tribal fighting and village antagonism, the mere fact that one village accepted Christianity was often a good reason for the neighbouring village to reject Christianity. Language differences also complicated things. It takes a long time to learn one tribal language. In Polynesia, one language often covered an entire archipelago, thus enabling the missionary or evangelist to travel from village to village. In Melanesia things were very different. The village a few kilometres up the coastline usually spoke a totally different language. This slowed the transmission of the gospel. The Polynesians too were more outgoing and accepting of outsiders, whereas the Melanesians were more withdrawn and suspicious of outsiders, and much slower in accepting the new beliefs (Forman 1982:7). The result was that, by the end of the nineteenth century, the Christian influence in Melanesia was very weak, and confined to little pockets near the isolated mission stations dotted along the coastline. Instead of widespread people movements, the Melanesian pattern was one of "slow village-by-village work with only small gains" (Forman 1982:9).

Expansion into the Highlands

In the 1920s, Melanesian Lutheran evangelists from Morobe Province entered the Eastern Highlands and began living and working in villages. In 1933, Jim Taylor and the Leahy brothers passed through Simbu and entered the broad, fertile Wahgi Valley. In 1934, the Catholic and Lutheran missionaries had both established mission stations in Simbu and near Mt Hagen. World War II brought many changes, predominantly to the coastal rather than the highlands areas. For the missionaries, there was a great loss of property and personnel. It is reported that "95 percent of the mission buildings in PNG and the Solomon Islands were destroyed. Churches, hospitals, schools, rectories, convents, and all the rest no longer existed, while 11 Anglicans died, 15 Lutherans, 24 Methodists, and 188 R. C. [Roman Catholic] Fathers, Brothers and Sisters" (Aerts 1991:63).

The war brought missionary expansion to a halt, but in 1947 the restrictions were lifted, and missions came back in force. World War II brought Papua New Guinea to the attention of many people in Australia, New Zealand and the United States of America becaues

48

their forces were stationed and fighting in PNG. Between 1950 and 1970, large numbers of evangelical missions entered Papua New Guinea. Lutherans came in with many evangelists from the Morobe area. Seventh Day Adventists came in with many missionaries and national workers from the New Guinea Islands (Forman 1982:144-148). The Methodists entered the Southern Highlands with missionaries from Australia and New Zealand, and also a large number from the Pacific Islands, as well as from New Britain and New Ireland.

Those who had been aeroplane pilots during World War II saw the value of aviation in the spread of the gospel, especially in a country so rugged. The Catholic Mission flew its first plane out of Wewak in 1948. Their most famous pilot was without doubt the "flying Bishop", Leo Arkfield (Huber 1988:138). The Missionary Aviation Fellowship (MAF) began in Papua New Guinea in 1951 and had a huge impact on the growth of the church, especially evangelical churches (Ambrose 1987). The rapid opening up of the highlands of PNG was due in a large part to the efforts of the MAF pilots. They often risked their lives in the interest of extending the mission of the church in PNG and Irian Jaya. The MAF now operates from seven bases in PNG, and provides access to many communities who would otherwise be totally isolated. Aeroplanes became to the highlands of PNG what ships had been to the islands of the Pacific in the spread of the gospel.

Aviation also highlights the huge technological differences between the Melanesian and European cultures.[15] This factor influenced the message that was heard by the people, as did the attitudes of the missionaries to the local cultures. In his studies of the Anglican Church in the Solomon Islands, Whiteman gives examples of varying types of missionary approaches: that of the reformer, for instance; the paternalist; and the empathiser (1983:205-217). There were differences between individuals within the same denominational mission structure and there were also broad differences between

49

one theological tradition and another. We will look now at four different approaches: Catholic, Lutheran, Evangelical and recent Pentecostal.

The Catholic Approach

The Catholic approach to mission is shaped by a very long church history, to which they look for inspiration and guidance. Pope Gregory the Great (590-604) was very interested in the conversion of the people of England. He sent a letter to St Augustine of England giving him the following instructions:[16]

> They should not destroy the peoples' temples but only the idols in them. Their temples should be consecrated, then altars be erected in them and relics placed there so that the people, when they see that this has not been destroyed, will wholeheartedly renounce their errors and eagerly gather in their customary sacred place to worship the true God.
>
> And since in former times it was customary for the people to slaughter many bullocks in the course of their pagan celebrations, this custom should also be given a new Christian meaning. Thus, for instance, the anniversary of the dedication of the church, or the anniversary of the martyr whose relics rest therein, could be celebrated with a religious banquet. In this way they would no longer sacrifice animals to the devil, rather they would kill them in honour of God and for their own consumption and, after the meal, render thanks to God the giver of everything that is good.
>
> If these external joys are permitted then they ought more easily find access to interior joy. (Pope Gregory the Great qtd. in Schaefer 1981:213)

The Catholic Church's representatives have seen that traditional practices are too deeply rooted to be totally discarded without leaving a vacuum of frustration (Nilles 1977:176). They have worked to inculturate by keeping traditional rituals wherever possible and pouring new meaning into them. But it is very difficult to disassociate the form of a ritual from its earlier meaning. They have tried to keep the ancestors as intercessors for the living community, while at the same time stressing that they do not have autonomous power over the living (Nilles 1977:183). How successful they have been remains to be seen; critics feel that this has often resulted in syncretism: that there has not been a clear understanding of biblical truth about spiritual powers (Rowsome 1993:53).

The Lutheran Approach

According to the 2000 census, Evangelical Lutherans make up 19.5 percent of the population of Papua New Guinea (Zocca 2004:41). Much of the reason for this following can be traced back to the influence of Christian Keysser, a missionary in Papua New Guinea from 1899 until 1921. After a very fruitful missionary career, he returned to Germany where he taught missions. Thirty of his students subsequently became missionaries in Papua New Guinea (McGavran 1980: viii). Keysser found that it was best that people could come to Christ as a group with their tribal structure intact. He wrote: "It dawned on me from the Holy Scripture that God does not only save individual souls but that he also wants to win entire nations. He had chosen Israel, saved, guided and reared her; not because she was pious but because of his own promise and grace" (1980:13).

This people movement to Christianity brought widespread change. It should be noted that the missionaries did not impose the changes, but rather the tribal leaders made resolutions about what was acceptable behaviour and what was not.

After long, hard discussions in the villages, they made joint resolutions on what henceforth should come to an end, and on what should take place in the future. Old customs were done away with by plebiscite. Blood revenge and all fighting were abolished in this way; they tabooed sorcery, prohibited

51

wife stealing, polygamy, feticide (abortion) and all theft, and they abolished the ancestor cult. (Keysser 1980:11)

The result was that, instead of the church being in opposition to the clan structure, and a tug of war developing between clan loyalty and Christianity, the reverse happened: "the whole congregation was the clan - the whole clan was the congregation" (Keysser 1980:21). Obviously not everyone was at the same place in their spiritual journey or exhibited the same level of Christian faith and practice; they were a "mottled and chequered society", but the clan structure was intact and now it was a people under God who worked together to bring their social life into conformity with the Word of God. This had a powerful effect on neighbouring tribes, who had not seen anything like it before. "There was no fighting, no killing, no distrust, no fear, no sorcery; peace and friendliness prevailed everywhere" (Keysser 1980:18). The approach of Keysser was to bring the people into the church and continue the disciplining process within the clan and tribal structures.

It is over one hundred years since Keysser began his ministry in PNG. Today nominalism is a huge problem in the Lutheran Church (though it is by no means the only denomination that has a problem with nominalism). Many who were baptised as infants have not progressed beyond a nominal faith in God and loyalty to the Lutheran Church.

Another problem is that the Lutheran Church did not have a strong theology of the Holy Spirit, yet Melanesian cultures are greatly interested in the spirit world. Keysser tried to downplay the activity of spirits as much as possible. He said in regard to spirits: "If one granted their existence, the Christians would never be liberated from their superstitious fear" (1980:179). Rather than trying to disprove the existence of spirits, it may have been more productive to have emphasised the power of God over all the forces of evil. In the 1970s, a series of revival movements swept through large areas of PNG and the Lutheran Church, along with other mainline churches, struggled to handle these movements. Today there are divisions in the Lutheran Church and some of these are related to differences about the work of the Holy Spirit.

The Evangelical Approach

Following World War II, there was a great influx of evangelical missionaries into Papua New Guinea. These included the Australian Baptist Mission, Church of the Foursquare Gospel, Assemblies of God Mission, Christian Missions to Many Lands (Brethren), South Seas Evangelical Church, Unevangelised Fields Mission, Evangelical Bible Mission, Swiss Evangelical Brotherhood Mission and many others. Many of these were located in the Highlands. The colonial ruler of New Guinea - the Australian government - was glad for the appearance of the missions, for they helped to build, staff and manage schools, health clinics, and vocational training, and did much to end tribal fighting.

The Church of the Nazarene Mission entered PNG in 1955. When I arrived in 1968 there were twelve Nazarene churches and a small Bible school. Most of the preaching was done by missionaries. Before long, Papua New Guinean pastors were doing most of the preaching, except in the town churches which were still led by missionaries. By the end of the 1990s, all of the three hundred and fifty churches were pastored by Papua New Guineans. For administrative purposes the Nazarene churches were divided into districts; initially most district leaders were missionaries, but again by the end of the 1990s each of the eleven district superintendents was an ordained Papua New Guinean elder and a graduate of the Nazarene Bible College. The Bible college staff was also largely Papua New Guinean, as were the tutors in the College of Nursing (see also Syvret 1999).

Missionaries worked hard at learning the local language, for without that they were unable to communicate their message. Organisations such as Summer Institute of Linguistics (SIL) and New Tribes Mission saw Scripture translation as their primary task. Many others were involved in Bible translation and literacy, teaching people to read so that they could become pastors and church leaders. Yet the evangelical attitude toward Melanesian culture was not as accommodating as was the Catholics' approach. Evangelicals saw their task as bringing the light of the gospel to people whose hearts and minds were darkened by sin.

Small people movements took place among the evangelical churches, although this was more as a result of the people insisting on being full members of the church, for the missionaries tended to be sceptical of people's sincerity and knowledge. Evangelicals had usually undergone a conversion experience themselves in which they accepted Christ as their personal Saviour. This was a very important life changing experience, and they want other people to come to experience God's love in the same transforming way. To evangelicals, the change that comes about through knowing Christ is seen in terms of contrast between the old and new, lost and found, light and dark, death and life, enemy and friend. The most significant of these metaphors in missionary thinking has been that of light replacing darkness. Light does not build on darkness, it replaces it. Many missionary hymns emphasise the imagery of light replacing darkness (for example, "The whole world was lost in the darkness of sin, the light of the world is Jesus").

Many festivals were declared heathen and so missionaries stayed away from them, unwilling to condone what was happening at the *singsings*. Yet by staying away they could not learn what was going on. It was only after eight years of missionary service that Don McGregor visited the fish festival in his area and tried to understand what was going on. Being there, and observing the festival from start to finish, gave him a much greater understanding of the people, their thinking, and their understanding of life.

In my view, it was a tragedy that for more than a decade missionaries thought of the Fish Festival almost entirely in terms of satanic activity ... And yet at the same time the

54

Western churches we missionaries came from accepted members who to a greater or lesser degree followed the gods of materialism and secularism and were in no ways disciplined. It may well be that behind both of these activities of the Wape and Western culture the "god of this world" is at work blinding people's minds. But to label one and not the other as completely "satanic" is, in my view, inconsistent. (1982:96)

McGregor asks, would it not have been better to work at Christianising the festival rather than condemning it completely? He traces this problem to the pietistic roots of evangelical missionaries and quotes James Packer, who wrote: "Pietism lacks interest in bodies as compared to souls, and heads as compared to hearts. This lack is its main defect. It is narrower than life" (Packer 1967:26).

The *Willowbank Report on Gospel and Culture* states:

Many of us evangelical Christians have in the past been too negative toward culture. We do not forget the human fallenness and lostness which call for salvation ... At the same time there are features in every culture which are not incompatible with the Lordship of Christ, and which therefore need not be threatened or discarded, but rather preserved and transformed. (Lausanne 1978:6,13)

In reality, light does not "remove" darkness - for darkness is merely the absence of light. The coming of the light brings transformation. Sometimes missionaries have been too impatient, unwilling to allow time for the transforming work to take place. The gospel needs to be understood as salt that penetrates and preserves, and as yeast that silently transforms from within (Matthew 5:13; 13:33). McGregor writes, "Let us continually seek out areas of their life which will serve as at least a temporary foundation for the Christian message" (1982:123). The Melanesian understanding of the importance of blood sacrifice, the reality of the spirit world, the belief that life continues

55

after death - these are all areas of similarity and points of contact that can be built upon in communicating the gospel.

The Pentecostal Approach

Several Pentecostal Churches arrived shortly after World War II (such as the Assemblies of God, the Four Square Gospel Mission, and the Apostolic Church), along with the many evangelical churches. In the 1970s a number of charismatic groups also arrived in PNG, became established in the towns and quickly branched out across the nation. The earlier groups were involved in pioneer evangelism and operated in many ways like other evangelical churches. They sought to learn the local languages, and were involved in schools and clinics, operated literacy programs and ran sawmills. They trained village pastors and operated Bible schools. The groups that came after independence (1975) started work in the towns with educated people, and concentrated on church planting and evangelism.

In the period from 1980 to 2000 there has been another rapid increase in the number of Charismatic and Pentecostal churches.[17] Some of these have started following revival movements that began among mainline churches in the 1970s; others are descendants of Pentecostal churches. There are also a growing number of evangelistic "ministries" that promote "healing crusades". Posters advertising a "healing crusade" or "evangelistic crusade" can be found publicly displayed in any town in Papua New Guinea.

Between 1980 and 2000 the number of people who identified as Pentecostal grew from being 1.5 percent to 8.6 percent of the population (Zocca 2004:41). In the same period, people who identified as belonging to the "Historical Mainline Churches" declined from 77.8 percent of the population to 61.2 percent (Zocca 2004:42).[18] Franco Zocca believes that the reason for the growth of these new religious groups is due to their emphasis on the infilling of the Holy Spirit, demonstration of supernatural power, emphasis on healing, enthusiastic singing and even dancing, on Bible teaching, loud dramatic preaching, strict moral regulations, and on an acceptance of dreams and visions as a way in which God communicates with ordinary people (1995:180-184).

The Pentecostals differ from the other groups in that they place a much stronger emphasis on the spirit world. Their stress on "signs and wonders" and spiritual gifts promotes healing miracles, people shaking, speaking in tongues, and falling under the power of the Spirit. The spirit world, Pentecostals argue, is very real, and they act to cast out evil spirits. These features fit very closely with the Melanesian world-view, and people have responded very positively to Pentecostals. Yet Pentecostal and Charismatic Churches often give very little emphasis to traditional culture. They emphasise Western music, songs in English and use electronic instruments, while local songs and bush instruments are seldom used. Videos of Western televangelists are widely distributed, and up and coming preachers try to imitate the styles of their American heroes. They acknowledge the reality of the spirit world, but make little effort to evaluate the traditional beliefs in the light of Scripture. Many of them seem to equate traditional ways with evil and modern ways with Christianity. A "health, wealth and prosperity" gospel, however, appeals to the Melanesian approach which does not separate the material from the spiritual.

The result is varied. There is rapid growth in congregations, but also a big turnover of people. The emphasis on spiritual gifts and the reality of the spirit world leads to what may be called "inadvertent contextualisation", but culture is not emphasised, and no deliberate attempt is made to contextualise. One notable exception is the Assemblies of God, for one of their missionaries, Kevin Hovey. Hovey, later their field leader, studied missiology at the Fuller School of World Mission. He worked within the clan structure and village leadership to create people movements into Christianity, and worked hard to create cultural awareness among missionaries and national leaders. His book, *Before All Else Fails ... Read the Instructions*

(1986), has been widely read and used by missionaries in PNG in helping them to understand the culture.

Cross-cultural communication is a challenge. Not only are the messengers' words interpreted in the light of the recipients' knowledge and experiences, but the messengers' lifestyle and methods of instruction also impact on the listener. We will now look at some of the ways in which Melanesians have responded to the coming of Europeans, and their messages.

Cargo Cults

The general plot of the cargo myth is that some time in the far distant past, the ancestors made a poor choice that has resulted in poor quality of life for the people. Now, however, the ancestors have learned the right way and soon they will share the cargo with us (1977:52). Strelan sees cargo movements as primarily religious in nature: "They are the external, ritualistic expression of genuinely-indigenous religious beliefs and hopes which existed long before the arrival of the gospel, and which will continue to exist unless there is a radical change in Melanesian religious orientation" (Strelan 1977:12). In short, cargo cults revolve around the theme of paradise lost and paradise regained. The loss is brought about more by foolishness, stupidity or lack of proper judgment, than by disobedience of some moral law. The paradise that the people are looking for is not a spiritual paradise in the future, but an earthly paradise here in this present life, as indicated by the term "cargo".

> Cargo is a symbol. It includes such things as money, freedom from hunger and death, release from the pressures and frustrations of work, the regaining of status and dignity as a man, and the effortless acquisition of knowledge and power. "Cargo" may be understood as the Melanesian word for salvation. (Strelan 1977:70)

58

Cargo cults are easier to describe than to define for they have appeared in wide variety of forms, from the western tip of Irian Jaya all the way to Fiji in the east. Trompf describes cargo cults as "typically ritualistic and agitated attempts by groups to prepare for the coming of these goods into the local people's hands ... often ... characterised by colonial authorities and expatriate settlers as unrealistic hopes to secure 'European' cargoes by bizarre and 'magical' means" (1991:189). Strelan claims that there have been more than 200 reported since 1860, and adds that there have been many others that were not reported or described (1977:13-50). Steinbauer reports that 150 authors have published more than 400 books and articles about cargo cults, and in the forty years since then numerous others have been added (1971:102).

Strelan lists ten components that are characteristic of conventional cargo movements (1977:52-53).

1. The myth of the return of the dead;
2. A revival or modification of paganism;
3. Christian elements;
4. Belief in the cargo myth;
5. Belief that Melanesians will become white men and vice versa;
6. Belief in the coming of a messiah;
7. Attempts to restore native economic and political control;
8. Violence or threat of violence against whites;
9. Unification of traditionally separate and hostile groups; and
10. An amazing tendency to revive after apparent failure and death.

Cargo cults come into existence because of religious beliefs and hopes which existed long before the arrival of the gospel and the white man. There are basic assumptions which are rooted in the people's world-view that give rise to this cargo mentality. We therefore need to look at the underlying assumptions in a Melanesian world-view and religious orientation that give rise to cargo cults.

Cargo cults start because of dissatisfaction with the present state of life. Europeans arrived with so much and continued to get more and more. They did not share their goods with the people around them. Melanesians believe strongly in reciprocity, but they saw cargo coming into their area that was not shared evenly. This inequality had a part to play in the development of cargo cults.

Cargo cults are a search for salvation. Melanesians do not distinguish between physical and spiritual, for all of life is integrated. Existence is a search for *gutpela sindaun* - a life of fullness, or abundant life. It is out of this drive and expectation that cargo cults come. Even when there is no apparent cargo cult present, the underlying theme ("cargoism") is still present. Many people are not searching for spiritual salvation, but abundant life in all of its dimensions here in the present world. I have heard pastors complain that in the coffee season when people have money, church attendance often drops. A few months later, when the coffee money is all spent, people start coming back to church. It is not difficult to see that cargoism is not far below the surface.

Myth is an essential ingredient. The coming of the white man and the coming of the gospel are intertwined in people's minds. The only way they can interpret such events is through the legends of the past. Douglas Hayward comments, "Numerous authors have noted the role of myth in the emergence of the various movements. Indeed, in some instances it was the reformulation of the old myths that gave occasion for the emergence" (1983:16-17). Of the many myths it was the myth of the return of the dead and the myth of the lost paradise that has made the cargo movements intellectually acceptable to the people.

Correct ritual will bring results. Closely associated with the presence of the cargo myth is the understanding that appropriate ritual correctly performed will inevitably bring the right results.[19] Symbolism, secrecy and ritual known only to the leaders and those inducted into the group are the keys to success.

Ancestors play a very important role in many of the cargo cults. Ancestors have supernatural knowledge and they will look after their people. Strelan explains,

> It is the ancestor or ancestors who will inaugurate the golden age, the age of salvation. Perhaps this expectation lies at the very heart of the cargo cults ... [C]argoism expresses and nourishes the hope that one day soon the ancestors, who have already gained access to the secret of the good life will share with the living the benefits and blessings they have already attained. (1977:74)

In this sense, ancestors are both part of the clan and yet outside of it. Through their death they have passed beyond the limits of this mortal world; they have access to the good life, and therefore will be able to share with the living the benefits and blessings they have already received.

Cargo cults are communal. The success of the cargo cult is dependent on the community acting together. It is the living people working together in conjunction with the ancestors that will bring in the new age. There is a strong emphasis on the solidarity of the group and therefore much pressure that everyone be involved. Salvation, cargo and the good life are not achieved by individual effort or action, but by the group acting together. In Melanesian thinking, unity of the clan is the source of life and strength. "Because the clan exists, I exist. If the clan is strong, I am strong. If the clan is weak, I am weak" is the Melanesian viewpoint. This thinking is seen very much in cargo cults as the clan, and sometimes a whole series of clans, join together in a common goal of bringing in a new age of divine blessing or cargo.

Cargo cults are focused on receiving the good life now. Melanesians are event-oriented and therefore are focused more on the past; they do not have a concept of a distant future. The message that Jesus will return is interpreted to mean, "very soon now Jesus

61

will return," for there is no concept of an indefinite future: in Melanesian thinking there is only an immediate future. This has had a part to play in some of the hopes of a whole new life with equality and riches for everyone. Trompf comments, "the events of the encounter with the whites and their possessions were themselves 'eschatological'" (1991:201). For many Melanesian peoples that event was the turning point of history, and life has never been the same since.

Cargo cults are complex movements, involving numerous cultural factors, as Melanesians have responded to encounters with Westerners and have tried to make sense of them. With the arrival of Western technology and resulting cultural imbalance, they have tried to remedy the situation, and obtain valued goods through the way that seemed most realistic to them, namely appealing to the ancestors through sacrifice and ritual.

Revival Movements

Revival movements have had a large impact on Christianity in PNG over the past thirty years. They have affected Catholic, mainline Protestant, evangelical, Pentecostal and independent churches throughout the country.

Associated with revivals, or "Holy Spirit movements", are a wide range of phenomena that have created a lot of uncertainty in the minds of both missionaries and nationals. Are these movements really of the Holy Spirit? Are they just mass hysteria? Do they involve evil spirits? Or are they a mixture of all three? If there is a mixture, then how do we divide the good from the bad?

The Melanesian Institute undertook a major study of these movements between 1980 and 1983.[20] It revealed that, common in all these revival movements are such phenomena as: "trance-like or ecstatic states, possession, dreams, visions, auditions, and the manifestation of extraordinary spiritual gifts and powers –

glossolalia, oratory, healing, prophecy, miracles, exorcism and divination among others" (Flannery 1984:117). If these things were happening in extreme Pentecostal churches, it would not be too surprising, but they were happening in Baptist, Lutheran, Catholic and United Churches as well as in Evangelical and Pentecostal Churches.[21]

Although there was much diversity in these movements, there were also common factors. Brian Schwarz lists these as:

1. An emphasis on spiritual experience, of immediate contact with the Spirit. This is manifested in such signs as shaking, falling down, crying, speaking in tongues, prophecy, dreams, visions, healing and other "enthusiastic" phenomena. Such manifestations tend to be especially prominent in the initial phases of the movement.
2. An emphasis on genuine conversion, expressed in such practices as the searching of sin, public confession, personal testimony of the new life in Christ, and the rejection of everything considered incompatible with a committed Christian life. The drinking of alcoholic beverages, smoking, involvement in magical practices and extramarital sexual activity are especially singled out for rejection.
3. Enthusiastic public proclamation of the experience of new life in Christ through the power of the Holy Spirit, and avenues for the expression of common joy and fellowship in this conviction.
4. A more lively and informal style of worship, providing opportunities for individual involvement and emotional and physical expression.
5. The knowledge and use of the Bible by all members.
6. Regular prayer promoted, especially group prayer.
7. The composition of new Christian songs, usually simple and involving repetition.
8. The imminence of Christ's return is emphasised, the signs of his coming, and the need to be ready for it.

9. A predominance of lay church members in the founding and the leadership of the movements; leadership roles and opportunities for service for women and youth.
10. Churches demonstrate a missionary zeal and develop outreach strategies. (Schwarz 1984:269-271)

When these features are listed out neatly like this, it is easy to sit down and evaluate them. But revival is not neat and tidy: revival is like a wildfire. It does not obey rules. It is unpredictable and breaks out in different places at the same time. In all the noise, confusion and excitement about so much power revealed at once, all sorts of things happen.

In the coastal areas where there had been more contact with Christian missions, the behaviour of those involved in revival movements tended to conform more to Western revival or Pentecostal patterns. In the Highlands, however, the behaviour tended to resemble that of traditional religions (Barr 1983a:3). Consequently, revival movements caused much controversy amongst missionaries. Some praised them as having brought new life into the churches. Those in leadership positions often felt threatened by these new movements they could not control, responded negatively, and often concluded that people were being led astray by evil spirits. They would point at wild abnormal behaviour and declare that it could never possibly be the result of the Holy Spirit, for it did not demonstrate the fruits of the Spirit (Galatians 5:22-23). As John White observes: "Revival is war, and war is never tidy. It is an intensifying of the age-old conflict between Christ and the powers of darkness" (1988:35). In all the confusion, divisions often took place with some supporting, and some denouncing, the revival movements. Pastors who had never studied such activities in the peace and orderliness of Bible college were at a loss as to what to do. Some packed up and left their church, feeling that things were out of control. Missionaries too were often at a loss to know what to do. The question we need to look at is how do these revival movements relate to the Melanesian context.

Power

One of the features evident in these revival movements is the presence of power made visible in people shaking, speaking in tongues, healing and other ecstatic phenomena. In the churches there had been much talk about the power of God but little demonstration. Now people were seeing God's power demonstrated in very overt ways. Part of the issue is tangible power. "The acquisition and control of supernatural power forms a major religious quest in Melanesia. Despite immense social changes, Melanesian religions maintain a high degree of continuity with the past" (Barr 1983a:1). Established churches which spoke of the power of God, but did not overtly exhibit that power, were perceived as being dead and powerless (Schwarz 1984:264). To many people, the presence of demonstrable power was the sign that they had the Spirit – and evidence that other people, including pastors and missionaries, did not.

Conversion at a Personal Level

One of the features of revival movements is a deep conviction of sin and a turning to God in repentance (Barr 1983b:147; cf Snyder 1989). There is a significant difference between a group accepting Christianity and an individual coming into a personal relationship with Christ as his or her Saviour. Keysser, who promoted village-wide movements of people in to the church, spoke of this distinction between collective and personal salvation.

> One must constantly bear in mind that people-movements are nearly always founded on the Old Testament and the first article of the creed. The Old Testament and the Ten Commandments concerned primarily *the tribes*; The New Testament, as a supplement and completion, brought salvation to the individual. Thus, the observance of the Old Testament pertains chiefly to the sphere of the folk life; trust in Jesus, on the contrary, belongs to the area of personal Christian experience. (1980:17)

Many people had accepted Christianity as a religion. They had accepted the Christian God as above all other gods and spirits. They had accepted the Bible as true and the church as their place of worship. This was a very significant event in their lives. But often there had been little realisation of sin, and people had not understood the significance of Christ's death for them as individuals. The possibility of a personal relationship with God through deep repentance and turning away from sin was offered in many of these revivals, in contrast to the more general welcome to Christianity given to groups.[22]

Emphasis on the Holy Spirit

All of these movements had a strong emphasis on the Holy Spirit. I have heard people say: "I was baptised in the 'Name of the Father, Son, and Holy Spirit' but then I never heard any more of the Holy Spirit. But now that the revival has come, I know who the Holy Spirit is." Some people thought of Jesus as being a "white man" like the missionary, but they thought of the Holy Spirit as being more Melanesian. Some said: "The missionaries came and taught us about Jesus, but we Papua New Guineans understand the spirit world and we can identify with the Holy Spirit" (reported to me by pastors in the Sepik area). This thinking may show a lack of spiritual knowledge, but it also reveals how important the spirit world is to Melanesians (and shows the potential for problems when the Holy Spirit is equated as a good spirit similar to the spirits of traditional religion).

Many of the phenomena associated with revivals (such as shaking from head to foot, speaking in tongues, prophecies, trances, dreams and visions) has been associated with the manifestation of the spirit in traditional religions. Simon Numanu writes:

> Supernatural phenomena are believed to be caused by spiritual power, but whose power they are not always sure of or concerned about ... They are most interested in power that manifests itself in supernatural happenings. For this reason

66

they expect the Holy Spirit to manifest power in the same way as their traditional spirits, regardless of their personal moral condition. (1983:113-114)

In some places, these movements led to a real desire to read the Scriptures and to know God in a deeper way. I have met people who have testified to the change in their life that came about through a revival movement, and how they developed a deep hunger to know God's Word. Even though they could not read, they bought a New Testament and then asked God to teach them how to read. They publicly testify that the Holy Spirit taught them how to read.

In some places, however, there has been a very different attitude toward the Scriptures. Some people have announced: "We do not need the Bible, or pastors, or teachers, for we have the Holy Spirit." Often this has happened in those areas where the pastors and church leaders have denounced the revival movement and semiliterate revival leaders have reacted against them. Often the illiterate and semiliterate have felt like second class citizens in the church. But in times of revival, God speaks to them in dreams and visions, in full colour, and in the *tok ples*. This is a powerful thing and people rejoice that God has been liberated from being imprisoned inside a book and has come alive to them. It is important that church leaders do not dismiss these people as ignorant, but humble themselves and as each learns from the other the church will be strengthened. As long as these dreams and visions are interpreted in line with Scripture, they can add a positive personal dimension to people's faith.

Worship Patterns

A common feature of these revival movements is a change in worship patterns and the incorporation of more indigenous forms of worship. This includes new songs and choruses, sometimes in Pidgin, but often in *tok ples*. Worship services often go for hours and prayer becomes extremely important. Women become more involved in leadership. A very common phenomena is for groups of people to go up into the mountains to pray, fast and receive the anointing of the Holy Spirit. In some areas in Baiyer River area and parts of Enga, people set aside prayer places. These are fenced off so that people can go there to meet with God (Cramp and Kolo 1983:103). In other places it has become a common practice to go up a mountain to meet with God. Much of this comes out of the significance of mountain top experiences in the lives of such people as Abraham, Moses, Elijah and Jesus.

Healing

Although the church may officially have a doctrine of divine healing, the missionaries demonstrate reliance upon modern medicine, which has been presented as the alternative to the village sorcerer or healer's work. But modern medicine at the village level is not very effective, with few medicines available and little trained people. Melanesian Christians have often been left without help, and can end up with a dual allegiance: believing in and worshipping God, but doubtful that he is really able to take care of their diseases. This has led to a conflict, a conflict that revival has addressed.

A common form of ministry among these movements is healing by the power of the spirit. This form of healing not only focuses on the physical manifestations of sickness but also, and more importantly, on the negative spiritual forces which are regarded as the cause of the illness. With the power of the Spirit these Christians feel equipped to combat sorcery and perform exorcisms ... Miracles are prayed for and regularly claimed. (Schwarz 1984:265)

Problem Areas

Confusion can result when people have not learned to discern the Spirit of God, but attribute every impulse to the Holy Spirit. In those

68

churches where little clear teaching has been given on the work of the Holy Spirit, there is often confusion about what behaviour came from the Holy Spirit and what came from some other type of spirit (Bartle 1998). Problems also develop when dreams and visions are substituted for Scripture and the written Word of God is neglected.

In some places, revival worship has consumed people's thinking, and gardens and families have been neglected. Without wise leadership, unsustainable patterns of prayer meetings and worship services can be entered into, until eventually movements exhaust themselves. For example, spiritual pride on the part of leaders can cause problems, as can *traim spirit* (testing the spirit). For *traim spirit*, men and women are sent off into an isolated place to pray. They are told to remove all of their clothes and spend the night in prayer. If no problems arise then they really have the Holy Spirit. (According to the reports I have received the success rate of testing the spirits has not been very high!)[23]

Reflections on the Current Context

Giving leadership to the congregation in times of revival is difficult. It is much easier to look back with hindsight and analyse what occurred, and what should or should not have happened. John White, writing from a Western perspective, comments:

> The excitement of power, of visions, of touching the fringes
> of a new dimension intoxicate the unstable and the unwary.
> Judgment goes by the board. And in the absence of good
> pastoral oversight, harmful excesses follow. The mainstream
> of the revival movement corrects its errors as it goes along.
> Power for holy living becomes more important than power
> for dramatic jerking. But in the early stages, the sight of
> powerful manifestations proves seductive, and so a sort of
> lunatic fringe develops along with the mainstream. (1988:129)

Bruce Blowers, a veteran missionary to Papua New Guinea, gives some words of advice from his many years of missionary experience.

I am no longer looking for what I was looking for in 1964. Then I was looking for the fire with no wildfire, God's working with no touch of Satan's working, the genuine with no touch of the spurious, the divine outpouring with no mixture of the human element or cultural propensities.

I can see more clearly the conflict between God and Satan. That conflict extends to times of revival. Revivals can be characterised as a period or periods of open conflict between these opposing forces. The struggle becomes visible. God will win, but where God is working Satan will also work. He will seek to undermine, to discredit, to cast the fruit God is intending to produce. We must not be ignorant of his devices.

From this vantage point I can accept and rejoice in all the positive aspects of a revival movement. It allows me to be involved, to encourage some features while withholding comment on others. At the same time it places the requirement on me to "try the spirits". It gives me the freedom to reject some aspects of a movement without becoming negative to the whole movement. I have the confidence to believe that in spite of some aberrations, God is going to be the victor. (1984:10)

Although many wild things happen during these times of revival, many good things also happen. Brian Schwarz lists five lessons that can be learned by the church as a result of these revival movements.

1. That the Christian worship of the established churches is generally perceived as being dull, lifeless and powerless by many Melanesians.
2. That the established churches are generally failing to provide Christians with experiences of fellowship and community.

70

3. That healing is an important ministry in Melanesia, and that this healing must be holistic, having physical, emotional and relational dimensions.

4. That there is a need for providing the laity with opportunities for meaningful involvement in worship and for developing leadership roles for youth and women.

5. That there is a hunger for Bible Study which the mainline churches are not satisfying. (1984:272)

Nominalism

At the beginning of the twentieth century, very few of the people in Papua New Guinea had any significant contact with any Christian church. 100 years later 96 percent of the people call themselves Christians (National Statistical Office: 25). Despite, or perhaps related to, the rapid evangelism of Papua New Guinea, nominalism is a great problem. Those who were baptised as infants have often received little nurturing in their faith (Schwarz 1984:268). Joshua Daimoi, Principal of the Christian Leaders Training College, comments: "The church in PNG is rich in evangelists, but poor in discipleship" (personal communication).

Although PNG calls itself a Christian country in its Constitution, Christian values do not seem to have made a big impact on daily life for many people. The media is full of reports of corrupt politicians; crime is rife; and HIV/AIDS infections are increasing rapidly. Tribal fighting continues to flare up, with high-powered rifles having replaced bows and arrows in many places. Robbery and rape are common, in urban and rural areas. These are some of the great concerns that affect the church in Papua New Guinea at the moment.

Today the church, although greatly influenced by its European roots, is largely in the hands of national leaders.[24] There has been a rapid change from churches controlled by missionaries to churches under primarily national control. The Australian Baptist Missionary Society is withdrawing all remaining missionaries apart from a few doctors

71

from Papua New Guinea. Other mission groups such as Christian Missions in Many Lands, Assemblies of God, and Asia Pacific Christian Mission have also greatly reduced the number of their missionaries until there are at most only a few remaining in-country. In the Highlands the change from pioneer missions and illiterate villagers, to established churches with national leaders, has taken place in the space of fifty years.

In the parable of the sower, Jesus says: "But the one who received the seed that fell on good soil is the man who hears the word and understands it. He produces a crop, yielding a hundred, sixty or thirty times what was sown" (Matthew 13:23). This image is true of the church in Papua New Guinea. There are thousands of strong Christians who have a deep love for God and faith in Jesus Christ. Their faith has been translated into a daily walk with God and an unshakeable faith in him. The majority of churches in Papua New Guinea were not started by missionaries but by Melanesian pastors and evangelists. Many are started by lay people who have a limited knowledge of the Bible, but have a deep desire to share with others the relationship that they have found through faith in Christ. Papua New Guineans have gone out from PNG as missionaries and are working in countries such as Sudan with Operation Mobilisation, in Bangladesh with Youth With A Mission, and in East Timor with the Church of the Nazarene, to name just a few.

Although much of the seed has fallen on good soil, nominalism is widespread. Trompf, who has specialised in the study of Melanesian religions, says that one crucial task of the church is to assert that its flock must feel free to "think out their Christian faith in a more decidedly authentically indigenous manner" (1991:263). Schwarz agrees that a part of the answer is to have a "relevant theology. Christ must be presented in terms that are culturally meaningful and impactful. He must be shown to be God's answer to the Melanesian search" (1984:247).

72

CHAPTER THREE

THE IMPORTANCE OF CONTEXTUALISATION

Contextualisation, it appears, is suspect. A contextualised theology is needed if the church is to make a lasting impact in the lives of Papua New Guineans. Yet when I mention contextualising theology to some denominational leaders, a look of concern crosses their faces. I am apparently not alone in discovering this. One missionary writes: "The term *contextualisation* is suspect among a number of classical theological scholars for there is always a danger of compromising biblical norms. The concern is valid" (Read 2000:36). The concern is that contextualisation will lead to syncretism.

"One of the greatest hindrances to contextualisation is the fear of syncretism", Schwarz comments (1985:111). *The Evangelical Dictionary of Theology* defines syncretism as:

> The process by which elements of one religion are assimilated into another religion resulting in a change in the fundamental tenets or nature of those two religions ... Syncretism of the Christian gospel occurs when critical or basic elements of the gospel are replaced by religious elements from the host culture. (Imbach 1986:1062)

The above entry lists three ways in which syncretism may come about. "The sender may introduce syncretistic elements in a [1] conscious attempt for relevance, or [2] by the presentation of a limited or distorted part of the message. It may [3] happen unconsciously as the result of an inadequate or faulty grasp of the message" (Imbach 1986:1062). Contextualisation done poorly may lead to syncretism, but failing to contextualise will without doubt lead to "an inadequate or faulty grasp of the message" and almost

73

certainly guarantee a syncretistic result. As Bruce Nicholls warns, we must not be "so fearful of syncretism that we fail to attempt the task of contextualisation" (1995:33). Let us therefore clarify what we mean by theology, why an understanding of culture is so important to theologians, and the relationship between contextualisation and syncretism.

The Contextual Nature of Theology

Classical theology has most often been understood as a "kind of objective science of faith" which originated in the university or seminary and was expressed in classroom lectures or some scholarly article (Bevans 1992:1,12). According to Stephen Bevans, this study of faith was based around two primary sources, Scripture, and the tradition of the church. Since God is unchanging then it was logically assumed that theology would likewise be unchanging and therefore unaffected by both history and culture. Scientific knowledge was seen as objective, proven, and true in an ultimate sense. The same qualities were attributed to theology. For example, the theologian A. H. Strong said, "Theology is the science of God and relations between God and the universe" (qtd. in Wiley 1943:15). As Hiebert says, it was thought that "[c]arefully crafted, theology could be totally objective and absolutely true. In the light of this other religions were seen as highly subjective and totally false ... The task of missionaries was to transmit his or her theology into new cultures unchanged" (Hiebert 1987:105).

For many church leaders, theology is not just an academic discipline or theory: it expresses the uniqueness and identity of a denomination. To these leaders, theology and doctrine are sacred. They are to be promoted, preserved and protected, but not to be altered or changed. The thought of contextualising implies change, alteration, and the fear that in the process truth will be diluted. There is also the fear that the unity of the denomination will be undermined. It is not surprising then that contextualising theology is looked on with some suspicion. Critics believe that whilst translation is needed, and some

74

adaptation to make it more readily understood in the receptor culture, work on theology should go no further than that. Church leaders feel that the role of the mission Bible college is to *teach* theology, not to *create* theology. The truths and doctrines of the church are established. Therefore, the great need is to help the students to learn them and then go out and preach them. It appears that churches of all theological persuasions have this perspective. Gerald Arbuckle, a Catholic anthropologist, describes a commonly held viewpoint: "The function of the seminary is not to educate a candidate to think, but rather to absorb the unchanging truths of the Church" (1985:185).

Although this approach is taken with the best of intentions, it has failed time and again to produce strong churches. Instead it has produced small churches, still reliant on missionary help and overseas money, with very little outreach, because the church and its message appear foreign to the people around them. Whiteman warns, "When we fail to contextualise, we run a much greater risk of establishing weak churches, whose members will turn to non-Christian syncretistic explanations, follow non-biblical lifestyles and engage in magical rituals. This is because a non contextualised Christianity seldom engages people at the level of their deepest needs and aspirations" (1997:5).

No theological statement or creed is culture-free. The educational, social, racial and economic background of the people involved influence all theology. It is important that we openly acknowledge the cultural influence in all theology. This is not a negative thing: God's truth is conveyed through human languages, which are a part of culture, and so it is impossible to communicate without using culture. It is important that the truth of God's Word relate to people, and to the problems and needs of their life. Although God is absolute and unchanging, our theology or understanding of God will never be absolute, and will continue to change.

"True theology is an attempt on the part of the church to explain and interpret the meaning of the gospel for its own life and to answer questions raised by the Christian faith, using the thought, values and categories of truth which are authentic to that place and time" (Gilliland 1989:10-11). This statement represents a major shift from seeing theology as an objective reality, to seeing its interpretation as contextual. "The time is past when we can speak of one right unchanging theology ... We can only speak about a theology that makes sense at a certain place and at a certain time" (Bevans 1992:2). Although God is unchanging, people's experience of God and consequently their understanding of God will vary considerably.

Theologians and church leaders of a wide variety of theological persuasions have argued for the need of contextualisation. Pope Paul VI emphasised the importance of contextualisation when he said,

> Evangelisation loses much of its effectiveness if it does not take into consideration the actual people to whom it is addressed, if it does not use their language, their signs and symbols, if it does not answer the questions they ask and if it does not have an impact on their concrete life. (Qtd. in Healey and Sybertz 1996:77)

Paul Hiebert, missionary anthropologist, writes:

> There is an offense in the foreignness of the culture we bring along with the gospel, which must be eliminated. But there is the offense of the gospel itself, which we dare not weaken. The gospel must be contextualised, but it must remain prophetic - standing in judgment on what is evil in all cultures as well as in all persons. (1987:109)

"Theology ... is the way religion makes sense within a particular culture" (Bevans 1992:7). It is both our own personal understanding and the way we explain it to others. Consequently, if truly dynamic and valid, theology will necessarily be culturally conditioned by both the questions it raises and answers, and the methodology and terminology it uses.

The Importance of Culture

Culture has been defined as: "an integrated system of beliefs ... of values ... of customs ... and of institutions which express these beliefs, values and customs ... which binds a society together and gives it a sense of identity, dignity, security, and continuity" (Lausanne 1978:7). God is the creator and God has made us in his image. He has given us distinctive human capabilities that are rational, moral, social, creative and spiritual. God told people to have children, to fill the earth and subdue it (Genesis 1:26-28). Human culture has its origin in these God-given commands and faculties. Unfortunately, we are fallen. Much of human culture is not beautiful but seems ugly, cruel and selfish, showing that human lives and human cultures have become tainted and blighted by sin. The fact remains that the ability to create culture is God's gift to us and it should be used for the good of others and for the glory and praise of God.

Some people expect that when people in another culture become Christians they will live and act just like Western Christians do. They see Christianity and Western civilisation as partners. No importance is given to the study of old or tribal cultures, for it is presumed that they will soon disappear. Does Christianity lead to the multitude of cultures being absorbed into one "Christian culture", or should it lead to cultures being renewed and transformed so that they reflect more of the glory of God? We will look at a number of stories taken from the Bible that show us God's attitude to culture.

Abraham

God makes a promise to Abraham in which he says: "I will make you into a great nation and I will bless you ... and *all peoples* on earth will be blessed through you" (Genesis 12:2-3). The term "peoples" refers to groups of people, such as tribal or language

77

groups. God says that as a result of blessing Abraham, these other groups will also be blessed. In the Old Testament, the term "blessing" carries the concept of God's favour being demonstrated in increased strength, health, fertility and well-being (Deuteronomy 28:1-13). God does not say that Abraham will become a great nation and all other nations will become lesser and be absorbed into one group. God's aim is not the destruction or elimination of cultural groups, but the blessing of cultures. This promise made to Abraham finds its fulfilment in Jesus the Messiah, and so we can say that the coming of the Messiah is to result in cultural groups being blessed. We should not restrict this to a spiritual blessing, for this promise referred to all of life.

Old Testament Vision of Multicultural Worship

The psalmist looks forward to the day when all peoples and even all the earth will worship the Lord in the splendour of his holiness (Psalms 96:3-9). As Solomon dedicates the temple at Jerusalem, he prays that foreigners will come to the temple and pray and that their prayers will be heard, "so that *all the peoples of the earth* may know your name and fear you" (2 Chronicles 6:33; 1 Kings 8:60; emphasis added).

Daniel has a vision of "all peoples, nations and men of every language" gathered together worshipping one, like the "Son of Man" (Daniel 7:14).

Jesus Ministered to People of Different Cultures

Jesus praises the faith of the Roman centurion (Luke 7:9), and the faith of the Syrophonecian woman (Mark 7:24-30). He makes a Samaritan the hero in one of his parables (Luke 10) and enjoys the hospitality of a Samaritan village for a number of days (John 4). Jesus associates with the marginalised people of his day, like the tax collectors. When he dies, the sign placed over his head is in three languages – showing there is room at the cross for all cultures.

78

Jesus' commission to the disciples is to take the gospel and make disciples of "all nations" (Matthew 28:19), "all the world" (Mark 16:15), "to all nations" (Luke 24:47) and "to the ends of the earth" (Acts 1:8).

Cross-Cultural Ministry in Acts

On the day of Pentecost the gift of languages reminds the disciples of their commission to go to all the peoples of the earth. It shows God's acceptance of the variety of cultural groups, as they declare: "We hear them declaring the wonders of God in our own tongues" (Acts 2:11). Peter explains the meaning of this at the house of Cornelius when he says, "I now realise how true it is that God does not show favouritism but accepts men from every nation who fear him and do what is right" (Acts 10:34-35).

Multicultural Worship Around the Throne

In the book of Revelation, there is a series of visions of the "big picture" that has been in the mind and heart of God all the time. The first scene shows the heavenly order of twenty-four elders and four living creatures praising the holiness of God and laying their crowns before them (Revelation 4:11). They are joined by millions of angels who encircle the throne and join in the song, "Worthy is the Lamb, who was slain, to receive power and wealth and wisdom and strength and honour and glory and praise!" (Revelation 5:12).

They in turn are joined by "every creature in heaven and on earth and under the earth and on the sea ... singing: 'To him who sits on the throne and to the Lamb be praise and honour and glory and power, for ever and ever!'" (Revelation 5:13). All of creation – both visible and invisible, the spirit world, animals, birds, insects, and fish – is praising the Lord. Finally we come to the climax as "a great multitude that no one could count, from every nation, tribe, people and language, standing before the throne and in front of the Lamb" (Revelation 7:9).

It is significant that it is not just a homogeneous group of redeemed individuals who appear before the throne, but that people come before the throne in cultural groups. Each of these terms, "nation, tribe, people and language", are cultural terms. These biblical stories show culture extending into eternity. They depict God as a creative God who delights in diversity. The physical, plant and underwater worlds, and the whole starry universe, are eloquent witnesses to God's love of diversity. God's desire is not to do away with cultural distinctions but to see cultures purified of all that is evil and self-centred, and to see those cultures brought into submission to Jesus Christ.[25]

This biblical understanding of culture is very important to our understanding of contextualisation. "The view we get of the kingdom is a multicultural view, not one of ethnic uniformity" (Whiteman 1997:4). Once we see that God enjoys and delights in cultural diversity, it can take away a lot of fear and hesitancy around contextualisation.

Common Misunderstandings Concerning Contextualisation

A person's world-view influences the way he or she understands God, but the question remains: "Won't contextualisation lead to syncretism?" For it is readily agreed even by those most strongly in favour of contextualisation that it potentially "compromises and betrays Christianity" (Bevans 1992:17).

Hesselgrave sees orthodox theology, contextualisation, and syncretism as points on a continuum with a strong emphasis on "[s]upracultural divine elements in biblical revelation" at one end, and on the "cultural human elements in biblical revelation" at the other (Hesselgrave and Rommen 1989:153). This view of contextualisation inevitably leads to a common question: "Where do we draw the line between contextualisation and syncretism?" There is a fear that if a person goes too far in contextualising, s/he will quickly end up on the slippery slopes that lead into syncretism.

Syncretism and contextualised Christianity are complex issues. Darrell Whiteman has drawn a diagram (Table 1) that is helpful in understanding the difference between these two, especially as it relates to form, meaning and rituals in the church.

Table 1. Relationship Between Form and Meaning

	Form	
	Indigenous	Foreign
Pagan **Meaning**	Indigenous Form + Pagan Meaning = **Traditional religion**	Foreign Form + Pagan Meaning = **Syncretism**
Christian	Indigenous Form + Christian Meaning = **Indigenous Christianity**	Foreign Form + Christian Meaning = **Foreign Christianity**

Traditional meaning and traditional form is *traditional religion*. Traditional meaning and Christian form is *syncretism*. Christian meaning with traditional form is *contextualised Christianity*. Christian meaning and Western Christian form is *foreign Christianity* in any culture other than a Western culture.

If we combine consulting the spirits of the dead through a medium with Christian songs and prayers, the result is syncretism. On the other hand, using traditional music and instruments to glorify God is indigenous Christianity for the form is traditional but the meaning is Christian.

Yet the relationship between theology and syncretism is more complex than that of a straight line continuum. The question, "Where do we draw the line between contextualisation and syncretism?" is misleading. The right question is, "How do we keep our balance?" For the failure to contextualise will likely lead to syncretism, just as easily as a careless lack of discernment and acceptance of all sorts of traditional religious attitudes and practices.

If people do not contextualise the gospel, and traditional beliefs are merely denounced as "superstitions" (such as the beliefs in the spirit world that Christian Keysser denounced), then traditional beliefs often go underground and people continue to practice them in secret. It is possible to go in two opposite directions, and still end up in syncretism. Promoting a non-contextualised Western form of Christianity will lead to syncretism just as definitely as an uncritical acceptance of folk religious beliefs and practices will lead to syncretism. When the gospel is not contextualised, old beliefs and customs do not die out. Because they are not consciously dealt with, they can become part of the Christian's "hidden culture". This leads to a form of syncretism that Jaimie Bulatao has called "split-level Christianity", which is an uneasy coexistence of "two or more thought and behaviour systems which are inconsistent with each other" (1966:2). For example, Christianity is often presented as offering eternal salvation, but does not address areas of daily life involving gardens, pigs, fishing and protection from vengeful spirits. People will go to church and worship God, but they see God as unconcerned about everyday problems, and so they use charms and magic to appease spirits in order to get the help they require. In this type of situation the failure to contextualise has led to syncretism.

"Uncritical contextualisation" occurs when people develop their own theology in isolation and the "contemporary cultural contexts are taken seriously but historical contexts are largely ignored" (Hiebert 1987:108). There is much that can be learned from church history and church tradition. Uncritical contextualisation also occurs when more attention is paid to culture than to Scripture, so that the resultant theology is based more on culture than on the Word of God. When this is the case, we lose the unity of the church: there is no common foundation for faith between one culture and the next. Culture often raises questions that theology must answer, and it may well determine how that theology is expressed, but it is not the foundation of theology.

The foundation must be the Word of God, for this remains unchanging across all cultures, even though human understandings will differ from one context to another.

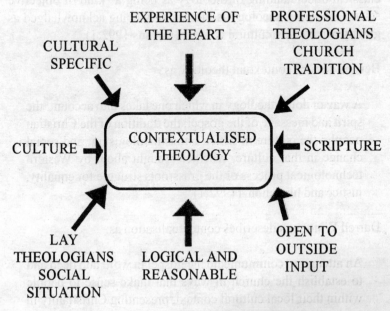

Figure 4. Keeping the Balance in Contextualisation

There are many factors that must be kept in balance as the church works in distinct cultures to develop contextualised theologies (Figure 4). We must keep in balance both cultural relevance and also fidelity to the Scriptures. We must look to the lessons of church history and at the same time look to the social needs of the present. We must listen to the questions, fears and concerns of local people and address these issues. At the same time, we must understand the Scriptures at a deep level. This is where the contribution of theologians and biblical scholars is so important. Theology should be logical and reasonable, and yet it must also be inspired and directed by the Holy Spirit so that it expresses a vital, heartfelt and experiential religion.

The Importance of Contextual Theology

Theology cannot be isolated from the cultural context of the people who formulate it, or from their intended audience. In contrast to the classical understanding of theology as being a "kind of objective science of faith", theology is increasingly being acknowledged as greatly affected by cultural context (Bevans 1992:1).

Bevans defines contextual theology as:

> A way of doing theology in which one takes into account: the spirit and message of the gospel; the tradition of the Christian people; the culture in which one is theologising; and social change in that culture, whether brought about by Western technological process or the grassroots struggle for equality, justice and liberation. (1992:1)

Darrell Whiteman describes contextualisation as:

> An attempt to communicate the gospel in word and deed and to establish the church in ways that make sense to people within their local cultural context, presenting Christianity in such a way that it meets people's deepest needs and penetrates their world-view, thus allowing them to follow Christ and remain within their own culture. (1997:2)

This description takes the process a step further to include not just theology, but the actual establishment of the church in ways that meet people's needs, with a minimum of social dislocation. This ties in with the underlying principle of contextualised theology – that Christianity is relevant to people's everyday life. Thus understood, contextualisation is a vital necessity if people are to grow and become established in their Christian lives.

Dean Gilliland gives a number of reasons why contextualisation is imperative if we want to see churches become strong and healthy (1989).

84

1. *Contextualisation Guards Against Foreign Domination of the Church*

It is possible for a church to be self-supporting, self-governing and self-propagating, but still be very much controlled by the overseas mission organisation (Smalley 1958:147). National church leaders often do not feel free to think for themselves, but instead they reinforce what they learned from pioneer missionaries. This is not always bad, but how much better if they had learned how to go to the Scriptures for themselves! Often national church leaders promote the status quo and are afraid of innovation. When questions arise they do not know how to search the Scriptures for answers, but remain silent, and old beliefs and practices continue in a secretive fashion. When this happens, the church remains weak. Contextualisation encourages Christians to think through its faith for themselves. Gilliland writes:

> It stands to reason that one who is proclaiming the gospel in
> another culture wants to hand over the experience, the full
> truth, without error, which has become his or her own. But it
> is this very spirit of domination and control which so subtly,
> so permanently keeps new Christians from discovering the
> Word of Truth in Jesus Christ for themselves in their own life
> and world. (1989:14)

Contextualisation helps a church become independent of foreign control and direction, and enables people to truly become the people of God, living out their lives under the direction of the Holy Spirit.

2. *Contextualisation Encourages People to Stand Upon the Scriptures*

Many churches founded by mission organisations have been taught beliefs but have not been taught how to go to the Scriptures to find the answers to their questions. Contextualisation encourages people in all places to go to the Word of God and, in dependance upon the

Holy Spirit, find the answers to questions and problems of their everyday lives. Where people have not been taught how to do this, nor encouraged to do this, the church remains weak and dependent on outside direction. Some people fear that contextualisation will mean that culture will take precedence over Scripture, but the model I am outlining here puts Scripture as the foundation and source of our faith.

3. Contextualisation Encourages People to Rely Upon the Holy Spirit

Jesus promised his disciples that when the Holy Spirit came he would "teach them all things" (John 14:26). Contextualisation relies heavily upon the work of the Holy Spirit in the church guiding people to a knowledge of the truth. We believe that the Holy Spirit is not given just to scholars and denominational leaders but to all of God's people - both men and women, young and old, and regardless of social class (Acts 2:17-18). The question is: Will we trust the Holy Spirit to lead and guide the church? Doing theology in a culture other than one's own involves study and a deep knowledge of God's Word, but it also requires a constant dependence upon the Holy Spirit, and the input and insight of indigenous believers, for they know the cultural issues and problems better than any missionary ever can. "Contextualisation, carefully implemented, honours the Holy Spirit and opens the way for believers to confront with confidence the questions raised in their own life situations" (Gilliland 1989:17).

4. Contextualisation Promotes the Growth of the Church

Where the gospel is not contextualised, the church has a foreignness about it that often causes people to reject the message. The foreignness can be so evident that people never understand or even hear the message. If people are to be won for Christ, then they must be approached in a way that communicates to them within their culture. Often it is not the gospel itself that people reject, but the foreignness of the gospel's presentation. The listeners feel that they must reject their culture in order to accept Christ. The missionaries and their converts can be viewed "with suspicion as cultural misfits and aliens" (Whiteman 1997:3). This is how Christianity comes to be seen as the destroyer of culture and the enemy of the people.

Contextualisation insists on taking seriously the cultural beliefs, fears, hopes, rituals and problems of people. It also challenges people, in reliance on the Holy Spirit, to search the Scriptures for answers to their needs. This results in a proclamation of the gospel that speaks directly and convincingly to people's needs. "Growth is inevitable where there is proper contextualisation" (Gilliland 1989:54).

5. *Contextualisation is Based on the Incarnation*

"The Word became flesh and made his dwelling among us" (John 1:14). When God wanted to communicate with us, he became a human - not by being born as some sort of generic human who was free from culture, for no such creature exists. Jesus became part of a specific human culture, born into a humble family in a very ordinary Galilean village. God communicates through culture; this is why contextualisation is so important. This same method of communication must be repeated again and again. Jesus must become "one of us" rather than a foreigner. Even in Papua New Guinea where Christianity has been accepted so quickly, I was surprised to find that many Bible college students thought of God as a "white man's God". They saw their culture as despised and useless. They felt that the more Western they became, the better Christians they would be. Bevans states that this is a common reaction amongst people living in countries that have been colonised (1992:6).

6. *Contextualisation Elevates People's Feelings of Self-Worth*

People need to feel that their culture is important to God, and that he has not come to destroy or pull down, so much as to renew and transform culture so that it reflects more of his love and beauty. It is true that there is evil in all cultures, but it is equally true that there is much goodness and beauty in all cultures. Culture is not merely neutral but can and must be used for the transmission of the gospel of Jesus Christ. As people learn how to think through the gospel within their own cultural setting, the church and the gospel come alive: they do not appear foreign, but become the people's own. It becomes "our faith, our church and our Saviour", as they think through the issues for themselves. Contextualisation is not concerned merely with presenting the gospel and leading people to faith in Christ, but goes beyond that, to help people live out their daily lives under the Lordship of Jesus Christ.

The Many Coloured Wisdom of God

Contextualisation is complex, and the question is not one of drawing a line between contextualisation and syncretism, but rather of keeping balance. All theology, even that which is considered "orthodox theology", is contextualised. John Hitchens argues that "we cannot choose whether or not we shall contextualise. We can only choose whether we shall do so well or poorly" (1992:30). If each group of people creates their own theology, where is the unity of the church? If we ignore the past, as we struggle to answer the questions of the present, we ignore the rich heritage of the church, and the church is weakened in the process. What guidelines do we need in order to develop a theology that helps people relate to God, and at the same time is culturally sensitive?

The *Willowbank Report* says: "The Bible proclaims the gospel story in many forms. The gospel is like a multifaceted diamond, with different aspects that appeal to different people in different cultures. It has depths we have not fathomed. It defies every attempt to reduce it to a neat formulation" (Lausanne 1978:12). Figure 5 shows the relationship between one God, and one set of Scriptures, but many cultures.

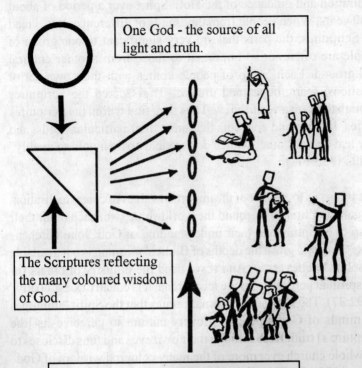

One God - the source of all light and truth.

The Scriptures reflecting the many coloured wisdom of God.

Worldviews act like lenses that make some truths very clear while causing others to be obscured.

People come with fears, questions, beliefs and practices that are conditioned by their cultural background. We "know in part" and "see but a poor reflection in a mirror" (1 Corinthians 13:12).

Figure 5. The Many Coloured Wisdom of God

There is one God, the source of all light and truth. There is one set of Holy Scriptures, written by many different authors under the inspiration and guidance of the Holy Spirit over a period of about 1500 years. When people from thousands of different cultures read the Scriptures, the parts that are very significant to one group of people are often not so important to those from another cultural background. Each group of people comes with their own set of questions, fears, hopes and dreams. They search the Scriptures through their own world-view. Thus they find within the Scriptures stories, lessons and concepts that meet their particular needs, and they leave aside "others which do not yield up their gold so readily" (Walls 1982:102).

This brings us to another of the important values of contextualisation. All gain as Christians around the world share with each other their grasp of Scripture and their understanding of God. John Hitchens says, "Power to grasp the depths of Biblical meaning is not available to isolated believers ... And if we need the ministry of others for our spiritual perception in the local arena, it is equally true globally" (1992:37). The Lausanne Covenant states that the Spirit "illumines the minds of God's people in every culture to perceive its [the Scripture's] truth fresh through their own eyes and thus discloses to the whole church ever more of the many coloured wisdom of God" (Stott 1975:10). This becomes what Whiteman calls a "form of mission in reverse", as we "learn from other cultures how to be more Christian in our own context" (1997:4). For it is not in isolation, either social or cultural, but it is "together with all the saints" that we are able "to grasp how wide and long and high and deep is the love of Christ" (Ephesians 3:17). As people from one culture share their understanding of God with people from other cultures, everyone is enriched as people see God and his salvation in a richer and fuller manner.

Who Produces Contextualised Theologies?

Contextualised theology takes very seriously the cultural context of the participants. Schreiter prefers the term "local theology" because it is produced in response to the questions, hopes and fears of the local congregations (1985:16). Mbiti describes this type of theologising as "informal, quiet, unwritten, unpolished theology, but nevertheless theology in its own way, and a theology which must be allowed a place in the church universal" (1976:15).

If this is the case, then what is the role of the trained theologian and biblical scholar? Are they no longer needed? In contrast, they remain very much needed, for they are also a part of that believing community. Bevans states: "The role of the trained theologian (the minister, the theology teacher) is that of articulating more clearly what the people are more generally or vaguely expressing" (1992:13). The theologian, biblical scholar and church historian then become parts of the process by providing people with a broader and deeper understanding of church history, the meaning of the Scriptures and theological thought.

Lay people and village pastors raise socio-cultural questions of their day to day life. As people listen to each other and interact, the church is able to synthesise a truly contextual theology. Out of this dialogue and interaction will come a theology that speaks to people's heartfelt needs while maintaining orthodoxy and proper scriptural interpretation. If there is no dialogue between the different theologies then the gap between the official theology (often imported from overseas) and the popular grass roots theology is very great. Cultural questions are not answered by the imported theology and so people look elsewhere for answers.

The issue of contextualisation is very important, for Christianity is not a "white man's religion". The majority of Christians today live south of the equator. However, theology continues to be the domain of American and European seminaries and universities. Mbiti said more than twenty years ago, "Christianity has exploded in Africa and theology too must explode" (1976:15). But what does an Asian or African or Melanesian theology look like? Is it a Western theology in "ethnic" clothing? Must it be expressed in abstract technical terms, or may it be expressed in such a way that Melanesians can sing, dance and dramatise their theology?

To these questions Taber replies: "What is needed now is for Africans and Asians to start afresh, beginning with the direct interaction of the cultures with the Scriptures ... and to restate the Christian faith in response to Asian/African questions, with Asian/African methodologies and terminologies" (1978a:10). Mbiti says that Western theology is "largely ignorant of, and embarrassingly impotent in the face of, human questions in the churches of Africa, Latin America, parts of Asia and the South Pacific" (1976:8). There is a need for a Melanesian theology that seeks to answer the questions of Melanesian Christians.

The Need for a Melanesian Theology in PNG

Christianity has been in parts of Melanesia for more than a hundred years. In the Highlands of Papua New Guinea it came much later, and has a history of fifty years or less. Regardless of when it came, it arrived with Western colonisation, and that association has had a profound effect on how Christianity has been perceived in the area. Bernard Narokobi, a Sepik man and former politician, describes the impact of that experience very graphically. PNG "has been invaded by a huge tidal wave from the West in the form of colonisation and Christianisation. Like any tidal wave, the West came mercilessly, with all the force and power, toppling over our earth, destroying its treasures, depositing some rich soil, but also leaving behind much rubbish" (1983:8). Narokobi concedes that it has brought some good but also much rubbish. How are these to be sorted out?

Part of the problem is that Christianity was equated with the ways of the white settlers, be they missionaries, plantation managers, government patrol officers or gold miners. Polonhau Pokawin writes, "To be a Christian, Papua New Guineans must forgo much of their culture and adopt a new one - the Christian way - which has been virtually identified with the new laws and values brought by the whites" (1987:25). Pokawin is concerned that Papua New Guineans have uncritically accepted "Christianity in its Western garb", and this has resulted in much superficiality, for the practices and rituals are imported and do not reflect the local customs or culture of Melanesia (Pokawin 1987:26). Papua New Guineans often describe people whom they feel are superficial as being "skin Christians", referring to the fact that although many have been baptised, only surface level behaviour has changed: there has been little transformation in their personal lives, and in the life of the community. Often those who are truly committed to Christianity feel they need to follow a very Western form of Christianity, with the consequent rejection of most of their traditional culture. Narokobi is likewise concerned that there has been "little or no attempt to differentiate Christ's teaching pure and simple, and the customs of foreign missionaries" (1977:11). This then becomes one of the big issues for Christianity in Melanesia today. What should Melanesian Christianity look like?

Trompf reminds us that in the first few centuries of the church's history, the church had no political or material strength: it was a persecuted minority (1991:262). It did not come as a tidal wave and it did not replace cultures. The church could best be described by the metaphors that Jesus uses: as salt, light, yeast or a plant that grows from a mustard seed (Matthew 5:13,16; 13:31,33). In the proclamation of the early church, they were not trying to replace one culture with another but to show how Christ was the fulfilment of pre-existing traditions. When Jesus speaks to Nicodemus he refers to Hebrew history and relates himself to the lifting up of the snake in the wilderness. John however, in writing to a different audience, describes Jesus by using the Greek concept of the Logos. Trompf writes, "Paul's epistles ... cannot be fully understood unless we learn ... what the beliefs and world-views of the recipients were like" (1991:263). The meeting in Jerusalem reported in Acts 15 is not just about the matter of circumcision. The bigger issue is whether or not the Gentile converts had to become followers of Jewish customs and religious practices in order to be accepted as believers

93

in Christ. The conclusion is that they do not have to follow Jewish cultural practices.

Unfortunately, this message has not come across very clearly in Papua New Guinea, for missionaries came with the support of colonial governments and their tremendous material and military might. The highly technological culture of Western people, missionaries included, clashed strikingly with the isolated survivalist cultures of Melanesia, and made many feel very inferior. Even though some foreigners came with good intentions and with hearts full of love, they were still people of their time. It was difficult for them not to be paternalistic and condescending, for "modern" historical thought at the time placed its civilisation as the epitome of a gradual evolution of cultures. The result of this is described well by Trompf: "The indigenous people have found it very difficult not to feel inferior before the whites and their new ideas, and have not found it easy to sense the free responsibility of developing Christianity in their own terms, without slavish dependence on white 'apparently superior' models." Trompf concludes that one of the crucial tasks of Melanesian theology is to make people aware that they now have the responsibility and the freedom to think through their Christian faith in a "decidedly authentically indigenous manner" (1991:263).

This was the philosophy of the Apostle Paul. He does not see the recipients of the message changing to his way of doing things; rather, he sees himself adapting to their way of thinking in order to bring them to Christ.

> To the Jews I became like a Jew, to win the Jews. To those under the law I became like one under the law (though I myself am not under the law), so as to win those under the law. To those not having the law I became like one not having the law (though I am not free from God's law but am under Christ's law), so as to win those not having the law. To the weak I became weak, to win the weak. I have become all

things to all men so that by all possible means I might save some. (1 Corinthians 9:20-22)

Contextualisation and the Use of Media

When the term "theology" is mentioned, people often think of thick volumes filled with abstract language and profound philosophical ideas. For many people it is a negative image. But Christianity is not just a system of beliefs; religion is a way of life, a system of symbols rather than a system of ideas.

Zahniser writes: "religions use symbols, stories and ceremonies to produce moods and motivations in believers that will keep life in harmony with faith" (1997:63). The building blocks of religion are not books or words, but symbols, stories and ceremonies. In contextualising theology, it would seem logical to give more attention to contextualising these elements, because this is how faith is primarily expressed.

In the Old Testament, people's theology is expressed in poetry, narratives of the actions of God in the lives of their ancestors, feasts and pilgrimages. The only real creeds are the Ten Commandments and the Shema, "Hear O Israel: The Lord our God, the Lord is one" (Deuteronomy 6:4). Faith is not expressed in carefully worded definitions, but through the narratives of the patriarchs and the exodus event. It is celebrated with processions, festivals, special meals, pilgrimages, temples and holy places; a priesthood with ceremonies, sacred clothes, sacrifices, altars and incense. In the enactment of these various rituals the narratives of the ancestors are re-lived and re-experienced. Traditional Melanesian culture is very similar to this.

Western Christianity, in contrast, is very cognitive and analytical. If theology is contextualised for Melanesia, it is important that we do not contextualise just words and propositional statements of faith. Schreiter says, "Theology as 'sure knowledge' looms so large in the

95

West, and is so often held up as the theological ideal elsewhere, that it is hard to think of it as being one form of theology alongside others" (1985:89). The truths of the gospel must be expressed through song, ritual, ceremony and symbols that are meaningful to people of Melanesian society. Melanesians need to feel free to innovate and experiment in contextualising Christianity through culturally relevant symbols and ceremonies.

However, in order for theology to be contextualised, we need to do more than rewrite the core beliefs of a particular denomination into a different language with a few culturally relevant or appropriate illustrations. The gospel must be expressed as the divine drama of redemption. The Bible must be seen as a book with an introduction, a long story with numerous interwoven themes and sub-themes and a thrilling conclusion. The creation, exodus and exile lead to the incarnation of Jesus. The cross, which appears to be a tragedy, becomes a triumph as Jesus is vindicated through the resurrection, and the story spreads as the church under the power of the Holy Spirit explodes across the Mediterranean world. This drama culminates with a vision of a cosmic celebration, as redeemed and reconciled people gather around the throne of God and live in perfect harmony with God on a new earth.

The gospel needs to be acted out and celebrated with drama, songs and a variety of rituals and ceremonies, including fellowship meals. We need to look for more rituals and celebrations other than just baptism and communion. We need to see which traditional rituals and ceremonies can be given new meaning and incorporated into the life and worship of the church. It is not enough that people in Melanesia believe the gospel: it must permeate their world-view, so that their daily lives and worship become a celebration of abundant life.

The message must also be expressed through art, using visual aids to prompt the oral recitation of stories. Writing out of their experience in Africa, Earle and Dorothy Bowen advise: "Use numerous visual aids - pictures, charts, posters, models - not only to boost learning, but to ensure that any learning takes place at all" (1989:274). The same applies to Papua New Guinea, for as Taber states, "Theology must always remember its true vocation, to serve the people of God; and it cannot serve its purpose unless it is intelligible to them" (1978a:67).

Contextualisation as an Extension of the Incarnation

One biblical truth that all Christians rejoice in is the Incarnation - that God became one of us. He did not remain aloof or distant but "the Word became a human being and lived here with us" (John 1:14 CEV). That which was eternal took on the confines of time and space limitations. As the apostle John says, "Our ears have heard, our own eyes have seen, and our hands have touched this Word" (1 John 1:1 CEV). This truth has important implications for contextualisation. When Jesus enters human history, he enters human culture. He comes into a Jewish family in Galilee. He is circumcised as required by Jewish culture and he follows Jewish customs and dietary laws. He is not an observer looking in from the outside, but is a real part of a real cultural setting.

Byang Kato explains that: "The New Testament itself has given us the pattern for cultural adaptations. The incarnation is a form of contextualisation. The Son of God condescended to pitch his tent among us to make it possible for us to be redeemed ... This in turn should motivate us to make the gospel relevant in every situation everywhere as long as the gospel is not compromised" (qtd. in Gaquare 1977:148). Just as Jesus becomes incarnate within Jewish culture, the gospel of Jesus Christ must also become incarnate within Melanesian cultures. Jesus disagrees with various aspects of Jewish belief and culture and for this he becomes a threat to Jewish leaders. At the same time he also says, "Do not think that I have come to abolish the Law or the Prophets; I have not come to abolish them but to fulfil them" (Matthew 5:17). Reflecting on this verse, Narokobi writes: "I have no doubt that had He been born in Melanesia, He

97

would have come to make more perfect the Melanesian religious experience" (1977:11).

Joe Gaquare, of the Solomon Islands, argues that the church must become incarnate within Melanesian cultures and at the same time bring about necessary reformation. Melanesian cultures should not be despised and dismissed as being evil and satanic, but appreciated for the good elements as God's gifts; people should work through these good aspects in order to reach the hearts of Melanesians with the gospel of Jesus Christ. He goes on to say, "The church at present needs to empty itself of all the unnecessary elements of Western heritage and pitch her tent in Melanesia. It needs to adapt itself to the cultural life of Melanesians, speak their languages and listen to their particular needs" (1977:148).

The call is not just for dressing up Western Christianity, "with *tapa* clothes, grass skirts, and *malo* and supplying it with spears, bows and arrows." Pokawin says we need something more radical that "will either develop something essentially in tune with prevailing Christian theologies, but distinctly Melanesian, or else something quite different from existing theologies but meaningful to our people" (1987:31). There is a danger in Pokawin's statement if we are not careful: in the search for something that is distinctly Melanesian, we must not leave aside either the authority of Scripture or the centrality of Christ.

Tuwere Sevati, from Fiji, also expresses concern for a relevant theology when he writes: "Carbon copy theologies from abroad still hang around our theological curriculum. They are simply rearranged here and there, all too artificially, to suit the current situation" (Tuwere 1987:149). Something more is required. If Christ is not to be perceived as being foreign, then the logical conclusion is that he needs to be seen as Melanesian. Can Christ be seen as the ideal Melanesian - the perfect man who completely meets all the ideals of Melanesian society?

98

CHAPTER FOUR

A MODEL FOR CONTEXTUALISING
THEOLOGY FOR MELANESIA

There is widespread agreement among missiologists today that theology needs to be contextualised; there is little agreement, however, about how the contextualising should be done. Are we to focus on the gospel message or on the cultural context?

Bevans argues that the key elements in contextualisation are: gospel, tradition, culture and social change. He outlines five main models of contextualisation in his book, *Models of Contextual Theology*. The following diagram (Figure 6) shows the various models in relation to each other.

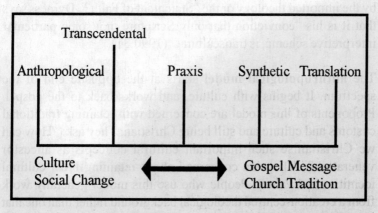

Figure 6. Bevans' Models Of Contextualised Theology (1992:27)

The **translation model** is concerned with transferring the gospel message as understood by the missionary and the sending church, into the language and thought forms of the people so that it makes sense to them. It is concerned with effective communication and seeks to preserve the content of the gospel and the church tradition.

Generally, evangelicals have taken the translation model approach. Culture is seen as very important, but the focus is on communicating the gospel as quickly and as effectively as possible to people within that culture. One of the key presuppositions of this model is that there is a central gospel core that is supra-cultural. There is no real agreement, however, as to what that core may be.

Papua New Guineans responded quickly and openly to Christianity, and often missionaries were overwhelmed with the initial response. The early emphasis was on translating Scripture, but that is a major long-term process, so missionaries tended to rely on a few Old Testament stories and some details of the life of Christ. The "Statement of Faith" or a basic catechism of that particular denomination was translated into the local language, and taught to the new converts. Most missions have continued in the same direction, usually by either translating or simplifying Western books or notes for use in Bible colleges. Is this the only approach to use? What do we do about the cultural questions that are not addressed by the imported theology or the "Statement of Faith?" Dyrness says that it is his "conviction that only Scripture, not some particular interpretive schema, is transcultural" (1990:31).

The **anthropological model** starts at the opposite end of the spectrum. It begins with culture, and works back to the gospel. Proponents of this model are concerned with retaining traditional customs and culture and still being Christian. They ask: "How can we Christianise such important cultural concepts as ancestor veneration?" They are concerned about retaining local cultural identities and values. People who use this model generally work from a creation-centred theological background rather than one that is redemption-centred. As Bevans explains, a redemption centred theology is: "characterised by the conviction that culture and human experience are either in need of a radical transformation or in need of total replacement." A creation-centred approach to theology works on the assumption that "culture and human experience are generally good" (1992:16). In this approach, "human experience, current events

100

and culture would be areas of God's activity and therefore sources of theology" (1992:17).

Ennio Mantovani has taken this approach. He calls it "celebrations of cosmic renewal", for "Melanesian religions in general could be defined as [having] 'An ultimate concern with *life*'" (1984b:29). He draws largely upon the *dema* myth, according to which "a being (human or animal) is killed violently and buried (or eaten). Out of his/her/its grave comes the item of culture which stands for life" (1984c:74). The strength of this approach is that it has a very positive view of culture and it starts where people are, with their real problems and questions. However, if people are not careful they can have an overly romantic view of culture, and not look closely enough at the evil in culture that must be addressed and dealt with.

A third approach is the **praxis model**, which focuses on the cultural changes going on within society. Its attention is not on knowledge about faith, but on commitment to positive action to bring about change in society. People who use this model emphasise the concepts of liberation and transformation. They seek to bring about change in society based on action with reflection. Sin is seen as a social problem that is closely related to social structures, rather than the concept of sin as personal evil.

The **transcendental model** emphasises individual human experience. God reveals himself "within human experience, as a human person is open to the words of Scripture as read or proclaimed, open to events in daily life, and open to events embodied in a cultural tradition" (Bevans 1997:99). Theology takes place as a person wrestles with his or her faith and then shares that faith with others within the same cultural context.

Midway between the approaches of translation and anthropology, is the approach which Bevans calls the **synthetic model** (Figure 7). In this model the four elements of gospel, culture, tradition and culture change are held in creative tension: culture and the gospel are

101

balanced with each other, and church tradition is balanced with the concerns of the local situation. Bevans describes the synthetic model as a "middle-of-the-road model":

> It takes pains to keep the integrity of the traditional message, while acknowledging the importance of taking culture and social change seriously ... It tries to preserve the importance of the gospel message and the heritage of the traditional doctrinal formulations, while at the same time acknowledging the vital role that culture has played and can play in theology even to the setting of the theological agenda. (1992:81,82)

The synthetic view sees culture as being a mixture of good and evil. Some of the culture is good and must be retained, some is evil and must be replaced; much is neutral and must be preserved and enriched.

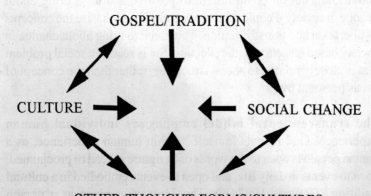

Figure 7. The Synthetic Model (Bevans 1992:86)

The synthetic model looks at the social situation and changes occurring there; according to this model the church must respond to social issues. It also looks to other cultures and other theological expressions to see what contributions they can make to the church.

102

This means that there is an ongoing dialogue taking place among all these different factors.

Dialogue is an essential feature of the synthetic model. This dialogue takes place between lay people, who bring the questions, concerns and fears of the local situation, and pastors, teachers and theologians who can bring biblical and church knowledge. In the Melanesian context, this means that issues such as ancestors and the spirits of the dead must be addressed, along with the whole spirit world. Another cultural question is the issue of spiritual power and the manifestation of spiritual power in revival.

Developing a Visual Model

Much of what is written about contextualisation is written with technical language in theological journals and textbooks. Taber suggests that much theology is doubly alien: "alien because it is Western in mode and form, and it is alien because it is highly technical and complex" (1978b:65). Theology is to serve the people of God and help them come to a greater understanding of God's goodness, love and salvation. Therefore, in dealing with the issue of contextualisation I have sought to develop a visual model that is easily comprehensible to lay people as well as to trained pastors.

The Wesleyan Quadrilateral

What are the essential features for effective contextualisation to take place? How can their relationship with each other be visualised? These questions led me to think about a simple model that has become known as "the Wesleyan quadrilateral" (Outler 1985:9). "Contextual theology" was not a term that was in use in John Wesley's day, but Wesley was very concerned with practical Christianity. He did not write a systematic theology as such, but he wrote a lot of theology in his sermons and letters. As Thorsen writes, Wesley focused "on issues having a more immediate and holistic impact on the life of faith in his day" (1990:63). It is obvious that real life situations of people were extremely important to Wesley, and so it is quite appropriate to speak of Wesley as doing contextualised theology.

Albert Outler points out that Wesley, in addition to the Anglican triad of Scripture, tradition and reason, adds a fourth factor - experience - when formulating his theology. Outler coined the phrase "the Wesleyan Quadrilateral" to describe this distinctive innovation. He writes: "We can see in Wesley a distinctive theological method, with Scripture as its preeminent norm but interfaced with tradition, reason and Christian experience as dynamic and interactive aids in the interpretation of the Word of God in Scripture" (Outler 1985:9).

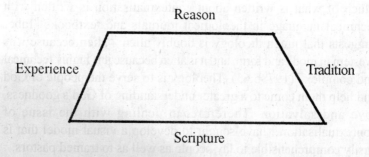

Figure 8. The Wesleyan Quadrilateral

Thorsen likens this method to a baseball diamond. Home plate is Scripture. First base is tradition. Second base is reason and third base is experience. "Presumably one must begin theological reflection with home plate - Scripture. But to 'score a run' one must cross the bases of tradition, reason, and experience before completing the return to Scripture - the start and finish of theological reflection" (Thorsen 1990:72).

Wesley saw Scripture as the basis and foundation of all true Christian belief. He said: "I lay this down as an undoubted truth: The more the doctrine of any church agrees with the Scripture, the more

104

readily it ought to be received. And, on the other hand, the more the doctrine of any church differs from Scripture, the greater cause we have to doubt it" (Jackson 1980: vol 10:33).

He placed great emphasis on "the early ecumenical creeds and the patristic writings of the Western and Eastern churches ... He believed that classical orthodoxy was the second most important source of Christian truth" (Thorsen 1990:239). He also drew from other sources besides the early church fathers. Wesley published a Christian library for the use of his pastors which included the work of writers from Christian antiquity, as well as extracts from Puritans, Baptists, Quakers, and Roman Catholics (Thorsen 1990:159).

Wesley wrote: "It is a fundamental principle with us that to renounce reason is to renounce religion, that religion and reason go hand in hand, and that all irrational religion is false religion" (Telford 1931: vol 5:364). He saw reason as a gift from God that we are to use for God's glory. He did not see faith as opposed to reason, but sought to lead people to a reasonable faith.

Wesley's greatest contribution was including personal experience as a valid way of knowing God and an important aspect of our theologising. Thorsen argues that Wesley was: "the first to incorporate *explicitly* into his theological world-view the experiential dimension of the Christian faith along with the conceptual" (1990:201 emphasis added). This is no doubt due in part to his own spiritual pilgrimage, including an event at Aldersgate Street. As he describes it in his journal: "I felt my heart strangely warmed. I felt I did trust in Christ, Christ alone for salvation: and an assurance was given me, that he had taken away my sins, even mine and saved me from the law of sin and death" (Curnock 1938: vol 1:475). Since this was so significant in Wesley's life, he made it a habit of interviewing people and learning about their personal Christian experience. He reflected that: "Christians cannot be satisfied with anything less than a direct testimony from his [God's] Spirit, that he is merciful to their

105

unrighteousness, and remembers their sins and iniquities no more" (Wesley qtd. in Thorsen 1990:219).

Let us take a look at Bevans' synthetic model for contextualised theology and Wesley's synthetic model and see if it is possible to combine them.

Bevans	Wesley
Gospel	Scripture
Tradition	Tradition
Culture	Reason
Social Change	Experience

Figure 9. Bevans' and Wesley's Models Compared

There are a number of similarities between the two models, especially in relation to gospel and tradition in Bevans' model, and Scripture and tradition in Wesley's. Wesley does not have a category for "culture", which was a term that was not common usage in his day. He was also working in what was a largely monocultural situation, though there were distinct class differences that he acknowledged: he stated that his intent was to speak "plain truth for plain people" (Wesley 1978: vol 5:2). He contextualised his evangelistic methods with such unorthodox practices as outdoor preaching, singing hymns to popular tunes, and appointing lay preachers, including some women.

He was also very aware of the social problems of his time and developed methods to address them. He provided basic medical care and wrote a simple medical manual to help those who could not afford professional care. He provided social services for widows and orphans. He started schools and produced all sorts of books to meet the needs of his constituents. He was aware of economic

106

problems and set up a loan fund for people with immediate financial needs. This religious and economic radicalism of Wesley laid the groundwork for later political involvement for Methodists, and he was a strong supporter of the abolition of slavery (Thorsen 1990:94,95). Because of this practical involvement, I do not feel that we are doing any injustice to expand Wesley's quadrilateral to include a fifth aspect of culture and social change. By combining Bevans' model and the Wesleyan quadrilateral, we end up with a fifth component of culture.[26]

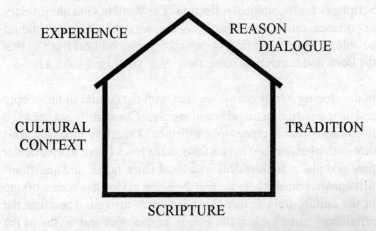

Figure 10. House Model for Contextualising Theology

It is not by accident that this diagram looks like a house. The image of a house conveys the idea of a theology that is constructed by the people, essential for life and providing stability, protection and security.

Scripture becomes the foundation and the base on which everything stands. Jesus says the person who listens and obeys his words is like a person who builds his house on a solid foundation (Matthew 7:24-27). Paul likewise emphasises the importance of Scripture: it is "God-breathed and is useful for teaching, rebuking, correcting and

107

training in righteousness" (2 Timothy 3:16). Numerous modern writers have emphasised the importance of Scripture as the basis of a contextual theology (Taber 1978b: 69-70; Gilliland 1989:11-12; Hiebert 1987:110; Hitchens 1992: 41). It is important that Christians are familiar with the Scriptures and are taught how to understand them, for there have been some "disastrous misunderstandings on the basis of insufficient and poorly selected biblical foundations" (Taber 1978a:57). Too often a denominational theology has been imported intact by Western missionaries. Contextual theology calls Bible colleges and seminaries to give students necessary hermeneutical skills and let them bring their own agendas to the Scriptures for theological reflection. The Word of God has primary importance, rather than a system of theology. All Christians should be able to "process, reflect upon and organise biblical truth so that the Book and the truth become their own" (Gilliland 1989:11).

In developing our theology, we start with the culture of the people and their questions, struggles and insights. Christianity is a life to be lived rather than a creed to be affirmed. Therefore theology must deal with what it means to be a follower of Jesus Christ in a particular time and place. It must deal with local fears, hopes and questions. Missionaries must recognise that the Spirit of God has been working in the culture long before the missionary arrived. Therefore the missionary must look at the rituals, ceremonies and myths of the people to search out those places where God has been at work preparing the people for the good news of Jesus Christ.

Cultural beliefs and values will influence people's theology. It is important that theology is not done in isolation, but in interaction with Christian believers in other times and places. If we neglect this "rich inheritance of Christian theology, liturgy and devotion" that has come to us through church history, we will suffer from spiritual impoverishment. However, this Christian tradition must not be "imposed on any church, but ... made available to those who can use it as valuable resource material" (Lausanne 1978:11).

The fourth component of our model is Christian experience, for it is very important that people's theology be tied in with their own experiences. Christianity is a life to be lived and knowledge is experiential rather than theoretical. Theology must be practical, it must give people a realistic view of the world in which they live, and of the intervention of God in their lives today. It must be relevant. The Scriptures are records of people's experiences as they respond to God and God interacts with them. People's individual stories are intertwined with the bigger cosmic story of God at work in the world. Individual and collective human experience is therefore a very valuable resource as we work to develop a theology that is truly contextualised and meaningful.

It is important that we combine dialogue and reason together. Reason by itself could give the impression that developing a contextualised theology was the responsibility of a professional theologian. But contextualisation involves dialogue as people reason together. Schreiter says:

> In cultures where ideas emerge and decisions are made on a communal basis, one now sees theology developing in that same way. While the professionally trained theologian continues to have a role in relating the experience of other Christian communities to the experience of the local group, the community itself takes much more responsibility in shaping theological response. (1985:4)

People come to the Scriptures with questions arising out of their cultural background. But the result is not merely answers, but more questions, for Scripture has a way of cross-examining us. "We find our culturally conditioned presuppositions are being challenged and our questions corrected ... We are compelled to reformulate our previous questions and to ask fresh ones" (Lausanne 1978:11). And so an ongoing dialogue between culture, Scripture and Christian tradition develops and continues.

Reason and logic have been important factors in shaping Western theology for they are a strong force in Western culture, but formal analytical theology is not part of the Melanesian tradition. Religion is an experience which one "feels" rather than thinks or reasons. One "feels into one's cosmos and its inhabitants through an organic process" (Trompf 1991:14). Melanesian theology will be rich in symbol, allegory and analogy. Dialogue is therefore an essential part of the theologising process. Charles Taber writes:

> It should be produced in dialogue: dialogue within the community of believers ... Dialogue with the world in which it is being evolved— the culture, the religion, the politics, the economics, the social system ... and dialogue with the church in the broadest sense ... It is important to maintain in a proper balance both the autonomy of the indigenous theologians ... and the interdependence of all parties of the body for the enrichment of all. (1978a:75)

The Pidgin Bible translates "Christ Jesus himself as the chief cornerstone" to read: Jesus Christ is the "number one post of the house" (Ephesians 2:20). This refers to the Melanesian style of building with posts from the bush. The centre post is usually a specially selected hard wood post that will out last all the other materials of the house, for it is the centre post that supports the roof and the house's structure. In the same way, Jesus Christ becomes the centre and focus of our theology (Figure 11). The diagram that we have is not sufficient. The heart of Christianity is not primarily a code of ethics, or a philosophy, but God's actions revealed in the life and death of Jesus Christ. Christianity without Christ is not Christianity. The essential heart of Christianity is that God reveals himself to humankind through the person of Jesus Christ. Taber insists that one of the requisites for Christian theology is that it be Christological (1978a:73).

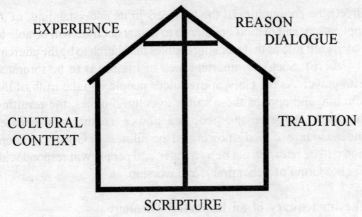

EXPERIENCE

REASON
DIALOGUE

CULTURAL
CONTEXT

TRADITION

SCRIPTURE

Figure 11. House Model With Cross

It is significant that the centre post is the cross, for the uniqueness of Jesus Christ is not primarily in his teaching, but in his death, resurrection and ascension. Paul says, "but we preach Christ crucified: a stumbling block to Jews and foolishness to Gentiles, but to those whom God has called, both Jews and Greeks, Christ the power of God and the wisdom of God" (1 Corinthians 1:24). We will readjust our model by inserting a cross in the centre of the structure (Figure 11).

There is an offence in the cross that contextualisation must not do away with. Jesus calls us to take up our cross and follow him. This involves turning from sin and self-centredness. He calls us to obedience and service to others. For many people this is not "good news" - but it is an essential part of the message. In many countries a foreign imported gospel is not good news, for the foreignness offends and turns people away from experiencing the good news of God's salvation.

Missionaries and church leaders need to trust the Holy Spirit to guide and direct the church in its theological reflection. Taber says, "The dynamic guide who leads the church into all truth is the Holy Spirit ... It is only as the same Spirit, who inspired the Scriptures,

111

directs the community of the believers in its understanding, in its application, and in their obedience to it, that doctrine will be able to play its full role as that teaching enables the church to be the church" (1978a:76). Such an important area of life needs to be saturated with prayer. As the Holy Spirit guides people into the truth of the scripture and applies those truths to cultural issues, the resulting theology will give the people a newer, fresher and greater understanding of God's power and the fullness of God's salvation. God will be relevant, not be a stranger, and people will respond with an outpouring of richer praise and worship.

The Inadequacy of an Imported Theology

This model shows how inadequate an imported non-contextualised theology is (see Figure 12).

The theology that is imported is biblical, orthodox and Christocentric, but it only partially relates to the questions, struggles and values of the culture. Because it does not adequately relate to local culture, it does not relate to the local people's experience. It is imported intact from another culture, and so the local believers are not involved in dialogue, reasoning and wrestling with issues. Christ is there and they have had experiences with him, but he is seen basically as a bit of a foreigner and not very involved in their world with their fears and struggles. Christ may have been presented as the Saviour from sin, but is he also the mighty conqueror who has defeated the powers of evil? Is Jesus seen as the friend of the poor and the down-trodden, or is he seen as the friend and ally of the Westerners with their comfortable lifestyles?

112

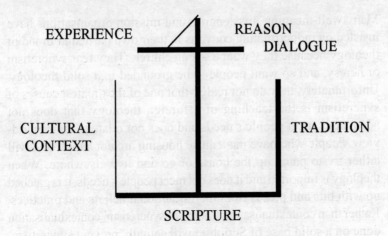

Figure 12. House Model Showing the Inadequacy
of Imported Theology

The model of theology as like a house carries the connotation that theology must be livable. When problems come, then our theology, i.e., our understanding of God, must be adequate to withstand the storms of life. Obviously the house in Figure 12 offers little protection from storms. It is biblical, orthodox and Christ-centred, but it is inadequate. The national Christian may conclude that God is not all powerful nor all knowing; God is inadequate to meeting the needs and problems of human life.

Indigenous theology must address itself to issues that are real to the people for whom it is done. It should resolutely ignore questions that do not emerge in the context, so as *to avoid irrelevance*. This may mean both that indigenous theology will say not a word about matters that in the history of the Western churches have caused endless controversy ... and that questions will be raised as burning issues requiring immediate solution that never occurred at all to theologians in the Western world. (Taber 1978a:67; emphasis added)

113

Many well-meaning missionaries and mission organisations have insisted on indoctrinating converts in their own particular brand of theology because they want a strong church. They fear syncretism or heresy, and so want people to be grounded in a solid theology. Unfortunately, they do not realise that one of the greatest causes of syncretism is the teaching of a foreign theology that does not adequately meet people's needs and does not relate to their world-view. People who have inadequate housing are not happy, and will either try to patch up the house or go and live elsewhere. When theology is imported and it does not meet people's needs, it is patched up with bits and pieces from their traditional beliefs and practices. Rather than contextualisation leading to syncretism, contextualisation done on a solid base of Scripture will actually prevent syncretism. Missionaries must be involved in working closely with the national church and *doing theology* with them, not merely teaching an imported theology to them.

Ongoing Theology

No model can do complete justice to a complex topic like contextualising theology. This house model does have one major problem: it suggests that the final product is the most important. From a modern viewpoint, a house is typically built by an expert and is expected to last for as long as possible with a minimum of attention. A more useful model is the traditional Melanesian house built by the people of the community. They work together, using local materials along with some imported items such as axe, hammer, saw and nails. Everyone knows that in five years time they will need to build another house.

We will not need a new theology every five years, but it brings us to the point that theologising must be open ended and on going.[27] Theologising is an ongoing dialogical process carried on in the church community that must be based on the Bible, focused on the cross, culturally relevant and related to the experiences of people in their social context.

114

Figure 13 is an expanded view of our model that sums up the major factors that are essential in developing a contextualised theology.[28]

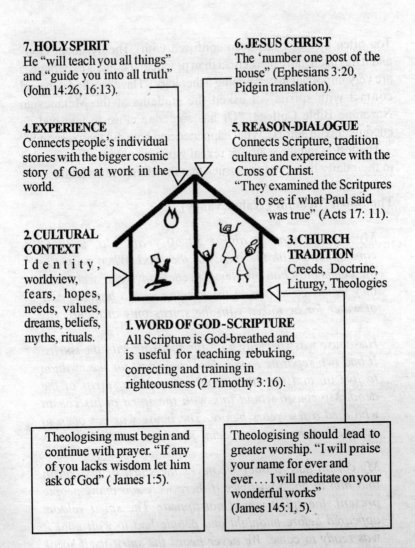

7. HOLY SPIRIT
He "will teach you all things" and "guide you into all truth" (John 14:26, 16:13).

6. JESUS CHRIST
The 'number one post of the house" (Ephesians 3:20, Pidgin translation).

4. EXPERIENCE
Connects people's individual stories with the bigger cosmic story of God at work in the world.

5. REASON-DIALOGUE
Connects Scripture, tradition culture and expereince with the Cross of Christ. "They examined the Scritpures to see if what Paul said was true" (Acts 17: 11).

2. CULTURAL CONTEXT
I d e n t i t y, worldview, fears, hopes, needs, values, dreams, beliefs, myths, rituals.

3. CHURCH TRADITION
Creeds, Doctrine, Liturgy, Theologies

1. WORD OF GOD - SCRIPTURE
All Scripture is God-breathed and is useful for teaching rebuking, correcting and training in righteousness (2 Timothy 3:16).

Theologising must begin and continue with prayer. "If any of you lacks wisdom let him ask of God" (James 1:5).

Theologising should lead to greater worship. "I will praise your name for ever and ever . . . I will meditate on your wonderful works" (James 145:1, 5).

Figure 13. House Model for Contexualising Theology for Melanesia

115

CHAPTER FIVE

SPIRIT WORLDS, DEATH AND BURIAL

Too often theology has been confused with "Theory about God" and it has been more theoretical than practical. People's experiences are very important in developing a theology. "Have you had personal contact with spirits?" I asked the students at the Melanesian Nazarene Bible College. "Or has someone close to you had an encounter with spirits? What happened and how did they respond?" [29] The following three stories reveal what people are experiencing in their daily lives, and the issues that the church must address.

The Spirit Medium (Wahgi Valley)

My cousin, who is about 50-60 years old, used to communicate with the spirits of the dead. When people in the community had problems, needed advice or were sick, they would go to him in the evening with a bamboo tube of water for he talked with the spirits only at night.

His house was specially built for speaking with the spirits. It had two separate rooms. One room was for the medium to live in, and the other room was for the spirits of the dead. My cousin would talk with the spirit of his cousin who died a few years before. The house was not open to anyone but those with special problems or burdens.

My cousin had to obey whatever the spirit of his cousin told him to do. Sometimes if there were too many people present, the spirit would not appear. The spirit seldom appeared before midnight and people had to wait until it was ready to come. We never heard the spirit itself speak but only the voice of the medium.

116

When it came close to the time for me to sit my grade six exam I wanted some help to pass, for this exam would determine whether or not I could go to high school. So I took a bamboo tube of water and went with my parents to my cousin's house. My cousin took the bamboo tube and placed it in the special room for the spirits. At this time I was attending the Catholic Church and my parents were both lay leaders in the Catholic Church. We began the session by singing songs from the Catholic Church and reciting prayers that we had learned. About midnight the spirit came and my cousin asked me to tell the spirit all my problems. I told him my concern about being able to pass the grade six exams so that I could go on to high school. After a while the medium told me that the spirit of my dead cousin had agreed to help me continue my education at high school. We stayed the night at my cousin's house and early the next morning the medium took the bamboo tube that had been kept overnight in the spirit's room and gave it to me to drink. I drank the water and went home satisfied and at peace, believing that I would pass my exams.

After a month we had the exams and I was confident that I would pass. When I got my certificate saying that I had passed and was able to go to high school, I was very thankful and praised the spirit of my dead cousin for helping me. I was accepted to go to Fatima High School, and was glad that I was a Catholic and had the help of the spirits as well as a good school to attend.

When it came towards the end of grade eight, I had to face another exam and if I was successful then I would be able to continue on for another two years. I prayed to my dead cousin, "Thank you for helping me to pass my grade six exam. Now I continue to pray that you will help me to continue my education to grades nine and ten."

117

But somehow I was unsuccessful, even though I had scored good marks. I was dropped from eighth grade and could not continue my education; I felt really upset.

When I came home and told my father, he was very angry with me. He had spent lots of money to pay my school fees, but now I was a failure and he chased me away from my home. I went to stay with some relatives who attended the Church of the Nazarene. While I was staying with them I gave my heart to Christ and my life was completely changed. Now I realise that calling on the spirit of my dead cousin for help was the wrong thing to do. I have a heavenly Father who loves me and cares for me and I should have gone to him for the help I needed.

Captured by Bush Spirits (Enga Province)

The church bell was ringing and people were going to the Lutheran Church for a midnight Christmas service. Lokan was a tall young man with long dreadlocks, of which he was very proud. He ran up the hill past the graveyard towards his friend Feal's house, for they were going to go together to the midnight service. He called out, "Feal! Feal!" Someone from Feal's house responded to the call. Just as Lokan arrived at the door he bumped into what appeared to be a huge man. Lokan yelled out "Feal Oh, Feal Oh." Lokan lost all sense of thinking and was carried away bodily by the spirit.

Feal heard Lokan call out, and ran out of the house with a lamp, and saw Lokan moving backwards through the air. Feal followed after him but he was travelling on foot while Lokan seemed to be floating in the air and moving over the tops of the pitpit reeds. Feal followed him down to the river, but there his lamp suddenly went out. Feal was terrified that the spirits would catch him also. He

118

turned and ran for his life back to the church. He rushed into the church yelling out that the spirits had captured Lokan and carried him away. The people grabbed the large Coleman lamps and rushed out of the church calling out Lokan's name.

They could hear him calling from the opposite side of the river. They rushed across to the other side of the river and called his name, but this time he answered from the side where they had just been. They rushed from one side of the river to the other and up and down the banks in the dark. They could never find Lokan because the spirits were always just out of reach. Eventually one of the older men got the people together. He said, "The spirits are playing tricks on you. He will not be far away. Search carefully for him along this side of the river."[30]

The old man was right. They were able to find Lokan. He was not far away in the swamp, but he had been turned upside down with his head and body deep in the mud and his two legs sticking up in the air. He looked like a tree trunk with two branches. They tried to pull him out but Lokan was struggling violently and would not allow them to do that. One went and got a rope and they were able to tie his feet and hands to a wooden pole and carry him home, but he was struggling violently the whole time.

The old men said, "It must have been the two spirits, Tipak and Titai, who lived between the karuka trees near the river who carried him away." The old men advised them to make a big fire and put the boy close to the fire. When they did this a very offensive smell filled the house. The men kept the fire going until morning. At daybreak Lokan appeared to be his normal self again. That evening however, when it became dark, the spirit took over and he was again very disturbed. This went on for a few days.

119

Eventually someone called for the Lutheran pastor to come. He brought the family together and told everyone to confess their sins. The pastor then laid his hands on the boy and told the evil spirit to leave. The spirit left Lokan and he became normal once again with no more problems. Lokan cut off his hair, as the people felt that his dread locks made him look like an evil spirit.

Death by Witchcraft (Simbu Province)

A man went to the Ramu Sugar plantation to visit his son and died as soon as he arrived. His body was taken to the local hospital to try and find the cause of his death but the doctor could find no apparent cause, and so the body was taken back home to Simbu Province. People were shocked by this sudden death and felt sure it was caused by witchcraft. They told people to cease their ritual wailing until they could find out who had killed him. They placed the body in the men's house and placed a tangket (cordyline) plant in his hand. They mentioned suspicious places and people to see if the coffin would move or not, but nothing happened. They then tried the local community and called the name of his wife. Soon a big noise came and the coffin was shaking violently. People knew without any doubt that it was his wife who had killed him.

The wife was brought before the assembled crowd. She was asked why she killed her husband and who had helped her to kill him. She replied that another woman who lived nearby had helped her. People asked these two women to give the names of all the witches. They did so, and other women were brought forward. They did not appear to be afraid of the people. The wife said that her neighbour had taken the heart and hidden it in the roof of the house. People went to look for it, but could not find it. The woman

120

who was responsible for hiding it went and found it. Then to everyone's horror and amazement she brought it forward for all to see.

The people decided that all of these witches should be burnt to death. But before this happened a witch doctor came from another area. People asked him if he could cast the witch spirits out of the women so that they did not need to die. The community wanted to live in peace and harmony. The witch doctor explained that the witches have different spirits and that the spirits have different functions. Some specialise in killing humans, some kill only animals, and some specialise in removing money from people. Also they have different types of spirits, such as cat, rat, dog, snake, bird, possum etc. They asked the women if this was true and each one told what sort of spirit she had and its special function.

The witch doctor said he could cast the spirits out but it would take a while. He would have to deal with them one by one. He added that the witch spirits are like babies living in the uterus and the women will have to go into hard labour before they can give birth to the spirits. The people wanted immediate action and were not prepared to wait for all this to take place. They therefore gave the alleged witches a warning and told them that if anything happened again it would be death for all of them. Everyone was dismissed and went home.

In these three stories we see Papua New Guineans dealing with three different types of spirit beings. The first story involves the spirits of the dead, the second story involves bush spirits, and the third story deals with witchcraft and familiar spirits that are attacking people in the community. The stories also show us several different ways people try to handle matters involving the spirit world.

The Spirit Medium. In this incident people are seeking supernatural help at a very important juncture in a young person's life and in a family's life. Getting into high school means a future possibility of getting a job with a salary. It therefore has a big impact upon a person's life, and on his/her parents' future as well. If their child has a job then the parents will have "social security" for their old age. In this story we have a combination of old practices and new Christian rituals. But is this contextualisation or is it syncretism?

There are Christian songs and Christian prayers, but the rest of the ceremony comes out of traditional religion and involves calling on the spirits of a dead cousin to give help and advice. This is a practice that is clearly condemned in Scripture (see Leviticus 19:31; Deuteronomy 18:10-11; or Isaiah 8:19). Since Scripture is the foundation of our model of contextualisation, this practice of calling on the spirits of the dead is unacceptable.

The Bush Spirit. Here is an encounter with an evil bush spirit who carries a person away bodily. Similar stories are told in Simbu and the Sepik provinces. There is a "trickster" element in this story, as the spirits continue to make the people run backwards and forwards from one side of the river to the next, trying in vain to retrieve their loved one. For the person concerned, and for the family involved, it is not a humorous event but a time of frightening anxiety. When they do retrieve the lost boy he is deranged, violent and has to be tied down. Light appears to settle him but as soon as it becomes dark the spirit begins to trouble him again and he loses his mind. The people eventually call the Lutheran pastor to help them. He tells them to assemble as a family and confess any anger, resentment and wrong deeds that they have committed. This practice is both traditional as a means of restoring harmony within the community, and Christian (James 5:16). After the time of confession, the people lay hands on him whilst the pastor prays and commands the demon to leave. The boy is healed and the problem is solved. We see in this example a belief that God is more powerful than the evil spirits; fervent prayer believing that God will raise the sick; and the traditional practice of family confession and conflict resolution. This is contextualised Christianity. The belief is Christian and the ritual is traditional, and there is nothing contrary to Scripture.

Dealing With Witches. In this incident, we have traditional means of divination: calling on the spirit of a dead person to reveal who is responsible for causing his/her death. The ritual is effective: the coffin rattles and shakes when the wife's name is called, thus revealing the witch. This is confirmed when the witch returns with the person's heart. The traditional solution is to get rid of the witches by burning them to death, but the people do not feel totally happy with this and look for an alternative. The church apparently has no answers to give and so the people turn to the traditional healer, who seeks to cast out the *sanguma* spirits by calling on a stronger spirit. This story ends with people calling a truce in the spiritual conflict, but with no clear answers. When the church does not know what to do, people will look for answers elsewhere.[31]

CHAPTER SIX

THE MELANESIAN SPIRIT WORLD:
A COMPARISON

I have struggled to know whether to use the past or present tense when describing "traditional" religious beliefs and practices. PNG is in the midst of change, and both traditional beliefs and the gospel have profound effects on people's lives. Some Melanesians may say as they read this chapter: "We used to believe that way, but not anymore." Yet it is also true that in many rural and remote areas people think the way I describe. What I have tried to outline is the world-view and culture into which the gospel entered. This still has a large influence on the way people live and think today, and although culture is constantly changing, people often revert to traditional ways and practices in times of crisis.

I will now compare the spirit beliefs of three cultural groups. The Simbu people are a large cultural group found in the Simbu Province; the Enga is the largest linguistic group in Papua New Guinea and much anthropological research has been done on it; and the Kobon are a small people group located on the fringes of the Highlands.

The Simbu People

The Simbu Province (also known as Chimbu) is one of the five highland provinces of PNG. I lived in Kundiawa, the main town in Simbu, from 1984 to 1994. Many of my closest friends are people who are proud to call themselves Simbus.

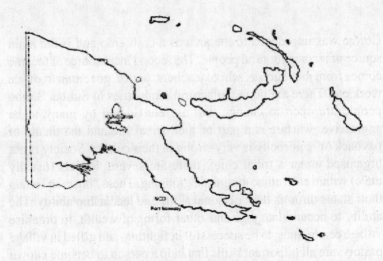

Map 2. Location of Simbu Province

The Simbu Province is very mountainous; Papua New Guinea's largest mountain, Mt Wilhelm (4,509m), is situated within it. People live at heights from 1200-2400 metres in scattered hamlets. They are skilled agriculturists and many make their gardens on very steep slopes. Their main foods are sweet potato, bananas, corn, greens, sugarcane etc. (Brown 1972:10-11).

Simbu has a population of about 259 703 people,[34] and the largest language group is the Kuman speakers. This is a linguistic grouping, not a social grouping, for the Kuman speakers are broken into many clans that intermarry and fight each other. The other language groups, such as Yongomugl, Sinasina and Dom, are all related to the Kuman group linguistically and culturally, and many of the people in these groups also speak Kuman. In many ways, the Wahgi people of the Western Highlands Province could be considered a subgroup of the Kuman people, for many of the Wahgi customs (especially those related to the great pig festival) are actually obtained from the Simbu Province (see O'Hanlon 1995). There are also very close similarities in traditional dress and dances of the two groups.

125

Coffee was introduced to the area as a cash crop and is the main source of income for rural people. The second main source of income comes from jobs such as school teachers, police, government office work etc. There are no manufacturing industries in Simbu. Simbu people are open to change, but are considered by many to be aggressive: warfare is a part of their tribal life and the theme of payback or reciprocity is very strong in their culture. Society is not organised under a tribal chief; there are several leaders (usually male) within each ethno-linguistic grouping. These "big men" attain their status through their personal skills and leadership ability. The ability to accumulate pigs and other forms of wealth, to organise village ceremonies, to be successful in fighting, and gifted in village oratory, are all important skills that help a person to become known as a "big man" (Brown 1972:43).[32]

Simbu people have migrated to many parts of Papua New Guinea; it seems that there is not a town in PNG without a group of Simbu people living there. They have been very active in politics.[33]

Supreme Being

The Kuman people believe in a Supreme Being known as *Ande Yagl* (literally sun-man) or *Yagl wano* (grandfather). The combination of *ande* and *yagl* indicates that the sun itself is not the Supreme Being, but is its symbol or "eye". The Sinasina people believe in a high power that has a dual nature, called *Yani-gela* – literally, "Sky-earth" (Brown 1995:121).

Today the practice of calling on the sun no longer exists. The term most commonly used in Simbu for God is *Neno kande* (Great father). John Nilles (a Catholic priest in Simbu for many years) observes that the sun used to be called on for the following help:

1. To give life and fertility to humans, stock and crops;
2. To protect and increase the quality of life and property;

126

3. To provide for the well-being of all living members of the group and success in all their activities; and
4. To help in times and places of natural disaster, especially in response to sacrifices of pigs. (Nilles 1969:12)

The sun was called upon to watch over a child during the naming ceremonies. When people were building a men's house, and the main post of a new house was being driven into the ground, people would call on the sun to provide warmth and security for the house. Sometimes in preparation of a new garden the sun would be called upon to provide protection and fertility for the crops.

Spirits of the Dead

For the Simbu people, supernatural beings – especially the spirits of the dead – control the affairs of the living. If pleased, spirits bring prosperity, fertility and success, but if displeased, they bring disaster, poverty and failure. Much time and effort were traditionally put into placating the spirits through sacrifices of pigs and correct ritual.

Each person has a *kuia*, which is his/her living soul. It leaves the body when a person is dreaming and returns before he or she wakes. It is the spirit that leaves permanently at death. The understanding is that the *kuia* may stay around for a few days after death until the completion of proper burial arrangements, when it becomes a *gigl*. A graveyard is known as *gigl pene*, literally "the place of the spirits", indicating that spirits live in the graveyard. The spirits of the recent dead are referred to as *neno manoma gigl* ("father and mother spirits") or a*lamo gawamo gigl* ("grandparent spirits"). The spirits of distant ancestors are known as *kowane aware gigl* (Nilles 1969:134).

To the Simbu people the dead are still present with the living. They do not depart but remain, and have a fuller knowledge of village life than they had before they died. As parents and grandparents provided for their children while they were alive, they will continue to do the

127

same after they have died, for they never cease to be part of the clan. Over a period of time however, as their age-mates die off and memories become lost, they fade away into semi-oblivion and join the collective ancestors of the past. They are not loved or worshipped as such, but they are considered part of the community that must be cared for. This is very pragmatic: if everything goes well, it is a sign that all is well with the ancestors. If sickness comes, gardens do not grow or other problems happen in the community, then the spirits are upset and appeasement needs to be made (Hughes 1985:80-81).

In contrast to the Engans, for whom the spirits of the dead live deep within the earth, the Simbu people believe the spirits live in the graveyard. Sometimes older people ask their children to bury them near the house so that they can keep an eye on them and protect them from harmful enemies.

Simbu people see the ancestral spirits as primarily helpful. In many ways they continue to provide the care and protection that a father or mother gave in life. An old man from the closely related Wahgi Valley says: "The spirits protect me from sickness and trouble. They help and care for my life, my family, my garden, and they answer when I ask them for something. If I do something that offends them, then they turn their backs on me and other wild spirits hurt me by giving me sickness and causing other troubles" (qtd. in Dorum: 3-4). This man says that other spirits cause the problems. If he maintains good relationships with his family members who are now dead, they will protect him from the attacks of other spirits.

Maintaining relationships with the spirits of the dead is very important. It is important that people be buried back at their birthplace, or at least with the other members of their clan. When a person is born, the placenta is buried in the village, and it is a good thing to be reunited with the placenta at death. Burial does not need to be in exactly same place as birth, but at least in the same clan area. In situations of violent death (i.e. a car accident or a tribal fight), it is

128

important that people return to the place of the death late in the afternoon, and usually with a chicken. The chicken is killed and its blood is poured on the earth. Some feathers may be burned in a small fire, and a ritual specialist will call the name of the dead. The spirit of the dead will respond with a clear whistle, often from a short distance away.[35] The ritual specialist will try to get closer to the source of the whistle and so capture the spirit. Others will announce to the spirit that they have come to take the spirit back home to the village. The aim is to get as close to the whistle as possible and capture it along with some dirt. Then it is wrapped in leaves like *tangket* leaves, and taken back to the burial place to be placed in the coffin. To leave the spirit outside in the cold and dark is disrespectful and would make it angry, and thus anyone passing the area would be in danger of attack. If left in a fight area, the enemy clan may capture the spirit, and that would be even worse.

A spirit remains in the village as long as the people who knew him or her are alive. When they have died, the spirit drifts away to some remote mountain top where he joins the unseen community of older ghosts. The spirits of the remote dead are essentially benevolent. They are tribal or clan spirits, and sacrifices are made in their honour at important events like the big *bugla gende* pig festival. Reay elaborates: "They bless the crops and ensure bountiful harvests. They give their descendants and living clansmen strength and success in war. To keep their goodwill, the living have to maintain their hostility toward, and seek every opportunity to overcome, the traditional enemies" (1959:134).

The *bugla gende* is a large scale festival and celebration centred around the killing of thousands of pigs. It is the biggest and most prestigious clan event that takes place (see Brown 1972; Knight 1979; Mantovani 1984d:147-168). Three to four years of preparation and planning precede it and the actual event takes a full week or longer. In the Wahgi Valley, it is known as the *kong gar* or *gol kerema* (Luzbetak 1954; Reay 1959; O'Hanlon 1995). It is a time of celebration and dancing that expresses tribal strength and vitality.

129

It is a time of economic exchange, as pigs are killed and given to friends, relatives and trading partners. It is also a time of securing the blessing of the ancestral spirits on the pigs, women and gardens. The theme of fertility is very strong and pigs are placed around the *mond* post or a *bolim* house, both of which are phallic symbols, or else around a special tree.[36]

Bush Spirits

This group of spirits live in mountains, away from human habitation, or near rivers and lakes where people only go when hunting. Some also live in those areas where pigs are left to forage, or where land has been left to fallow. They are of non-human origin, yet have some human characteristics and can appear as humans.

Gigl kangi is a bush spirit with shape changing powers and is able to appear as a man, animal or tree, while its footprints are those of dogs or marsupials. It is capricious and able to possess the souls of people, especially when humans displease the *gigl kangi* by trespassing on its land (Hughes 1985: 84). People who trespass and incur the wrath of the *gigl kangi* can become mentally deranged and wander around lost in the bush for days.

The *gigi kangi* can steal babies from mothers' *bilums* and replace them with deformed, weak or sickly children.[37] The *gigl kangi* are the protectors of pigs. When pigs are killed, there is a special acknowledgment that the *gigl kangi* has looked after the pigs. If this is acknowledged by offering a small portion of the meat to the spirits, then the *gigl kangi* will continue to look after the rest of the herd. This practice is not as strong as it used to be.

Dingaan (also spelt *Dingan*) is another spirit that is similar to the *gigl kangi*, but has no positive features and never enters into reciprocal relationships with people. *Dingaan* is a term also used to describe serious illness, such as leprosy, swollen abdomen, insanity and a dirty unkempt person. The *dingaan* gain control over a person

130

by eating the person's bodily waste. It is important that mothers are very careful to dispose of children's faeces so that this does not happen (Hughes 1985:87). Again, this practice and belief is in decline.

Sanguma and Kumo

The Kuman word "*kumo*" refers to an animal-like spirit entity. It is always evil and inhabits its host – often a woman, but men are also susceptible. A similar spirit is known of in many areas of PNG, but is stronger in some places than others. The Pidgin expression is *sanguma*. The *sanguma* is thought of as a small animal, such as a rat, snake, bird, bat or cat (Hughes 1985:89).[38]

Sanguma is always antisocial. From interviews with a *sanguma* woman, Jenny Hughes describes the *kumo* as being: "a small animal, most commonly a rat, snake or bat. When not engaged in its evil activities, it resided inside the host's body" (1985:90). The *sanguma* spirit acts as an alter ego, and people who have *sanguma* have reported having conversations or even arguments with the *sanguma*. It appears that the *sanguma* is not able to act on its own free will and requires some degree of cooperation from the human host.

This agrees very closely with the information I have received from numerous informants over many years. *Sanguma* have an unquenchable desire for meat, especially the liver, and will eat both pigs and human flesh. They cause the death of humans by removing their organs, especially heart and liver, through psychic means. The victim then drops dead a few days later. *Sanguma* exhume and eat bodies from graves; for this reason, some people will light a lamp and keep watch during the night at a new gravesite to see if anyone or any animal comes near the grave. Any animal that approaches the grave is a *sanguma* spirit, and will be killed. *Sanguma* people are able to fly through the air either as a bat or a bird, or as a bright light travelling above the tops of the trees. In one night they can easily travel from one village to another, kill someone and return home. Some people who have *sanguma* powers leave their bodies

131

at home in a deep, almost comatose state, and their spirits travel at night, often in the form of some sort of animal. They travel in the spirit dimension and so are not hindered by physical obstacles. Therefore, they can consume a body even though the earth on top of the grave is undisturbed. Any sudden sinking of the ground above a grave is often taken to mean that the body has been consumed. Many people in the Highlands of PNG are buried in simple thin plywood coffins, so it is quite common for graves to sink. The ample rainfall also contributes to this problem of sinking graves, and the *sanguma* stories grow.

Sanguma people do not usually use any physical substance to kill a person. They may kill simply by gazing intently at a person. Someone may stand outside a house at night, and project their force through the walls of the house to the people on the inside.[39]

The Kobon People

The Kobon people are a group of 5000–6000 people living in the Schrader ranges on the border between the Madang and Western Highlands Provinces of Papua New Guinea. The Schrader ranges are located midway between the Jimi River to the south west and the Ramu River to the north east. Closely related to the Kobon people are the Kalam people, located to the east of Kobon; the Kalam are a much larger group of 15,000 people and are based at Simbai. Further east are the Maring people.[40]

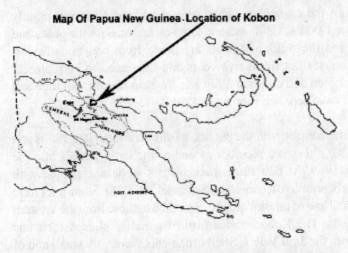

Map Of Papua New Guinea - Location of Kobon

Map 3. Location of Kobon People (Schendal 1978:6)

The Kobon people are of small stature with an average height of about 1.5 metres. They do not live in organised villages; their houses are spread out among garden areas. "Settlement is dispersed and the only persisting groups are of household size" (Jackson 1975:9). The population is very scattered and large ceremonies are staged by small groupings of two or three households. In contrast to the Simbu, who have a "big man" style of leadership, the Kobon have a style of leadership that Jackson calls "anarchic", in that there is an absence of any tribal structure, for there is no social group larger than the household (Jackson 1975:160). Instead, life is regulated by a large number of taboos that must be observed. "All Kobon are subject to large numbers of taboos, notably kinship taboos, life cycle taboos, local inherited taboos, and taboos associated with bleeding and death" (Jackson 1975:11). There is fear that if they do not observe these taboos, then various "wild spirits" will bring sickness upon them.

The Kobon people are gardeners, hunters and gatherers. Sweet potato and taro are their staple foods, along with a variety of bananas. They raise pigs and hunt for marsupials and a wide variety of birds,

133

including the cassowary. They live at various altitudes, mainly between 1,000 – 1,800 metres. Houses are made with poles and vines, and the walls and roofs are made from pandanus leaves. These houses last up to five years and then need to be replaced. Men, women and children all live in the same house, but men and women have separate rooms (Jackson 1975:46).

Their first contact with the outside world was in the late 1960s and early 1970s. I was a member of one of the early patrols into the area in 1969. At that stage, they were a stone age people with extremely primitive technology (Schendal 1978:28). Stone axes were very small and of inferior quality compared to those from the Western Highlands. The Kobon traded bird of paradise plumes for stone axes from the Jimi Valley. Shell ornaments were very small and of poor quality. Although many people lived at 1,800 metres where it is very cold at night, they did not have bed or sleeping platforms in their houses, but slept on the bare earth. The women wore skirts of bark drapes that covered the front and back, but left the thighs bare. Men wore a string net at the front attached to a waistband of cane and leaves covering the buttocks. Today, the sale of coffee enables them to buy Western style clothes, many of which are secondhand, imported from Australia and sold in small trade stores.

There are no roads or vehicles into the area. Contact with the outside world is by aircraft (mainly Missionary Aviation Fellowship aeroplanes) operating from small grass airstrips. There are only two primary schools (grades 1-6) in the area and so literacy rates are low. The main outside influence is the Church of the Nazarene, which has about thirty churches in the area and also operates a health centre.

Rumualye

The Kobon people believe in a Supreme Being whom they call *Rumualye*. The literal meaning is "thunder" (*Rumu*) "calls" (*alye*). *Rumualye* is "he who speaks with thunder". Thunder is identified as his voice, and as a warning against possible enemies approaching. A lightening strike is his divine intervention to destroy an unseen enemy. He is greater than all other beings, supreme over all spirits, and is all-powerful.

Rumualye is called upon in times of tribal fighting. People will call to him: "Our enemies are coming against us. *Rumualye* are you watching us? We need you to help us in our fight." The men then gather and confess any grievances, disagreements etc. They place all their shields and weapons together and sprinkle them with water, calling upon *Rumualye* to cause the enemy's spears to miss them, and enable them to kill their enemies. If thunder rumbles, it is a clear indication that *Rumualye* has heard and will help them in battle. A rainbow is another positive sign.

Rumualye's assistance is also sought in times of sickness. The family members gather and any problems or grievances are settled. The leader takes a bamboo tube of water and says: "*Rumualye*, are you watching over us or not?" Then the sick person takes the water and drinks it.

Rumualye also helps care for pigs. When a big pig is about to be killed, the people place a dish of water near the pig and tie some small pigs nearby. The head of the family then says: "*Rumualye*, we want to kill this big pig that you have been caring for. Now we want you to care for the little pigs as well. We want you to protect them so that they do not get sick, or die, or become weak and malnourished." Then they pour some of the water on the large pig, as well as on the little pigs. In this way the strength of the big pig and the blessing of *Rumualye* is transferred to the small pigs. When the pig is cooked, there is always plenty of pork for everyone to eat.

When Nazarene missionaries first went into the area, they tried to find out what understanding the people had of God as a creator. Some local people said they came from the egg of a cassowary, and others said that they came from some other type of bird or animal.

135

The missionaries concluded that these people had no concept of a creator God. This, however, was only partially true. They had a concept of God, but related it primarily to thunder, rather than to creation. It was mainly the translation of the Old Testament in Pidgin that led the people to realise that *Rumualye* and God were one and the same. Verses such as these from Job and from the Psalms were very significant:

> Listen! Listen to the roar of his voice, to the rumblings that come from his mouth. He unleashes his lightning beneath the whole heaven and sends it to the end of the earth. After that comes the sound of his roar; he thunders with his majestic voice. When his voice resounds he holds nothing back. God's voice thunders in marvellous ways; He does great things beyond our understanding. (Job 37:2-5)[41]

One informant, a village leader and a strong lay leader in the church (James Sambal), said that he personally visited many of the old men and told them that the God of the mission was not a new or different God, but really the same as *Rumualye*. He also told me that there used to be a group of people who were very devoted to *Rumualye* and who kept themselves separate from the rest of society and did not participate in tribal fighting. This group has died out and no longer exists.

The reference of thunder and lightning associated with the giving of the Ten Commandments was especially significant. The people identified the Ten Commandments with many of the instructions that they had received from the tribal elders during the initiation ceremonies:

> 1. You must not steal. If you see someone's papaya tree with a ripe papaya, you must not steal it. If sugarcane is hanging across the path, you must not take it. You must not steal other people's pigs or food items.

2. You must be hospitable. If someone comes to your house, you must feed him. Even if he or she is a person who has mistreated you in some way, you should still feed him or her.
3. You must always respect your parents and do whatever they tell you.
4. You must care for the elderly and the widows by giving them food, and helping to repair their houses or building new houses.
5. If an elderly woman accidentally exposes herself in some way, you are not to laugh or ridicule her.
6. You are not to touch other women. If you meet a woman on a path, you must not touch her. When she goes past you, you should not turn and look after her. That will only bring trouble.
7. If you obey all these instructions then you will have a long and happy life.

Before the initiation ceremony began, a village leader would go up onto the roof of the house and sprinkle water on the house and on the gathered boys who were watching. While doing this, he would ask for *Rumualye* to give his blessing. Inside the house, a long narrow fire pit was dug and a place made for each boy. Each boy had to stay in his own place and not move around. They were seated in front of the fire, and the heat of the fire engraved the lessons on the minds of the boys.

The initiation ceremonies faded out for a combination of reasons. Young people left and went to work on plantations in coastal areas. Sometimes this left the Kobon people very short of manpower, thus upsetting the traditional pattern of village life. The missionaries spoke against the initiation ceremony because of its connection with spirits. As far as I know, no anthropological study was ever done of the initiation ceremony. Some of the pastors, however, have now expressed thoughts about restarting initiations as they feel that the people have lost a lot from not having these ceremonies. They feel that young people are not as obedient or respectful as they used to be.

Graham Jackson, a medical doctor, did anthropological research among the Kobon people from 1965 to 1972. This was the beginning of contact between the Kobon people and the outside world. His research thus involves beliefs of pre-contact time. He talks about "thunder men" who live high on the mountain, who come with the thunder and take people's souls. They are associated with cassowaries; when a cassowary is killed, there is thunder. I did not hear any stories about this type of being. I did, however, hear legends about people who live in a paradise up in the sky, who are similar to the sky people of the Enga Province.[42]

Spirits of the Dead – *Wiwanj*

The spirits of the dead play a very important part in the life of the Kobon people. The dead body is placed on a platform in the house during the initial mourning period. If a man has died, then his wife has to sit on the floor under the corpse while the people cry. She is often covered with white clay and beads to indicate that she is in mourning. At the conclusion of the mourning period, the body of the dead person is placed on a platform about 1.2m off the ground, not far from the house. Fingers are often removed from the dead person, dried and worn on a string around the neck of close family members. The body is left to decompose. Food is placed in a raised basket-like receptacle beside the burial platform.

When the body has completely decomposed, the jaw bone, right arm bone and right leg bone are collected and kept in a *bilum*, along with hair from the head. These are kept in the men's house and are consulted for information and appealed to for help. Sometimes the *bilum* is held out and allowed to swing like a pendulum. Questions are asked and a positive answer is confirmed if the *bilum* suddenly stops its movement. Thus, it can confirm the name of the person who has caused the sickness or death. The remaining bones are

138

taken and placed in a fork of a large tree in the forest. Sometimes food offerings are placed at the foot of the tree in honour of the dead person.

The Kobon people speak of an unseen spirit as *wiwanj*, and of a visible ghost as *wiwana*. There is no name for distant ancestors. It appears that when the bones of the dead are removed from the house and taken to the tree, the spirits disappear. They follow the streams down to the Jimi River to the south, or if on the north side of the Schrader range, then down to the Ramu River. In warm climates (e.g. down near the big rivers), the spirits of the dead are visible even during daylight hours. If someone hunting near the Jimi River encounters a python, they believe it is the spirit of a dead person. There is no term for the collective ancestral spirits of long ago, as is found among the Wahgi and the Simbu people.

According to Jackson, ghosts are the most common cause of illness (1975:229). They maintain the same relationship with the living as they did when they were alive. They are thought to be close by and have a benevolent influence.

Wild Ghosts – *Wiyip*

Jackson mentions seventeen varieties of a supernatural being called *wiyip*, which he translates as "wild ghosts" (1975:357-366). They are similar to ghosts, but not derived from dead people. They are closely associated with the keeping of certain taboos and look after the welfare of gardens, game animals and pigs. This type of spirit inhabits diviners and speaks through them when they are trying to find out the cause of illness (Jackson 1975:255-258).

Bush Spirit – *Kinjaki*

"*Kinjaki*" is the term given for all bush spirits. Some are located in the rainforest high in the mountains, others are located near pools of water, and some are believed to live in whirlpools or deep places in

139

the streams and rivers. These spirits, if encountered in the bush, can cause people to become disoriented and mentally deranged.

Kinjaki spirits are also believed to steal children who sleeping in *bilums* while their mothers are busy working in the gardens. A deformed or sickly child is considered the child of a *kinjaki* spirit. How the *kinjaki* spirits reproduce is not discussed. Fear of the *kinjaki* has the positive effect of encouraging mothers to keep an eye on their infants while they are working in the gardens. Kobons have adopted this term as their term for Satan, who is known as *Kinjaki Satan*.

Divination and Magic

The Kobon people place great emphasis on magic in obtaining supernatural powers for healing and personal success. Divination is very important. The diviner smokes a native cigarette and begins loud intense chanting. This chanting has a definite pattern and intonation. It goes on for twenty minutes, during which time the person enters a semi-trance and is unaware of what is happening around him. The spirit (wild ghost) enters the smoker. It works its way up the body, makes sweat appear on the smoker's forehead and causes him to shake a little. The spirit then speaks through the mouth of the smoker. The smoker looks for an offence to some ghost or some other being. If the sickness is caused by a ghost, then the smoker will say a spell commanding the ghost to leave the sick person alone (Jackson describes these spells as shouted commands that tell the spirits to leave; 1975:254-262). In one example, the person performing the spell called the names of each person who had died in the community in the last few years and told them to leave. This was repeated three or four times, and each time the spell was concluded when the sick person was told to get up. When it was believed that the sickness was caused by a wild ghost, the ghost was instructed to go outside and look after the taros, yams, bananas and sugarcane (Jackson 1975:263).

140

Another practice associated with curing illnesses is the rubbing of the ill person with stinging nettles. The nettles are rubbed up the legs, down the arms and chest to the abdomen. The healer concentrates on the area that is thought to be the seat of the trouble.

During a recent revival in the Kobon, people who "had the Spirit" showed behaviour that was very similar to traditional practices. The person who received the spirit went into a semi-trance and talked in a loud monotone. The message was usually one of exhortation. Sometimes it was a description of a trip to heaven and back; the beauty of the river of life and the tree of life were described, the person met Jesus and then retraced his or her steps and returned to earth by coming out of the trance. During these times, people sat around and listened. I listened to one girl who had never been to school and normally spoke only in Kobon - yet under the influence of the Spirit, she spoke in perfect Pidgin for about twenty minutes. She spoke with a sense of awe of the beauty and holiness of Jesus, and wonders of heaven evidenced in flowers that smile, trees that wave their arms, and a river of life that jumps and skips. There was no mention of streets of gold, but everything that she described revealed abundant life in a biocosmic sense and parallels passages such as Psalm 96:10-11.

Other people who were also "used by the Spirit" seemed to be play acting and the message seemed artificial. Some Christians questioned whether it was the Holy Spirit speaking, or were some people pretending and trying to get their own message across.

One of the most powerful rituals is seldom talked about, and never to women. Prior to a *singsing* or other important event, a man may scrape a certain shell ornament in order to obtain a small amount of fine white powder. If fortunate enough to have a crocodile's tooth, obtained from the Ramu River area, he uses that for the scraping. Then he takes a leaf with a serrated edge and cuts the skin of his penis to cause it to bleed. This blood is collected on a leaf, and the white powder and certain other special leaves are added. Over this

141

he utters magical words that he has learned from older men. The men believe that this gives them success in whatever endeavour they are seeking to undertake, whether that be a *singsing*, to seduce women, to have a great garden, to pass school exams or to win in an election. This ritual is very secretive. The pastor who told me this information did so in a whisper lest someone over hear what he was saying. He said many people, including Christians, still hold on to this ritual.

The Kobon do not have a highly developed social structure, and the big pig kills that are common in the large Highlands societies (such as Enga and Simbu) do not exist among the Kobon. The "big man" concept is much less prominent in Kobon. The concept of taboo, however, is a very strong force. There are a wide variety of taboos that regulate and structure life. The wild ghosts mentioned above are believed to have a large role in enforcing the taboos.

Witchcraft

Kobon beliefs regarding *sanguma* are similar to the Simbu beliefs, involving night flying, nocturnal gatherings and cannibalism. The description given by Jackson about witchcraft also reveals similarities (1975:240-251). This subject will be treated in more detail in the chapter "The Christian Response to the Spirits of the Dead and to *Sanguma*". The Pidgin expression is either: "*Em i sanguma man*", "*em i sanguma meri*" or "*em i gat sanguma*". Literally: "he is a *sanguma* man" or "she is *sanguma* woman" or "he or she has *sanguma*". The Kobon *tok ples* also makes this distinction. *Sanguma* is not an action, but part of a person that may come and go. Fear of *sanguma* is very strong in Kobon.

The Enga People

Enga is the largest language group in Papua New Guinea. Varying dialects of Enga are spoken by almost all of the people of the province, which makes it unique, for it is the only province where

142

one language is spoken throughout. Consequently, Pidgin is used less in Enga than in any other Highlands province. In the centre of the province, the population is dense and land disputes are quite common (Meggitt 1965:105). Like the Simbu, the Enga people are renowned for tribal fighting, as is described by Meggitt in *Blood Is Their Argument*. They have a similar social organisation as the Simbu and other Melanesian societies (i.e. "big man") (Meggitt 1977:8). They live at an altitude of 1,200 - 2,100 metres above sea level. A big gold mine at Porgera has brought many changes to a small section of Enga, with an instant town and foreigners at the mine site and wealth to those directly involved in the mining activity, but the majority of people still gain their income from the sale of coffee. The main food crop is sweet potato, and people give much attention to raising pigs for village ceremonies.

In this section, we will look at their understanding of the spirit world and the forces that control their lives. When one asks about the spirit world, people tell stories of events that have happened to them, to a relative or to their tribe. Their concern is not so much about beliefs as practices. It is possible, however, after listening to the stories, to pick out common themes and practices, and from these to determine the underlying beliefs on which they are based. We can divide attitudes regarding the spirit world into four main types of spirits. They are the High God, sky people, spirits of the dead and forest spirits.

143

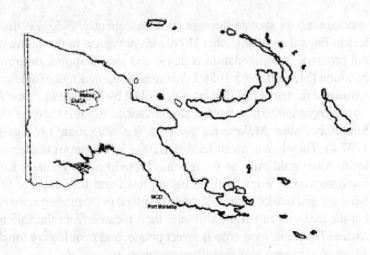

Map 4. Location of the Enga Province

The High God

The Enga have a concept of one supreme being who is higher than any other being. In some places, this supreme being is referred to as *Aitawe* (Brennan 1977:15, Dlugosz 1998:53). Among the Laiapu Enga (Wapenamanda area), it is known as *Weapo* (Kambao 1989:385), and in western Enga as *Tae* (Rusoto 1980:7). One of my informants from Kompiam referred to him as *Yalya*. He is always good and never harmful, and is a preserver of life. All of Enga cosmology is controlled by *Aitawe,* for as creator he is superior to all other forces or powers. Normally he is not called on for help, only in times of great distress. Sacrifices are not made to placate him for he is always benevolent, but ceremonies are made in his honour in order to remind him of the problems of this earth and the need of his care and provision (Brennan 1977:16-17). He can be compared to the sun in that he looks on us, warms us, and gives us good things. Nothing is hidden from his gaze. These all agree with a Christian understanding of God. It differs, however, in that *Aitawe/ Yalya* is seen as almost passive. "It is hard to imagine *Aitawe* getting excited when something happens which disrupts his creation or his

144

creatures" (Freund, Hett, and Reko 1970:143). Although *Aitawe* is all powerful he does not place any specific moral requirements on people. In many ways, he is comparable to the Western concept of luck or providence. Thus, when someone narrowly escapes an accident, their good fortune is attributed to *Aitawe*.

My informants tell me that *Yalya* does have laws of moral behaviour which people are expected to obey. These laws include no fighting within the clan, respecting the rights of others, caring for and respecting the elderly, and observing sexual taboos etc. The people at Lakemanda, near Wabag, showed me the sacred grove of trees where they used to sacrifice to *Yalya* in times of tribal distress. If the people were not living well, the pigs were thin and sickly, or the gardens were not producing well, then the people would take some of their best pigs to the sacred grove. They would offer them to *Yalya*, and call on him for his blessing on their clan. When they did this, there would be an immediate and spectacular change to the productivity and well-being of their clan: the gardens would flourish, the bananas would bear, the pigs would get big and fat, and the children would thrive. These sacrifices to *Yalya* were not observed on a regular basis, but rather at times of special need. It is also reported to me that not everyone could go to the sacred grove to sacrifice to *Yalya*: people who were spirit mediums and communicated with the spirits of the dead never went. In fact, if they did attempt to go, they could not enter the grove, for the trees would always block them. There was some sacred power present that prevented them from entering the holy ground.

The Sky People - *Yalyakali*

According to Brennan, the sky people (*yalyakali*) were created by *Aitawe* who is symbolised by the sun (male), with the assistance of the moon (female). *Yalyakali* comes from two words - *"yalya akali"* - and literally means "sky man", but is generally regarded as "sky people", although some places also refer to *"yalya enda"*, meaning "sky woman". The sky people are spirit beings that are semi-human:

145

they appear as human and yet are divine. It is thought by some that the sky people were responsible for creating the first human beings, or at least determined where the various tribes should live.

The sky people express themselves through such events as rain, lightning and earth tremors. Many of the early churches were built in or near the sacred groves where people had once made special sacrifices to them. They are often associated with legends that explain how humans lost the good life and are now relegated to earth with its constant struggle of providing for daily life, and where death comes to all people. The following story describes this relationship:

In the land of the Yalyakali Sky-People, so the story goes, there is no hunger or pain, no tension among the people, no sickness or death, no fighting or destruction. All is in perfect harmony and peace. In times past, the Yalyakali set about the task of peopling the earth. The first man found a wife, and they lived together in a land of plenty without the cares, problems and pain that mark life today. At the birth of the first son, the father knew that he would have to go and draw water from the source of the "Water of Life" to give to the baby. Before he left, he warned his wife not to give the baby any breast milk, even if the baby cried, but to wait until he returned with the water which would ensure the continued prosperity and happiness of all. The trip was rather long, however, and the young mother could not deny the hungry wail of her son, so she fed him from her breast. With this action, humankind was now bound to this earth with all its troubles, anxiety and death. The Water of Life and the way to paradise was lost. People were left with only a longing to return and to be made whole once more. They had a hope that one day someone would find the way, and would discover the yalya toko, the ladder to paradise. (Wagner and Reiner 1986:302)

146

The myth of the lost paradise is a common theme in Melanesian legends. The loss is generally due to human carelessness, greed or vanity.

According to Dlugosz, the sky people live in a paradise in the sky. They interact with people on earth and - according to Enga legend - sent their representatives to populate the earth (1998:56). These sky people married, raised pigs and grew crops (Brennan 1977:16-17). Some people think of them as being like angels. They are not feared, are usually good, and may help pigs to grow and help in other ways.

An old man was building a house and other people of the clan were helping him to thatch the house. Rain came in the afternoon and they were unable to finish the task of thatching. There were other activities planned for the next day and the old man would not have the same number of helpers, so he went to sleep wondering how he would get his house finished. The next morning there was a heavy mist that covered everything and people stayed inside the warmth of their houses waiting for the sun to rise. Eventually, when the mist disappeared, the old man went to the house to discover that the thatching was almost finished. Someone had added a lot more thatch to his house during the night. People were convinced that it was the sky people who came to help them. The sky people wanted cloud cover so they could work without being disturbed, and that was the reason everything was so misty in the morning.

It is not hard to see why people associate them with angels. One person said to me: "If angels are real, then angels have been here in PNG all the time. Missionaries did not bring angels, they were already here, and they helped our ancestors in the past."

The Spirits of the Dead - *Timongo*

According to Dlugosz, the spirits of the remote dead, which she calls ancestors, are believed to "pass on the wisdom of life, speaking through dreams, signs, animal forms, etc. The ancestors were mediums of blessing that they channelled from the supernatural. They were also mediators of curses, which fostered right relationships among the living, and loyalty in obligations towards the dead" (1998:60). There is a two-way exchange going on between the living and the dead. The dead are dependent on the living to keep their memory alive and to nourish them with offerings of food. The dead reciprocate by providing good fortune and prosperity to the clan. "It is the wisdom of keeping harmonious relationships that leads to an abundance of life. Thus, broken relationships are responsible for sickness, death, and other misfortunes" (Dlugosz 1998:60). The ancestors function in many ways as a social conscience. This respectful fear has a controlling influence upon clan relationships and morality.

The relationship is different to the spirits of the recent dead. When a person dies, his *imambu* (breath-soul) becomes a *timongo* ghost or spirit of a dead person (Wagner 1970:247). The spirits of dead relatives cause an intense fear. Brennan quotes a common saying, which when translated says: "I must obey my father in life so that he won't bite me after death" (1977:13). Their presence is expressed through dreams and misfortune, such as death, sickness and accidents. They may reveal themselves by whistles and shadowy images, and are most common at dusk or at night.

Ghosts may reveal their presence with a bird call like the hoot of an owl, as in the following story:

> *A family is sitting around the fire at night, having eaten a meal of sweet potato. They are quietly talking about the events of the day when suddenly they hear a bird call. Immediately, all talking ceases. No one moves. Everything*

148

is deathly quiet. People break out in a cold sweat and fear grips them. Mothers hold their babies close, making sure they make no noise at all. They wait in silence wondering: "Will it come again, or will it go away?" That bird call means death to someone. They hope it will go away. If the bird (spirit) hears no noise, perhaps it will think there is no one around and will fly off to some other place. If the bird calls again, there is great fear. Sometimes one of the men may run out, grab a chicken, and quickly ring its neck in hope that this will satisfy the spirit and the family will be left unharmed. If there are no more bird calls, the people slowly relax. But big questions remain. Whose spirit was it? Why did he come? What could the problem be? If someone becomes ill, it is quickly associated with the bird that called in the night.

Engas believe that these ghosts, when not appearing around the village, live in the depths of the earth, generally in their clan territory. Sometimes the ghosts of women are thought to return to the place of their birth. They are seen as basically evil and destructive; however, their assistance is sought to foretell the future, overcome an enemy's magic, reclaim lost property, and gain wealth from other clans (Wagner 1970:248-249).

There is a fatalistic attitude towards the power of the ghosts. "The triumph of the *timongo* is as sure as death, because his ultimate victory is death. His power may be modified through magic ritual, he may be appeased temporarily by sacrifice, he may be tricked or frightened away for the time being, but ultimately he must win. The power of these feared beings is very great" (Wagner 1970:250). Wagner feels that this fatalism carries over into people's understanding of Christianity in that the expression *"Satan i pulim mi"* (Satan tempted me) excuses sinful behaviour: people blame Satan, instead of taking personal responsibility. The powers of evil are seen as being too strong to resist.

149

The belief in the spirits of the dead is used to help reinforce inner clan obligations. People who neglect their responsibilities are open to attack by the clan spirits.

Bush Spirits - *Pututuli*

Bush spirits are believed by Engans to be some sort of half-human, half-animal, hairy creature/spirit with red eyes that will attack people in the forest, steal and eat their hearts. They are believed to live in caves, waterfalls, pools, trees and isolated spots of high mountains. One of my friends told of meeting one of these bush spirits out in the forest. He was frightened and began to run. As he ran he could hear the sound of the spirit running after him. He jumped over logs and across streams. He twisted and turned in an effort to escape the pursuing spirit, and did not stop until he reached his house. It was a long time before he went back to that part of the forest. Even though it had happened ten years before, he never forgot it and today he thanks God for sparing his life from certain death.

Although greatly feared, bush spirits are sometimes seen as guardians of the forest; consequently, before cutting down a big tree, an offering of possum meat would be made to *ambon*, one of the forest spirits, to placate the spirit so that disaster would not come on the people cutting down the tree. *Pututuli* are considered to be usually evil and malicious, and consequently they are greatly feared (Wagner 1970:259-260).

Wagner lists a number of different "female spirits" which are a sub-group of the forest spirits. These stories seem to differ from place to place. Some spirits are reported to kidnap children who are unattended, substituting the healthy child with a sick or weak child. This fear encourages mothers to check on children while working in the gardens. Another female spirit is associated with rivers and seduces a young man, forcing him to marry her and then destroying him and his wealth.

Ritual

People use various rituals to restore and maintain harmonious relationships between the living and the spirit world. There are ritual specialists known as *topoli* who assist in divination or in conducting a ritual of appeasement. The diviner's task is to find out which ghost is attacking, why it is attacking, and what is needed in order to placate that ghost. In Engan thinking, ghosts have the same basic emotions as living people. Clan-wide misfortunes are attributed to the ancestral ghosts, whereas the ghosts of those who have died recently are responsible for individual attacks (Dlugosz 1998:71). These two situations are treated differently. If the problems relate to an individual, then that particular family can deal with it. If the problem exists throughout the clan, then a ritual involving the clan is needed. The *Yainanda* is a ritual designed to restore harmony back into the social environment. It involves the killing of many pigs and the offering of food towards the ancestors who are represented by sacred stones (Brennan 1977:38-40).

Missiological Implications

As we look at these three systems of religious beliefs, we notice some distinct similarities and differences.

1. The High God

All three have the concept of a high God who is located in the heavens. This is more than just a geographical location; it is associated with some sort of celestial paradise. Many tribal legends speak of a time in the distant past when there was communication between the two realms, but this has been broken. The people are still looking for the ladder that will lead them to paradise or to the tree of life which they can climb to get there. This Supreme Being is good, but is generally remote and only indirectly involved in the affairs of everyday life. People do not sacrifice to him, for he is always good and never angry; so he does not need to be placated or appeased.

151

In times of tribal calamity, however, offerings are made to remind him of the people's needs. When these offerings are made, positive changes came about.

I believe it is very important that the church ties in its message to these traditional beliefs, just as Paul relates his message to the "Unknown God" of Athens. Paul says to the people there: "Now what you worship as something unknown, I am going to proclaim to you" (Acts 17:23). Unfortunately, this has not happened a great deal in Papua New Guinea. When teaching a class on "Gospel and Culture" at the Nazarene Bible College, I found that most of the students had not thought much about any connection between traditional beliefs and Christianity. As we studied the names for God in the Old Testament - *Yahweh*, and *El Elyon* - and then the name *Theos* used in the New Testament, they saw that God has many names (Richardson 1981:8-9; 41-42). They were surprised to discover that the word "God" actually came from the German "*Gott*", the Supreme Being of German traditional beliefs. They began to see their traditional beliefs in a new light. Although "the world around us is under the power and control of the evil one" (1 John 5:19), yet "The light keeps shining in the dark, and darkness has never put it out" (John 1:5 CEV). This light is the "the true light that shines on everyone" (John 1:9 CEV). They began to realise that the missionaries did not bring God to PNG, but that God was already here, albeit largely hidden. It was God who brought the missionaries so that people could know God better. Instead of learning about the "white man's God", they could instead see God as the God of all nations and also the "God of our Melanesian ancestors". This God, although partially hidden in the past, is revealed in greater clarity and power in the Scriptures. Simon Apea, writing about the belief in Yakili, the Creator God of the Southern Highlands, says: "Christianity should use these 'footprints of God' as a foundation for its teaching about God" (1985:253).

Having said this, we do have to face the fact that not every tribe in PNG knew of a high god, and where it did exist, such awareness was very limited and vague. Many of the Sepik tribes, for example, had no knowledge of a Supreme Being who was above all other spirits. Instead, they have a localised god who is responsible for a certain territory or controls a certain function, like hunting (McGregor 1982:9-10). This is similar to many parts of the Old Testament, where there is Dagon, the god of the Philistines, Chemosh, the god of the Moabites, Ashtoroth, the goddess of the Sidonians, and Molech, the god of the Ammonites (Judges 16:23; 2 Kings 23:13). According to my informants, in the Sepik each of these tribal gods competes against the gods of other tribes. One informant said that in the Highlands, although magic and the help of the ancestors are involved, tribal fighting is primarily a contest in the physical strength of tribes. In the Sepik, tribal fighting is primarily a battle between the tribal gods (Bruno 2000:13).

2. The Spirits of the Dead

Of the three major types of spirits, it is the spirits of the dead that have the greatest impact on the world of the living. People believe in life after death, but it is basically a shadowy continuation of this present life. There is no glorious future, and eventually the spirits fade away into oblivion. The spirits of the recent dead - or the remembered dead - are feared the most and are blamed for causing most illnesses. On the other hand, if they are remembered and cared for, then they will protect and care for the living. The distant ancestors are generally more benevolent. The primary means of re-establishing harmony between the living and the dead is through an animal sacrifice, which is usually the killing of a pig. This is one of the major themes that binds Melanesian religions together (Trompf 1991:14).

This relationship between the living and the world of the spirits is a precarious one. Things go wrong and there is much uncertainty to life. Problems come, diviners seek to find the cause, sacrifices are made and taboos are followed, yet the dream of an abundant life, though often hoped for, seems far away.

153

3. The World is Full of Spirits

It is evident in these three cultures that spirits are very important; there is hardly an aspect of or event in life that is not affected by spirits. Wherever one goes, and whatever one does, spirits are not far away. Unfortunately, Christianity has come to PNG from countries that have a secular focus, and which have basically ignored the spirit world. This secular orientation has influenced Christianity. If we look at any standard theology book, we will find very few references at all to Satan and almost no references to demons. For example:

- *Systematic Theology,* by Charles Hodge, has only eleven pages out of 1380 to cover the realm of angels, demons, Satan and the problem of evil (1871).
- *Christian Theology,* by H. Orton Wiley, gives thirteen pages out of 1686 to deal with angels, demons and Satan (1940).
- *Christian Theology,* by Millard Erikson, gives eighteen pages out of 1250 (1983).
- *Systematic Theology,* by Wayne Grudem, gives forty out of 1200 (1994).

In this list, it is the more recently published books that give more attention to the spirit world. Hopefully, this is an indication that scholars in the Western world are beginning to pay more attention to this topic. We have seen that the spirit world is very important to Melanesians, and Western theology gives minimal attention to it, or treats it as a remnant of a primitive culture that Christians should soon outgrow. This approach can be very frustrating to Melanesians. One Bible college student wrote: "I had some experience with encountering spiritual powers, but at Bible college, I observed a 'big silence' regarding this subject. I became reluctant to pursue Christ's ministry and Paul's ministry regarding this area." The spirit world is very important and Christians need to have a biblical understanding of the spirit world.

The Bible is full of references to the spirit world.[43] There are twelve different terms referring to Satan, various gods and spirits, with a total of 749 references. We can add to this list a further 292 references to angels, and 67 references to cherubim, seraphs and archangels, giving a total of over 1100 references to the spirit world. Also listed are nine different types of religious practitioners and practices with 113 references. This list is not exhaustive, for it does not include verses such as Paul's classic statement in Ephesians 6:12: "Our struggle is not against flesh and blood, but against the rulers, against the authorities, against the powers of this dark world and against the spiritual forces of evil in the heavenly realms."

Wiley states that theology in a "general sense is the science of religion" (1940: vol.1:17). It would appear, however, that Western theology is not objective: its focus and emphasis is affected far more by a modern scientific world-view than is usually admitted.

Clinton Arnold argues that there is a conflict between two different world-views, and that differing world-views affect people's theology. According to Arnold, there is no doubt that people of the first century, including the apostle Paul and the other New Testament writers, believed in evil spirits. The problem is that "the modern scientific world-view stands in direct contradiction to the first century world-view and also to the biblical world-view" (1992:176). He calls on the academic community "to rethink the part of the Western world-view that denies the actual existence of spirits, demons and supernatural powers" (1992:177).

As part of his argument, Arnold points out that while modern science denies the reality of evil spirits, they do remain an integral part of the world-views of most other cultures. He adds that Christians from other parts of the world "often express disappointment that the Western church has not been able to help them develop a

155

Christian perspective on the realm of the spirits" (1992:180). I agree wholeheartedly with Arnold, and feel that Arnold has highlighted one of the biggest failures of Western Christianity. Because it has largely denied the existence of the spirit world, it does not relate to many of the questions that people in other parts of the world are asking. Consequently, it has no answers, and so people look to other sources for help. A contextualised theology that deals directly and specifically with the spirit world in all of its dimensions is very important, because this is where Western theology is so lacking. Merely condemning traditional beliefs as superstitious and primitive will not help people. It will lead only to a "conspiracy of silence", in which people no longer talk about these beliefs and problems because they know that the missionary does not understand (Henry 1986:33).

4. The Importance of Ritual

In each of these three cultural groups, there are a large number of rituals including sacrifices, spells, divination, taboos to be observed, dances and festivals. I have not described the multitude of ritual activities that are such a vital part of Melanesian religions, as the rituals are many and the details vary greatly from place to place. Nevertheless, it is possible to list the types of rituals that take place. Traditionally, religious rituals were connected with almost every area of life. I asked Bible college students to divide into small groups and make a list of the various activities for which supernatural help was sought in previous times. They took only a few minutes to put together the following list:

- Gardening, planting, harvesting, hunting, fishing, pig raising.
- Child birth, child naming, girls first menstrual period, initiation for boys, obtaining a wife/husband, marriage, sickness, counteracting sorcery, at time of impending death, and at burial.
- House building, canoe making, warfare, tribal dances, peacemaking, trading, safety on journeys.

We discussed the various types of spirits and sources of power. I asked them to write down the types of things that link the various sources of power (i.e. the spirit world) with the events they had listed as needing supernatural help. They listed the following: *singsings*, sacrifices, songs, chants, dances, spells, food offerings, prayers, healing rituals, eating special foods, divination, talking to the spirits, confession, use of leaves and herbs.

Rituals can be thought of as bridges that link the sources of power in the spirit world with the needs of everyday life. This relationship is depicted in the diagram below (Figure 14).

Traditional Melanesian religion is very rich in its use of rituals to channel the power of spirits into events of everyday life. How will Christianity respond to this challenge? Protestants as a whole, and evangelicals in particular, have tended to shy away from rituals. They do not want people to take a magical view, whereby people's faith is in the ritual rather than in God himself. When Christian missionaries fail to express the Christian faith with symbols and ceremonies, worship may not be fully satisfying to people used to such ways. It leaves a vacuum, which is often filled with magical practices inherited from the traditional religion (Zahniser 1997:74-75). Sometimes we forget that the Old Testament is full of all sorts of rituals, songs, sacrifices, feasts, pilgrimages, festivals, ceremonial washing etc. Correctly used rituals can be a valuable asset in teaching and in building up people's faith.

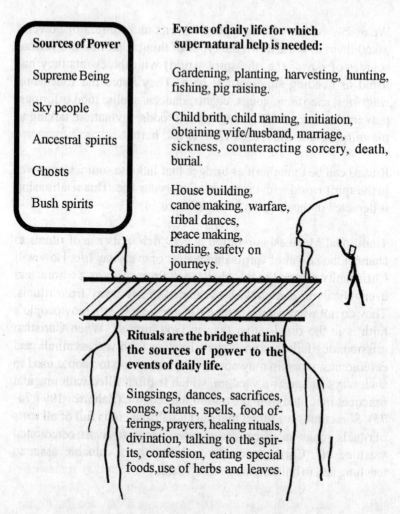

Sources of Power

Supreme Being

Sky people

Ancestral spirits

Ghosts

Bush spirits

Events of daily life for which supernatural help is needed:

Gardening, planting, harvesting, hunting, fishing, pig raising.

Child brith, child naming, initiation, obtaining wife/husband, marriage, sickness, counteracting sorcery, death, burial.

House building, canoe making, warfare, tribal dances, peace making, trading, safety on journeys.

Rituals are the bridge that link the sources of power to the events of daily life.

Singsings, dances, sacrifices, songs, chants, spells, food offerings, prayers, healing rituals, divination, talking to the spirits, confession, eating special foods, use of herbs and leaves.

Figure 14. Rituals as a Bridge Between Sources of
Power and the Events of Daily Life

Figure 14, which shows the "bridge of rituals", helps us to understand the situation from the Melanesian perspective. Bridges in PNG are often two logs with a number of planks or even just split lumber nailed or placed on top. Sometimes the planks come loose or go missing, and crossing the bridge can be an alarming exercise. Western Christianity has removed many of the old rituals (planks) and replaced them with a bridge that has only a few planks (few rituals); missionaries are surprised when people are not satisfied and feel insecure. In times of revival, there is a rapid increase in the practice of rituals that were not part of people's Christian worship. Dreams, visions, fasting, nights of prayer, shaking, trances, prophecy and miracles of healing are all activities in which people can feel the sources of power impacting in their daily life. Alan Tippett, in *Solomon Islands Christianity*, writes that when Christianity arrived in the Solomon Islands, the contest was not between a pagan deity and the Christian God. "The encounter had to take place on the level of daily life against those powers which dealt with the relevant problems of gardening, fishing, war, security, food supply and personal life crisis" (Tippett 1967:5). The church must deal with this area of life.

Too often the modern division between religion and science has resulted in many missionaries - and those they have trained - taking a largely secular approach to medicine, agriculture, etc. As a result, issues which were once religious have become secular. As a result of contact with modern culture and Western Christianity, people have often ended up less religious than they were before. How much better if the church would provide Christian rituals, songs and prayers to help fill this gap, for: "Christianity will remain Western unless it expresses its faith through abundant rituals" (Mantovani 1984e:189). People feel much more secure when the bridge has many planks to it. George Hunter has pointed out that the Celtic Church provided abundant prayers and rituals to connect the power of God with the needs of everyday life (Hunter 2000:33).

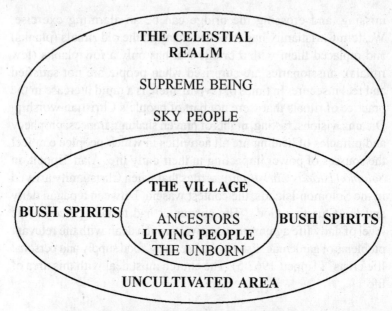

Figure 15. The Realm of the Spirits

5. The Cosmic Dimension of the Spirit World

We have seen the three main categories of spirits. There is the Supreme Being, who often manifests himself through the sun, or moon, or thunder and lightning. Some cultures have sky people who are supernatural beings who come to the assistance of humans. There are the bush spirits that exist on the edges of society. Finally, there are the ancestral spirits, who are mainly concerned with social relationships within the clan. This complex of relationships can be seen in Figure 15. This diagram is adapted from Jentsch and Doetsch (cited in Dlugosz 1998:51). It is divided into three realms:

1. Above is the sky realm, the place of the supreme being and the sky people.
2. Below is the forest that is inhabited by bush spirits.
3. In the centre is the clan settlement, inhabited by people, ancestors and ghosts.

160

There is no part of life that is not controlled or influenced by these spirit beings. This whole universe shares in a common life and "true life is experienced through the establishment of relationships through a reciprocal exchange with people, with spirits and with nature" (Dlugosz 1998:52). This fits with *gutpela sindaun* as the goal of Melanesian religion. This world-view is similar to that of the Bible. Paul states that it is God's desire and purpose "to reconcile to himself all things, whether things on earth or things in heaven, by making peace through his blood, shed on the cross" (Colossians 1.20). There is a cosmic dimension here that is often missing from Western Christianity. The reconciliation which Jesus brings affects more than individual people's relationships to God: it should extend beyond that to bringing peace and harmony to societies and people groups, and should also include people's relationship to the environment.

How does the triune God relate to this world of spirits and how do they relate to God? How did the death and resurrection of Jesus affect the spirit world and especially the spirits of the dead? These are important theological questions. In Melanesia, all of life is pervaded and influenced by spirits, and it has therefore been described as cosmic (Mantovani 1984b:32). This cosmic dimension is biblical, and if theology is to be meaningful to Melanesians, it must deal with this.

6. Harmony in Relationships

One feature that comes through each of these cultures is that life depends on harmonious relationships between people and the world around them, including the spirit world. Harmony in relationships is a biblical concept; in the first few chapters of Genesis we read of the disruption of these relationships. The final chapters of Revelation speak of the restoration of harmonious relationships between humans and God, a renewed universe and God dwelling among his people. One group that is using this approach very effectively is the Nazarene Community Based Health Care team. In their approach to health care and village development, they emphasise health as being right relationships with:

1. God;
2. Other people in the community;
3. The environment and the world around us; and
4. Ourselves.

People have responded enthusiastically to this holistic approach. They emphasise: "The earth is the Lord's, and everything in it, the world, and all who live in it" (Psalms 24:1). Deuteronomy 23:12-14 has become an important verse for health teaching: "Designate a place outside the camp where you can go to relieve yourself ... for the LORD your God moves about in your camp to protect you and to deliver your enemies to you. Your camp must be holy, so that he will not see among you anything indecent and turn away from you." They have emphasised that the earth is the Lord's. God is present and involved in his creation and we are to care for it. They have brought the teachings of God into the daily issues of village living. As people have realised God is not remote, but here among us, and have cleaned up their villages, the change in health and in church life has been dramatic. Again and again, village leaders have said to the health team leaders: "This is good news. This is what we have been looking for." They are dissatisfied with a "disembodied Christianity" that deals with one's relationship with God and a heavenly future, but largely ignores life here and now. Too often health care has been left to the government, or when done by the church, has been institutionalised and separated from the life of the church. In either case, health care has lost its spiritual dimension - which is so much a part of the Melanesian world-view. It would help the Community Based Health Care teams if they were to incorporate clear teaching about the spirit world in their presentations, and show how being united with Jesus Christ can enable people to overcome the fear of sorcery and witchcraft.

162

7. Blood Sacrifice

All three of these groups rely on blood sacrifices in order to restore relationships with the spiritual realm. The concept of blood sacrifice is widespread throughout all Melanesian cultures, and it is commonly accepted that reconciliation can only be made through a blood sacrifice. It is therefore not difficult for Papua New Guineans to understand the concept of Jesus' death and his blood being shed in order to reconcile us to God.

In developing a contextual theology, it is important to present Christianity so that it deals with these beliefs. They must not be ignored, but may be used as points of discussion. Jesus Christ comes to restore relationships between individuals, between us and God, between ourselves and our neighbours, and other clans as well. He does this through his sinless life and sacrificial death. Through his death and resurrection, Jesus is now "the Lord of both the dead and the living" and is seated at God's "right hand in the heavenly realms, far above all rule and authority, power and dominion" (Romans 14:9; Ephesians 1:21). "Christ must be presented in terms that are culturally meaningful and impactful. He must be shown to be God's answer to the Melanesian search" (Schwarz 1984:247).

In concluding this chapter, these words, from Don McGregor writing about the Wape people in the Sepik Province, are very appropriate:

We missionaries must realise the need for the Wape Christians to eventually develop from Scripture a theology which speaks a word concerning their various classes of spirits along with the innumerable daily tensions all tied up with their world-view, spirits, magic, and sorcery. Their relevant theology will not be a static thing, but will change as their understanding of the world changes and as they grow in their Christian experience ... Their Wape theology adequately spelled out will address itself to the problems of existence in their world and will have much to say about

163

sorcery, ancestral spirits, sickness and death ... A relevant
theology will accept the existing world-view, and in so
doing will be an instrument for changing it gradually. In
addressing itself to the tensions and fears of everyday
life it will show the Christian way to life in their world –
without fear and with love to God and fellow man. A
relevant theology thus spelled out can emerge only from
the people themselves. (1982:122)

A relevant theology is definitely needed, but what form should this
theology take?

CHAPTER SEVEN

MELANESIAN MYTHS

Myths are multi-functional. They explain the universe, nature and the customs of society in ways people can easily remember and understand. Stories are entertaining. They are told around the fire at night. The glow of the fire reflects off the face of the story teller, and the faces of the listeners. They do not hurry, for the sweet potatoes roast slowly in the depths of the accumulated ashes. The stories stretch out to fill in the evening, with no breaks for commercials. These stories are written stories, but are part of an oral culture. Told and retold, they endure because they provide meaning and hope to life.

The Importance of Myths

Melanesian spirit world beliefs are not organised by Melanesians into a systematic theology. Unwritten but woven into the fabric of life, they are contained in the multitude of stories that are basic to a people's knowledge of who they are, how they live and how they relate to the world around them. They may be embedded in *singsing* festivals, acted out and dramatised by the clan. In thinking about how to express theology in the Melanesian context, the importance of myth in Melanesian societies must be understood. Rituals and religious practices do not exist in a social vacuum. Very often they relate to myths that provide a foundation or basis for a people's view of life. Malinowski writes: "Myth fulfils in primitive culture an indispensable function: it expresses, enhances and codifies belief; it safeguards and enforces morality; it vouches for the efficiency of ritual and contains practical rules for the guidance of man. Myth is thus a vital ingredient of human civilisation; it is not an idle tale, but a hard worked active force" (1948:79). Stories can provide people with a sense of identity and bring meaning to the world around them.

165

Many Papua New Guinean cultures have a vast reservoir of myths and legends that are very important to the people.[44] The Simbu people do not place a big emphasis on legends from the past, for Simbus are focused on the present and see change as being inevitable. Even so, the legends that tell the origins of the tribe, where they came from and the battles they have fought, are very important to the Simbu people. These stories give them a sense of identity and belonging (Brown 1995:14-20).

Basic Themes in Melanesian Mythology

Strelan suggests that there are four major themes that are found in Melanesian mythology (1977:60):

1. The division of people. A situation is presented in which a choice is made, and this choice serves to separate one progenitor from another, and one group of people from another. This helps to answer the question: "Who are we?"[45]

2. Two brother myth. The theme of two brothers is one of the most widespread in Melanesia. This myth shows the importance of material goods (cargo) and seeks to explain the reason for inequality between different peoples. At the same time, it speaks of the importance of community. A very well known myth is that of Manup and Kilibob, which comes from the Madang Province (Pech 1979). (I have heard versions of this same myth in West Sepik and Middle Ramu.) In this myth, there is an act of hostility or stupidity by one of the brothers, causing the two to separate and go their own ways. One prospers and gains much cargo, but the other has very little. The hope is expressed that one day reconciliation will be made, and harmony and peace restored between the brothers (Steinbauer 1979:40-41). This myth is used to explain why Europeans have so much more cargo than Melanesians. Consequently, it has become the underlying story behind many of the cargo cults along the north coast of Papua New Guinea.

3. Lost paradise. This theme has countless variations, and tells how an idyllic life style was destroyed by one person's foolishness, disobedience or greediness (see also Aerts 1998:31-34).

4. Coming deliverer. The theme of a messiah or saviour-hero who will return and bring the ancestors with him. This will usher in the golden age of peace and prosperity.

There is another very common myth that Strelan does not mention, but which is very important: the *dema* myth (Jensen 1963:88). In this myth, a cultural hero either offers himself in death to save his people or family, or is killed tragically; very quickly out of his grave comes new life that benefits the people. From the death of one comes life for many.[46]

The following myths were told to me by PNG pastors. They believe these stories are very significant and see them as similar to the stories of the Bible. The myths recorded here are shortened versions, and have lost something of the original flavour being told to me in Pidgin (instead of the *tok ples*) and then translated and written down in English.

Paradise Lost[47]

Many years ago, a man went out hunting for a cuscus.[48] He knew where to find the big fruit bearing trees which were the favourite food of the cuscus. He found a tree and settled down to watch. It was a clear night and the tall tree seemed to stretch up to the sky. He waited and waited until his keen eyes picked up the form of a big white cuscus coming down the tree. He fitted an arrow to his bow, waited until the cuscus came in range, and then pulled back on his bow. The hunter was about to let the arrow fly when suddenly the cuscus began to change form. Instead of a white furry animal, it changed into the most

167

beautiful, gorgeous woman he had ever seen. Instantly his hand relaxed on the bow and he lowered the arrow. He could think of nothing else other than to capture the woman and make her his wife.

Using all of his skill and cunning, the hunter crept close to the tree. He caught hold of the woman and persuaded her to come home to be his wife. He was very happy, but there was one problem. What would he need to give as a bride price? Her father lived up in the sky and the only way to reach him was by climbing up through the big tree. The woman said that her father demanded a large fat pig for the bride price. The big day was set for giving the bride price. The man, however, was rather selfish, and instead of obtaining the biggest, fattest pig he could find, he brought along his own pig which was skinny and malnourished. The man in the sky was upset that the earth man should think so little of his beautiful daughter and offer such a miserable little pig. In his anger, he swept his daughter back up into the sky and pulled up the rope ladder that dangled from the sky to the top of the tree. Ever since then, the way to paradise has been lost, all because of one man's selfishness.

Sumisama and Paradise Lost[49]

Sumisama is a cultural hero who is renowned in the Kagua area of the Southern Highlands. *"Sumi"* is the name of the area where he lived and *"sama"* means man. This story also deals with the problem of "why we missed out on the good life".

Sumisama lived at Wosuma, where he had a house and gardens. Nearby was a mountain and often in the late afternoons, he would hear the sound of young women laughing. He wondered who they were and where they came from. One day Sumisama went to investigate. He

168

found an area where people had been digging out yellow clay, but, strangely, although there were marks of people's hands, there were no marks of people's feet. Nearby were large trees and he noticed clay on their branches. He was puzzled by the strange sight.

The next day he went back early, hid in a clump of pitpit reeds very close to the yellow clay, and waited and watched. Then he heard voices - women's voices, and looking up he noticed the branches of the tree moving. There in the branches of the tree, were the most beautiful women he had ever seen. They all sat in a line on the branches of the tree. He looked at each one until he came to the last one, who appeared to be the leader. She was the most beautiful woman he had ever seen. One by one these heavenly women came down out of the tree and gathered handfuls of the yellow clay. Sumisama looked at the last one and his heart was smitten. "I must get that woman for myself," he said to himself.

The last one spoke to the others: "Sisters, please get some for me." They laughed, "Come and get your own," they said. "No. I feel something strange, and I do not think I should." But when none of the others were willing to help her, she cautiously approached the clay pit. Sumisama waited for his opportunity. He tensed every muscle. She reached down her hand to scoop up the clay and as she did so, Sumisama grabbed her hand. She struggled with all her power, but Sumisama held on with all his might. The other women fled back into the sky for they were sky people. "What do you want of me," she demanded.

"I want you to be my wife. You are the most beautiful woman I have ever seen and I will never be happy unless you are mine." The woman struggled. Lightning flashed, the wind roared, and the earth shook. She struck him

169

with thorns, but Sumisama held on. He would not let go.
Eventually, Sumisama prevailed and the woman agreed
to go home with him.

Sumisama was filled with joy. His life had never been
better. The garden blossomed and flourished, as did his
pigs. They lived in happiness and harmony, and Sumisama
was the happiest man in the world. Everyone envied him
because of his beautiful wife and the prosperity with which
he was blessed.

Some time passed and Sumisama heard of a singing
festival coming up. He was determined to go, so he
prepared his best decorations and plumes for going to
the singsing. The woman, however, was not happy. "Lots
of bad things happen at singsings," she said.

"Oh, you do not need to worry," he laughed at her.
"Nothing will happen to me. But I must go for I am an
important man in the village."

She said: "You may go and singsing, but do not look at
other women, and come straight back." The woman had
prepared a long fine string that she fastened to his
finger.[50] "I will fasten this to you, and then if anything
happens, I will know immediately."

Sumi went off to the singsing. As he walked away from
the house, the woman allowed the fine thread to unwind.
Many people were at the singsing; Sumi and his
decorations were outstanding, and everyone commented
on his beauty and splendour. Then word came that a
famous woman and her tribe were coming. People were
beating their drums and singing their chants as they
danced in circles. The woman's group came in, formed a
large circle, and began to dance. During the afternoon,

170

the large very black woman noticed Sumi. She watched him and was greatly attracted to him. She approached him and took his stone axe from his hand, thus showing that she was very attracted to him. Immediately, the thread that was on Sumi's finger slipped off and sprang back to his sky woman wife who was sitting at home. Instantly she knew that Sumi had disregarded her instructions and had not been truly faithful to her.

The singsing went on and Sumi enjoyed the woman's attention. At the end of the singsing he walked back home. As he came to the top of the hill and looked down toward his house, he was surprised to see no sign of a fire. When he came to his house, he was shocked, for his house was old and falling to pieces. There was no fire, no wife, no pigs and no garden. Everything was empty, cold, deserted, and in disrepair. He remembered now the words and the warning his wife had given to him. He sat down in despair. "What have I done?" he said. "She has left me and now I have nothing."

As time went by, he became increasingly lonely and sad. One day as he went to the water hole to get some water, he looked down and saw the woman sitting in the deep pool, making rope for a bilum. "At last I have found her," he cried. He set to work, diverted the little stream coming into the pool, and drained out all the water. It took all day to get it done, but when all the water was gone, he found nothing but sand. He went home dejected, but determined to try again the next day.

The next day he returned to where he had diverted the water. Now there was a new pool, and looking into the pool he saw the woman he loved. He set to work and diverted the water again in the hope that this time he would find the woman of his dreams. But alas, he found nothing

171

but sand. This happened again and again. He felt frustrated and his back ached from all his digging. One day after a full day of digging, his back was aching so badly that he lay back on the grass to rest. As he did so, he looked up and saw the woman far above him in the sky. He realised now that the woman in the pool was only the reflection of the woman in the sky. All his hard work had been in vain. He had been digging furiously, trying to catch her reflection. He looked at her and his heart ached after the good life he once enjoyed, but now had lost. He thought long and deeply. He looked and there to the west he noticed a mountain that seemed to touch the sky. "If I could climb that mountain then I would be able to reach her," he decided.

The next day, he climbed and climbed, but when he got to the top of the mountain, he found he was still short of where he needed to be. As he studied the surrounding area, he noticed another mountain (now called Mt. Sumi), that seemed to touch the sky. He decided to build a ladder which he would take to the top of the mountain and use it to reach the sky world. He worked for days cutting trees and carrying them to the top of the mountain. He joined the pieces of wood together, and made the longest ladder in the world. He climbed to the top of the ladder and when he was about to reach the woman, the ladder collapsed and he came tumbling down. Both of his legs were broken, he never did recover, and he died in that place. His bones can still be seen there, even to this day. He was a giant of a man and most of the bones have been removed, but his two thigh bones which are about 1.8 metres long can still be seen. Because of his foolishness and pride, he lost the good life. Life has been full of hardship and struggles ever since.

An Alternative Ending

I heard this same story from a number of other people, but Pastor Vincent Puringi, who first told it to me, said that his father's version has an ending that others do not; his father's version has a happier ending.

The man reached the feet of the woman and she said: "If you want me to come back, you must give a bride price of 100 white pigs." Sumi searched high and low and eventually collected the 100 white pigs. He came back to the woman and said: "I have obtained the pigs you required." She said: "I will talk to my father, but you cannot come to where he is or else you will die."

Vincent's father believed that the father in the sky was Yakali, the one who is above all other beings and the father of all things. He believed that only by sacrificing a white pig could he gain the blessing of God and obtain healing. Vincent's father has made it a practice to obtain a white pig, if at all possible, for offering to Yakali.

Pastor Puringi's Analysis

This story is very similar to that of Adam and Eve. Because of disobedience, we missed out on the good life that we could have had. Sumisama had eternal and abundant life, but he lost it because of disobedience. The woman represents the Word of God, God's truth. This parallels the book of Proverbs, where "wisdom" is personified as a woman (Proverbs 2:5-9). The story also emphasises the futility of trying to get right with God through our own strength. White pigs are similar to the Old Testament requirement of a lamb without mark or defect, and represent God's requirement of righteousness.

These two stories are very similar, even though they come from different areas of the country. In each story, there is a sky person

173

who descends, becomes a wife and brings great joy and happiness. In both stories, the beautiful relationship is destroyed through man's greed or disobedience. In the second story, all human efforts to repair the relationship are fruitless. This theme occurs in a number of legends, and shows the significance of relationships, their fragility and their need to be protected and maintained.

One Melanesian pastor said: "Our stories do not end with everyone living happily together, but usually have sad endings." The *gutpela sindaun* seems to be lost forever. Part of the missiological task can be to suggest alternative ends and interpretations to the story. There is good news, we can offer: the price has been paid, the road has been opened so that we can return to God and relationships can be restored.

Dema Myth - How We Got Our Vegetables

This story comes from the Kobon area.

> *Long, long ago, we had very little food to eat, and certainly did not have the variety of foods that we have today. One man went to the bush to clear the jungle and to plant a garden. He chopped down a number of trees with his stone axe and cut them into short lengths. At last when he was finished, he went home to his house. The next morning, he came back to the new garden area, only to find that things were very different from the way he had left them. Someone had come in the night and had reassembled all the trees he had cut down. They had been put back together and were growing just as they had been before.*
>
> *This puzzled him, but he went to work and cut them down again. By the end of the day he was very tired, so he picked up his stone axe and went home. When he came back the next day, the same thing had happened. All the*

174

trees had been put back together and were standing up in the garden. He wondered who was playing tricks on him. He was tempted to give up, but he needed the garden to grow food for his family. He went to work and cut them all down again, just as he had done on the previous two days. This time however, instead of going home, he pretended to leave, but carefully circled back, hid and watched. As it became dark, he saw an old man with a big stomach climb down out of a very tall tree. The man began to pick up the branches and pieces of trunk and reassemble the trees.

The gardener was very angry at seeing this old man destroying all his hard work. He put an arrow into his bow, pulled it back with all his strength and shot the old man. His aim was direct and the old man fell to the ground with the arrow wound. He rushed up, killed the old man and decided to burn him. He gathered dry branches and other firewood together, put the body of the old man on top of the firewood and lit the fire. The flames blazed up and burned the old man. As he was burning, the old man's abdomen began to expand greatly. There was a tremendous explosion, like the sound of a gigantic exploding bamboo, as the old man's abdomen burst open.

The man was shocked; he rushed home, but told no one what he had done. After a few days, however, his curiosity got the better of him and he returned to the garden. He saw the ashes where he had burned the old man, and to his surprise he saw all sorts of new plants growing up out of the ashes. He decided to leave them and see what type of plants they would become. The plants grew rapidly, and he watched them eagerly to see how he could use each one. A taro plant grew; he tried eating its leaves, but found they were too tough. He left them and some months later discovered that the big starchy root was

175

excellent food. He tried the leaves of another one, the cucumber, but the leaves were rough and raspy. He left that one also and eventually found that it bore fruit which were full of water and very refreshing. And so it was with bananas, sugarcane, sweet potato and all sorts of edible greens. From death and ashes came life-giving food.

That this old man climbed down out of the tree speaks of his heavenly origin. His actions of putting the trees back together shows him as the one who cares for creation. The man of the earth misunderstands his actions and kills him, but out of his death comes life and blessing to many people.

This type of story has come to be known by anthropologists as a "*dema* myth", a name that comes from the Marind-Anim people in Irian Jaya (Jensen 1963:88, Mantovani 1984e:184-185). The new thing may be vegetables, as in this story, or the first coconut, or the ancestors of all pigs, or some other essential part of life. This reminds us of the words of Jesus: "unless a kernel of wheat falls to the ground and dies, it remains only a single seed. But if it dies, it produces many seeds" (John 12:24).

The Defeat of Evil

Told by Joe Pindipia, pastor of the Church of the Nazarene in Mendi, Southern Highlands.[51]

Long, long ago, there was a father and two sons. The father's name was Limbo and the two boys were named Ole and Ale. One time there was a big singsing celebration and the two young men wanted to go. The father was a bit reluctant, but they really wanted to go and so he allowed the two boys to go by themselves. The father tied a string to each of their hands and fastened the other end to his own fingers. They dressed up in their finest feathers and rubbed oil on their bodies until their skin shone. They were truly magnificent and outshone everyone else at the singsing.

They had a wonderful time and enjoyed themselves thoroughly, but in the afternoon it became dark. Rain was threatening, and so they found an empty house in which to spend the night. They started a fire to keep themselves warm, and then a big old woman came into the house. She claimed to be their aunt. She was big and ugly. The two boys were afraid of her and didn't trust her. They were afraid that she might do something to harm them while they were asleep, and so they decided to take turns staying awake and keeping alert. However, some time in the early hours of the morning, they both fell asleep. The old woman spotted her chance and picked up Ale and stuffed him into her bilum, slung it onto her back and set off with him. Ole woke up some time later to discover that his brother was gone. He set off in pursuit, but this was no ordinary woman: she was a wicked witch. Ole walked and walked until he came to a big river, but there was no bridge by which he could cross it.

Brokenhearted, he returned to his father with the sad news that his brother, Ale, had been abducted. Father and son cried together. The father said: "I knew something had happened for I felt the string on my finger break." Together they planned a rescue operation to save the missing brother.

They killed a big pig and cooked it in a hole in the ground with hot stones. They also shot and killed an eagle and plucked it. The father fastened the feathers to Ole's arms and body and he practiced flying. First he flew up onto a fence, then he flew up and landed on a tree, then he became so good he could fly high in the sky like an eagle.

177

Ole removed the feathers and placed them carefully in a bilum. He also put the cooked pork into a bilum and set off on his rescue mission. He walked for a long way until he came to the big river. He wondered how he would cross the river. As he wandered along the bank, he spotted an old house with an old man and woman living in it. They were friendly and offered accommodation. He told them of his errand and they said: "What you say is true. We see people going down that way, but they never return." Ole took out some of his pork and sprinkled it liberally with traditional salt and gave it to the old couple. They were delighted with his kindness and generosity. In the morning they sent him on his way. But before he left, the old man gave him a present which was wrapped in leaves. He said: "If you come to special difficulties, this will be very useful."

When Ole came to the river, he opened the present and found a walking stick. He struck the river with it, it parted, and he was able to cross easily. When he got to the other side, he struck the river again and the river resumed flowing, just as it had done before. He walked all day until it was dark and came to another house where an old man was living. He befriended the old man, gave him some of his pork, and shared his story. The old man said: "Over the next mountain range, you will find a big deep valley with a lot of smoke coming up from many fires. That is where you will need to go. Be careful, for that is a place where they eat people. Many people go there and never return." Before Ole left, the old man gave him a small parcel and said: "You will find this very useful on your journey." Ole thanked him and went on his way.

Ole walked to the top of the ridge and there before him was a big deep valley with many fires. He saw many women, and also the big bad witch who had stolen his

178

*brother. Ole opened his bilum and took out the eagle
feathers. He carefully fitted them to his body and flew up
into the sky. He circled high overhead calling out: "Ale,
Ale, Ale, your father is looking for you." Down below
him, the women were cutting the bush and burning the
scrub to make a large garden. The women heard the bird
calling out as it flew overhead. The girls said: "Old
Mama, look at that big bird calling out." Ole alighted on
a tree not far from the old woman and watched what was
happening. It was a very hot day and the heat from the
fires made everyone thirsty. The old woman told one of
the girls: "Go and fetch me a bamboo tube full of water."
Ole opened the present the old man had given him, and
discovered a mosquito inside. Quickly he changed into
the mosquito and flew down to the stream where the girl
was filling up the bamboo tube. Without her noticing, he
flew into the tube and landed on the water. The girl
brought the water to the old mother who quickly
swallowed it and in doing so, swallowed Mosquito Ole
as well.*

*The next day, the old woman felt that something had
happened to her. She realised that she was pregnant with
a baby growing within her. The baby grew very rapidly
and soon a baby boy was born.[52] The women and girls
were delighted, and the old mama was thrilled that she
had a son. He quickly grew up and the old mama took
him everywhere she went.*

*One day she said: "Let us go and check the animal traps
and see how the pigs are doing in the pig house. It is a
long journey and will take all day." Ole and the old mama
set out, crossed mountains, forded rivers, and walked and
walked. Eventually they came to a place where lots of
sugarcane and bananas were growing. On the way, they
had checked the animal traps and had filled their bilums*

179

with many possums. At this place there were many spirit houses. In the middle was a huge house, bigger and higher than all the others. "This is my pig house where I keep all my meat," the old woman said. The old woman told Ole to take some of the possums and cook one of them in front of each of the spirit houses. Ole quickly did this and while the old woman was working in the garden, he ran to the big tall house. He opened the door and sure enough, it was just as he expected. There was not a single pig inside. Instead, there were hundreds of men inside, all of them tied up with strong canes and bush rope, and there was his brother Ale. He told them to be very quiet as they must not alarm the wicked witch. He quickly cut their ropes and set them free. He ran outside and collected sugarcane and bananas, and gave them food to renew their strength. He handed out his feathers to the people and told them to quietly practice their flying skills inside the house. He went back to the old woman who told him: "Take all the food out of the pits and we will parcel it up and take a parcel home to each of my daughters." Ole knew that the old woman's favourite daughter was her eldest and usually received twice as much as all the others, so while the old woman was busy, he hid the largest parcel under some banana leaves. Loading all the other parcels into the bilums, the two started walking home. They walked for hours until their home was almost in sight. Ole said: "Mama, maybe we should check to make sure that all the parcels are here. It would be terrible if one was missing and the girls became upset." They opened the bilums and sure enough, the big parcel of food for the eldest daughter was missing.

Ole immediately volunteered to run back and find it. Leaving the old woman with all the bags of food, he ran back. He opened the door of the big house and released all the people who were inside. Now they could really practice their flying. They quickly set fire to all the spirit houses and the big house where they had been imprisoned.

The old woman was waiting impatiently for Ole when she noticed the smoke rising up from all the burning houses and saw all the eagles circling over head. She ran back to see what had happened. Ole, who had also put on his eagle feathers, called out: "Mama, you thought I belonged to you, but I am not your child. I am my father's son, and I came back to free my brothers. You will never catch us again." The old woman was very angry and chased after the birds. The birds teased the old woman by flying a little distance and then landing. She kept chasing after them, but as soon as she got almost close enough to catch one, they would fly off again. In this way, they led the old woman back to their home place.

Ole sent word ahead to his father. He said: "I am bringing all those who were imprisoned and the old woman as well. Dig a deep pit on your side of the river as for catching a wild pig, and fill it with sharpened spears. Also build a big fire and heat lots of big rocks." The old woman followed them all the way back to the river. The birds landed on the other side of the river and she rushed across the cane bridge. She was so eager to catch her escaping prisoners, that she did not see the trap. She fell headlong into the pit and was impaled on the sharpened spears. Now the people took all the rocks out of the fire and dropped them down on the old woman until she was burned alive. The people then had a great celebration, for now the wicked witch was dead and would never trouble them again. They were free at last and back home with their father.

Interpretation

The hero in this story has to overcome many difficulties as he seeks to save his family and clan. Through a miraculous birth, he becomes a baby and grows up within an evil cannibalistic household. He does not forget his mission. He destroys the wicked witch/cannibal, saves his brothers and they are happily reunited with their father.

This is how Joe interpreted the story: the father represents God the Father, Ale represents the human race that has been taken captive and Ole represents Jesus who comes to find his lost brother. The old woman represents Satan. When Ale is taken away by the wicked woman, the father feels the tie broken and is immediately concerned. The father and son plan a rescue operation to reclaim those under Satan's control. There is a parallel between Ole using the stick to divide the river, and Moses using his staff at the crossing of the Red Sea.[53]

Respect for the elderly and generosity are both important characteristics of good people. Ole gives generous amounts of the pork to the old people and, as a result, is blessed by them. The eagle, which is the largest and strongest of all birds and which also flies the highest, is a symbol of divine help.

The incarnation is seen in Ole becoming a mosquito so that he could be born as a baby, and thus be able to rescue his brother and all those in captivity. Even though Ole lives under the woman's influence, he does not become like her, but remembers his objective to find and release his brother, and ultimately be reunited with his father.

Ole persists until he finds his brother and all the other captives, and brings them release. They fly away and return to the father; however, the wicked woman ends up in a deep pit and is burned with hot stones (Revelation 20:10). Ole is the saviour who conquers evil and rescues his brothers.

There are, however, some distinct differences to the biblical story. Ole is born to an old ugly wicked witch, which contrasts greatly to the biblical story where Jesus is born of a young virgin. In the stories from Enga and another parallel story from Tari in the Southern Highlands, the hero becomes a mosquito and goes into a beautiful young virgin and is born. Ole won the victory by tricking the old woman, whereas Jesus did not defeat the devil through trickery, but by perfect obedience to the Father.

The stories from Enga and from Tari have a resurrection scene at the end. In the Tari version, the hero takes the bones of his brothers, who have been killed and eaten, and places them in a stream of running water (the river of life). As the water flows over them, flesh grows back onto the bones and then skin covers them. (There is a parallel here to the valley of dry bones in Ezekiel 37:8.) Eventually they become alive again and are reunited as a family. In the Enga version, the bones of the family members who have been killed and eaten are covered with the healing leaves of a special plant. The people come alive again and the family is reunited and live happily ever after.

Pastor Joe's story does not have a resurrection end to it, however it is possible to see a distinct parallel between this story and that of Jesus going to the place of the dead, defeating the evil one, announcing good news to the prisoners and leading many captives to freedom. The end result is the same: the family is reunited, evil is destroyed and the family live happily together.[54]

Missiological Implications

These stories are reminders that God "has not left himself without testimony" (Acts 14:17). Don Richardson has written about "redemptive analogies" and the way that God has prepared people's hearts so that they may turn to him and accept him (1976:234, 1984). Richardson gives numerous examples from a wide variety of countries, of legends and rituals that prepared people for the gospel.

In many cultures there are rituals and myths which can be used to open up people's hearts and minds to the gospel. It is important that missionaries and national pastors use these stories. When the good news is communicated using stories and rituals that people are familiar with, it ceases to be seen as foreign and is more easily understood and accepted.

Narrative

Recently, I was sitting in a Bible college chapel service. A Papua New Guinean Bible college teacher came to the pulpit. He said in Pidgin: "I must apologise for my sermon this morning, for it is not really a sermon, but a story that my grandfather told, and yet it is a story with much truth in it. I must also apologise, for it is a long story and some of you have heard this story before. But people who have heard me tell it remember it well and have asked me to tell it again." He then launched into a story about an evil bush spirit that steals a baby and replaces it with its own evil malnourished baby. The baby is cared for and nurtured by the family, but it is always greedy and eats all of their food.

I noticed that the congregation listened intently, and the mothers kept their children quieter than normal. I was intrigued by the complex story, but wondered how a tale about an evil bush spirit could possibly relate to the spiritual needs of the Bible college students. The story was long, and at its end the baby, who had by now grown quite big, turned on his parents and killed both father and mother. The teacher brought out a dramatic analogy, comparing it to the sinful nature that is hostile toward God and leads to death (Romans 8:6-7). He invited people to come to the altar to pray, and in minutes the altar was lined with students praying that God would cleanse their hearts from all that was hostile towards God in their lives.

This sermon and the previous stories are dramatic, captivating and easily remembered. It was a wonderful service, but I was

184

disappointed that the teacher felt that he needed to apologise for telling a story, rather than preaching a "proper sermon". Bible teaching must not be minimised or restricted, for the Bible is divinely inspired and has a historical validity that these stories do not have. All truth is God's truth, and so cultural stories can highlight truth and be used to apply the biblical truths in a powerful way.

Much Western style preaching uses an expository style and the monologue lecture is not easily remembered. If we are to be good communicators of the gospel, we need to use the styles of communication appropriate to local contexts: that are familiar to people, and so effective. The traditional myths are points of contact that God in his sovereignty has preserved within a culture. They prepare people's minds for understanding and accepting the gospel story. As people respond to the gospel story, they see their traditional myths in a new light, and see new truths in them that they had not seen before. Myths open the door for the acceptance of the gospel, and the gospel in turn sheds new light on the myths.

Stories are foundational to many people's world-views. "It is story that gives meaning to history and world-view" (Snyder 1995:261). One of the things that sets humans apart from other animals is the fact that humans tell stories. "We dream in narrative, daydream in narrative, remember, anticipate, hope, despair, believe, doubt, plan, revise, criticise, gossip, learn, hate and love by narrative" (Harding 1968:5). If we, as Christian communicators, want to change a people's world-view so that it reflects Christian values, then we will have to tell them a life changing story. It will need to be a true story that links the power of God with human problems. It must be a story that is cosmic and yet relates to local issues. It must be a story that people can identify with, remember and which will have a life changing impact. Christ's incarnation, death and resurrection is such a cosmic drama. It is dramatic, historically true and cosmic in scope (Hiebert et al. 1999:260).

185

Tom Steffen emphasises the importance of storytelling in communicating the gospel (1996, 1998). He argues that we must get rid of the false ideas that story telling is "just" entertainment, or mainly suitable for children, and that Bible stories and theology are unrelated. He lists seven reasons why story telling is extremely important:

1. Story telling is a universal form of communication.
2. More than half of the world's population prefer the concrete mode of learning. He says this on the basis that more than half of the world's population is either non-literate or semiliterate.
3. Stories connect with the imagination and the emotions. "Stories unleash the imagination, making learning an exciting life-changing experience" (Steffen 1996:122).
4. Every major religion uses stories to socialise its young, convert potential followers and indoctrinate members.
5. Approximately 75% of the Bible is narrative. Poetry covers a further 15%, and thought-organised format comprises the remaining 10%.
6. Stories make it easier for people to share the gospel, for people find it easy to repeat a good story.
7. Jesus taught theology through stories. He used stories to "tease audiences into reflecting on new ways of thinking about life" (Steffen 1996:120-125).

Given that 75 percent of the Bible is written in the narrative genre, why is it that seminaries require numerous courses in systematic theology, give little attention to biblical theology and virtually overlook narrative theology? Change is coming. Michael Lodahl writes:

A growing number of Bible scholars and theologians are arguing for the importance of seeing the Bible as an over-arching story (with many and various little stories along the way, to be sure) and of understanding that the primary task of theology ... is to unravel and make sense of the

186

biblical story, that is to "tell the story" afresh in a new age filled with its own questions and anxieties. (1994:13)

Lodahl is writing for a Western audience; if this is the situation in Western countries, then how much more important is it in countries who have always communicated in story form? People in Africa are recognising the importance of story.[55] Unfortunately, Bible colleges and seminaries in Melanesia do not emphasise story telling or drama as a means of communication. They teach classes on homiletics and analytical thinking and try to get students to prepare structured sermons with an introduction, three points and a conclusion. We still have a long way to go here for Christianity to be truly contextualised.

It is time to re-emphasise the telling of the story in such a way that it captures people's minds, hearts and imaginations, as they focus on the wonderful drama of redemption. In this drama, Jesus Christ is the centre of the story and we are also actors in the ongoing drama of redemption. Dyrness says that the story of the kingdom of God is a drama in five acts: creation, exodus, exile, Christ and consummation. God himself is the chief actor and playwright (1983:14,15; cf. Snyder 1995:272). God is a story teller and people are story telling animals (Steffen 1998:485). A contextual theology for Melanesia will have to be a narrative theology. It should focus on the drama of God's acts in history, rather than prepositional truths about God, which is the way in which theology has typically been presented. It will rely more on images and metaphors, rather than on systematic statements of faith presented in a carefully reasoned, logical format.

CHAPTER EIGHT

DEATH AND BURIAL: AN ANALYSIS

Death is a part of life, and is a very important part of the religious life of the people of Melanesia. It is a feature of many Melanesian myths and spirit beliefs. In Melanesia, death is not hidden away as it is in modern cultures, but is experienced in public view. Children are not shielded from it, but sit with the rest of the family around the corpse of the loved one. A funeral lasts from three days to a week, and death is obvious. At the end of the mourning time, people are exhausted and their throats are often hoarse from wailing.

In 1999, I led three week-long conferences for Nazarene pastors in which we discussed the subject of death. There were approximately thirty pastors at each conference. These conferences were held in Simbu, the Kobon area of the Madang Province and in the Southern Highlands.[56] Their purpose was to develop a theology related to death, dying and the spirits of the dead. To do this, we first described cultural practices. We divided into four groups of seven or eight and discussed cultural practices, including:

1. What happens in the family shortly before someone dies?
2. What happens immediately afterwards and during the time of mourning?
3. What happens at the time of burial?
4. What happens after the burial?[57]

At the end of the week, after studying Bible passages related to death and the resurrection, the pastors reviewed the practices that they had listed at the beginning of the week. They discussed them, considering which practices were good and acceptable and should be retained, which practices needed to be modified and which should be replaced. In this chapter I will present the findings of the three groups and their evaluation of these practices.

Simbu

Before Death

When a person is very sick, particularly if it is thought that death is near, the family gathers together. They encourage the sick person to confess any ill feelings toward others and to talk about anything that he/she thinks could be making him/her sick. At the same time, the other family members are also encouraged to confess any anger and resentment that they may have. Trompf explains that, "deaths, like particular sicknesses, are almost always the effects of negative payback - sorcery ... the vengeful dead, disturbed *masalai* (place [bush] spirits) or a wrathful person driven by a power beyond himself" (1991:71-72). The goal of the family sharing together is to uncover the problem so that they can bring about a sense of harmony. If problems are confessed, then reconciliation must be made. This can be settled by a gift of cash or a chicken. It is not enough to merely shake hands and forget about problems: some gift must be made. A pig may even be killed to cement and celebrate the unity, to show that all problems are cleared, and that there are no unsettled concerns. Any unpaid debts are settled, for they could be the cause of a person feeling angry and so make the family sick.

If the sick person does not improve, then people will look deeper for the cause of the sickness. This may involve calling in a diviner known in Pidgin as a *"glasman"* or a *"posin man"*.[58] The job of the diviner is to find out which spirit (or, more accurately, whose) is causing the sickness. The diviner encourages people to talk and share their various ideas as to who may be causing the sickness, and think about anything which could have upset the spirit of some relative who has died in the past few years. Sometimes the diviner will take a small piece of sharpened bamboo, no thicker than a pencil, and use it to try and pierce the root of a ginger plant. As he does this, he

189

calls the names of people who have died in recent years. If he calls the name of the one who is causing the sickness, the spirit will seize the bamboo spear so that it can no longer pierce the root of ginger (Trompf 1994:139). Once the offended spirit has been identified, the next step is to identify which pig needs to be killed in order to appease that spirit, and thus allow the person to be restored to health.

Sometimes, in place of the diviner, Christians will be called to come and pray that God will heal the sick person. When Christians are asked to pray for a sick person, they will begin with singing and Bible reading, and people will be reminded that they need to be right with God. They will be encouraged to repent and confess their sins, especially the sick person and his or her immediate family. Then people will pray. Usually all pray at the same time and then, if a pastor is present, he will conclude the prayer time.

People may try modern scientific treatment and medicine if available. Seldom, if ever, will the sick person be taken to the hospital before the family meets together to reconcile their differences. If all else fails, people may decide that the sickness is due to *sanguma* and that a more powerful form of treatment is needed. If that is the case, they may call in a *sanguma* doctor. A *sanguma* doctor is usually from some distance away and is credited as having more power than other *sanguma* people. He is willing to use his power to discover who is causing the sickness and so break the power of the disease.

During this time, the family stays near the sick person. When it seems that, despite all the efforts of the people, the person is dying, word is sent out for all family members to come. The family members listen for the last words of advice or blessing. If the father of the family is dying, then instructions will be given relating to division of the land, and how the money, pigs and other possessions should be divided among the family. The person may give instructions about where he or she would like to be buried. Pastors like to take the

190

opportunity at this time to strengthen the sick person's faith and make sure that the person is ready to meet the Lord.

The Mourning Process

As soon as someone dies, loud wailing begins to let people around know that there has been a death. Immediately, members of the extended family gather together, if they have not already done so. People buy a coffin, which may be a very simple box made from thin plywood, or, for those with more resources, a more elaborate coffin from town. The body will be dressed, wrapped in a new sheet or blanket and placed in the coffin.

The body is taken out of the house and placed in a cleared area under a large plastic tent. Word is sent to family members who are away from home (working in one of the cities, for example, or at a mine). It is very important that as many members of the family as possible be there for the burial. Burial may be delayed for a couple of days in order for family members to return for the funeral.

People show their grief by loud wailing, tugging at their hair and daubing or plastering themselves with mud. People wear old clothes and do not wash. They sit near the body, touch it and rub the face or other parts of the body with their hands. In the past, close relatives would cut off one of their finger joints, or cut an ear lobe to demonstrate deep grief. This still happens occasionally.

If a person has died in a tribal fight or car accident away from the village, then people will return to the place of death. They will call on the dead's spirit, enticing it with offerings of food in order to capture it and return it to the village.[59] They believe that to leave the spirit alone in an unfamiliar area could cause problems for any people walking through that area.

People who come to cry will come as clan groups and not as individuals. Generally, they will congregate out of sight of the funeral

191

area and, if they have not already done so, they will apply mud to their faces and clothing. When all are present, they will make their entrance with loud wailing; some who are very close to the one who has died might roll on the ground while wailing.

Each group of mourners will be greeted by the immediate family. They will be hugged and then escorted to the place where the others are seated around the body. The mourners who are already present, other than immediate family members, will make space for the new mourners.

The dead person's maternal clan is very important at the funeral. They come as a large group and demonstrate almost uncontrollable grief. Wild destructive behaviour is very common. They may enter in force, slashing down sugarcane, banana palms and coffee trees with their bush knives. Some may be dripping in mud, and their wailing is very intense. If a young child or a teenager dies, then the angry relatives (maternal clan) may beat up the father of the child and the immediate family in their rage. (It is thought that the parents did not take proper care of the child, and so are largely responsible for the death of the child or young person).

If a young man has taken a wife, but has not given the bride price or only a part of it, and the woman dies, there may be a lot of violence. The girl's tribal brothers are very angry, and her mother's clan are also very angry.

Once things have settled down, the mother's clan may bring pigs and bunches of bananas as well as hundreds of kina in cash for the people who are mourning. There are, however, a lot of "strings" attached to this "gift". It is expected that whatever is given will be doubled and returned to the givers. For example: if four pigs and K500 are given, then eight pigs and K1000 will be given back to the mother's clan.

During the time of mourning, people are seeking to determine the cause of the death. Death is seldom, if ever, attributed to natural causes, old age or a medical reason given by a doctor. People look for signs that may indicate *who caused* the death. Such signs include:

- Unusual behaviour of people in recent days.
- The body of the deceased. Sometimes, when only the immediate family is present, the body will be asked to reveal the name of the person who killed him or her. The body is watched to see if there is any movement when the names of possible culprits are mentioned.
- The body is also watched as the various groups of mourners approach the body. People will watch the body for any sign that would indicate a response. For example, any discharges of blood from the nose, mouth or ears, or a discharge of urine, are signs that the guilty person is near. The persistent buzzing of a blowfly that appears when a certain group approaches the body can be interpreted as a sign that the guilty person is nearby.
- Dreams of the immediate family and mourners.
- People who do not appear to be showing sufficient sorrow.

During the times of less intense mourning, people relive the stories of that person's life. They talk about the good things the person did, the funny things he or she said, and his or her generosity, hard work and all that was accomplished. Plans are finalised for the burial. The mourning period in the Highlands generally lasts three days to a week. During this time, particularly during the evenings, there will be services held in the large men's house where the coffin is kept at night. Pastors will come and pray for the people, read the Scriptures and give an exhortation.

Burial

Prior to the 1930s, the dead were buried in limestone caves high up in the rugged mountains of Simbu or under sacred trees (Trompf

193

1991:42). Then people started to bury them closer to the village and under little hous :s near the *singsing* ground. The spirits of the dead were thus expected to live there in these houses, and be fed and nourished by their clan members. In turn, they would provide protection and strengthen the tribe.

Before death, a person may often express a wish to the family specifying where he or she wants to be buried. Some will be buried in the graveyard with other clan members. Most of the Simbu people do not live in clearly defined villages, but in houses scattered over hillsides. A man may therefore wish to be buried near his house so that he can be close to the rest of the family and look after them. If the person was an important member in the community, he may be buried in a prominent position near the roadside so that people passing by can see the grave.[60]

As mentioned earlier, the body is dressed, wrapped in a new sheet or blanket and placed in a coffin. A funeral service will be held there in the village. Very few are held in church buildings as most village churches could not hold the hundreds of people who come to join in the mourning. There will be singing by church people, prayer for God's peace on the people, a Scripture reading and an exhortation to the people. The content of the exhortation will depend on the life of the person who died. It may be a message giving thanks to God for the person's life, or it may be a message of warning to repent. The theological background of the pastor or priest will make a big difference to what is said. If the leader believes that one's salvation is based on baptism, then that will come through; if the pastor believes that one must have a clear testimony of salvation, then this will greatly influence what he says. After the service, the body is taken to the gravesite for burial.

Concluding the Mourning Period

On the day of the burial, pigs are killed and cooked in the ground with sweet potatoes, bananas and various types of greens. The food

194

is divided up very carefully and distributed amongst the people who have come to cry. Special attention will be paid to those who were very involved in the death and burial process. For example, those who have handled the body of the dead person and those who helped dig the grave are publicly thanked and their appreciation demonstrated with gifts of pork.

Years ago, a pig would be killed specifically for the spirit of the person who died. There were strict taboos to be observed, and only the immediate family would be allowed to eat this pig. The Catholic and Lutheran Missions did not agree with this practice and these days this is no longer done. Today the pigs are killed for all the mourners to eat.

Community leaders will give speeches of appreciation and thanks to those who came and shared in their grief, and also give thanks for those who donated food to the mourners. Speeches may include warnings if they felt that the death had been caused by irresponsible behaviour. If it was felt that the death had been caused by *sanguma*, then warnings are made: the cause of death will be found out and revenge will be taken against whoever caused the death.

Pigs and money will be given to the mother's clan. These ties of relationship are very important and must be maintained and strengthened.

The period of mourning now over, the visitors leave, and life slowly goes back to normal. People are allowed to wash and the normal routine of life once again takes over. For the widow of the dead man, or the parents of the young person who died, it takes longer and the family continues to share their grief and comfort each other.

Care of the Grave

The gravesite will be decorated with flowers, *tangkets* and limestone rocks. A small wooden cross is often erected with the name and the date written on it.

If it is thought that *sanguma* is responsible for the death of the person, then a makeshift plastic shelter will be set up where people will do grave duty. They will camp out with a Coleman lamp, bows and arrows and even guns to watch over the grave. Any dog, rat, bird or possum that ventures near the grave will be interpreted as a *sanguma* witch in disguise and will be shot (Hughes 1985:446).[61]

It is common to erect a small house over the grave. Many of these houses are quite small, being about 1.5 metres long, a metre high and less than a metre wide. They are built with wooden posts and have a peaked roof of corrugated iron. This practice probably arrived from the concept of the grave as the place of the dead. The purpose is to keep the rain off the grave and so protect the coffin and body. Also, it is a way of showing respect to the dead. The size of the house reflects the person's importance and status in the community. Some houses are quite elaborate, with a cement floor, and may be almost 2 metres long, 1.2 metres high, and 1.2 metres wide. They are painted and some are surrounded with a little fence.

Spirits of the Dead

It is believed that the spirit stays nearby and has immediate and complete knowledge of everything that happens. If the spirit is unhappy, then life is full of problems. This will be revealed in sickness, poverty, natural disasters and poor crops etc. If, on the other hand, the spirit is happy, then life will go well and everything will continue as normal.

Spirits may be contacted through spirit mediums. The main question that is asked of a spirit is: "Who caused your death?" The pastors told me that some people will go to a public telephone late at night and dial 000 000 and ask to speak to the spirit of their loved one. Other people have said that if one dials 666 (number of the anti-Christ) one can be put through to the spirits of the dead. These stories suggest an understanding that the dead are still alive, but living in a shadow or parallel world.

If people are finding many problems in their lives, it is possibly because there is unfinished business between them and the spirit of someone who has died. They solve this problem by going to the gravesite and confessing the problem, thus restoring the broken relationships so that life will improve.

People do not call upon the dead as much as they did in the past. Life is changing with new influences from around the world. However, the belief is still there, and in times of crisis the help of the dead is still sought.

The Kobon

Before Death

When someone is very sick, the family comes together and asks the sick person what s/he thinks is causing the sickness. They ask if s/he has anything on his or her mind that s/he wants to talk about. Other family members also talk about anything that could be related to the sickness. If there are apologies to be made, or debts to be settled, then these are taken care of. The first step is to remove all possible causes of ill feelings. This does not refer only to problems existing between the sick person and other living relatives, but to those between the sick person and the spirits of the dead.

A diviner may be called on to find the cause of the sickness. The diviner smokes and chants. In the process, s/he is taken over by a spirit being which then speaks through him/her (Jackson 1975:255). If it is thought that a ghost is causing the illness, then a chant will be made by the diviner in which the names of all the people who have died in recent time are called; they are instructed to go away (Jackson 1975:263). The diviner may also kill a pig and call on the ghost in order to placate the ghost so that the person will get better. It is believed that the ghost will consume the "life" of the pig while they consume the meat of the pig (cf. Glasse 1965:31).

If the people think the sickness is caused by a "wild ghost", they will instruct it to go back to the gardens and look after the yams, bananas, sugarcane and other garden produce (Jackson 1975:264). If the family feels that the sickness is caused by *sanguma*, then they will attempt to find out the name of the *sanguma* person. They will threaten that person, and demand that the *sanguma* person restore the organs s/he stole from the sick person. If it is a long lingering illness and the person looks like s/he will die, then the family may have a small feast to show appreciation and gratitude to the sick person. This is also the time when the sick person can have the family around him or her, give his or her last words, distribute property and give a blessing to the children and grandchildren.

These are traditional remedies. Now that most of the people have identified themselves with the Christian church, people may call the pastor to come. This may be in place of the above or in addition to it. His approach will be similar to that as practiced among the Simbu people.

Death and Mourning

When a person dies, especially if an adult, there is loud wailing and calling out so as to let all the relatives and family members gather. People express their grief by smearing white clay on their faces and bodies. Tufts of hair are tugged out as people cry over the dead body. People, especially the immediate family, do not eat. The wife of the dead person will rub white clay on her body and also put strings of beads (made from seeds known as Job's tears) around her neck.

The body is placed on a raised platform inside a large house. Partitions within the house are removed so that people can come inside and gather around the body. If a man has died, his widow is required to sit underneath the body of her husband and do nothing else, to show sorrow.

As in Simbu, people watch the body for signs of movement or bodily discharges that may indicate who caused the death. If they see dirt on the body, it could be interpreted that there was a dispute about land. A pig's hair on the body may indicate that the death was caused by a dispute about pigs.

When the mother's clan comes, a mock battle erupts as they attack the immediate family for being so thoughtless as to allow this person to die. Although this is a mock battle, it can get rough and people can be injured (Jackson 1975:301).

Again, the big concern is: "Who caused this person to die?" It is important to answer this question, for if the problem is not solved then other people will continue to die. If the family feel that another clan is offended, then it is important to give compensation to that clan as quickly as possible so that harmony can be restored and no one else will die. It is important to give the compensation before burial. Usually three days pass before burial, but sometimes it is five (Jackson 1975:300-301).

Sometimes a close relative will be overcome by grief and go into a trance-like state. When that happens, people listen closely, for they believe that the spirit of the dead will speak through the mouth of that person and may reveal the name of the person who caused the death. During the time of mourning, there will be morning and evening Bible readings, songs, prayers, and the pastor will speak to the people.

Burial

Until the 1970s, when the mourning period ended the dead body would be placed on a small platform about one metre off the ground, not far from the houses. Often fingers or, in the case of a child, a whole hand would be removed from the corpse. They were dried and worn on a string around the neck of a close relative (Jackson 1975:302; cf. Trompf 1991:41-42). A small fence would be built around the body to prevent animals such as dogs from eating it, and the body would be left to decompose. Food would be placed at the burial enclosure for the dead.

When the body was completely decomposed, the jaw bone, the right arm bone and the right leg bone would be collected and kept in a *bilum*, along with hair from the head. This *bilum* would be kept in the men's house. These bones would be consulted for information and appealed to for help. For instance, the *bilum* could be held out and allowed to swing like a pendulum; questions could be asked and answers interpreted from the *bilum's* movement. In this way the name of the person who had caused the sickness or death could be discovered. The remainder of the bones were taken and placed in a fork of a large tree in the forest (Jackson 1975:305). Sometimes food offerings would be placed at the foot of the tree in honour of the dead person.

Things have changed greatly in the past forty years. The government ordered the people to bury the dead underground, and forbade wearing fingers on a string around the neck. Now the body is washed and dressed in clean clothes. A grave will be dug near to where the person lived. The body will be wrapped in a blanket and placed on a small stretcher (plywood coffins are not available in the Kobon area). A funeral service will be conducted along with songs, prayer, Bible reading and exhortation from the pastor. Then the body will be buried.

Some pigs will be killed and cooked along with sweet potato and taro, and given to the people who have come to mourn. Speeches are made, recognition and gifts of pork are given to the members of the maternal clan and to others who helped in special ways, such as those who helped to dig the grave.

Care of the Grave

The gravesite is decorated with flowers, stones and shrubs are planted, especially *tangkets*. Often a small wooden cross will be erected on the grave. The gravesite is kept clean and tidy as a mark of respect for the loved one.

It is believed that the spirit of the dead will, after some time, leave the home area and follow the river down to the Jimi River, or if the death occurs on the northern side of the Schrader ranges, down to the Ramu River (Jackson 1975:227). There is no belief concerning the collective ancestors of the past being involved in the daily life of the village. There does not appear to be a name for the collective spirits of those who have died in the distant past.

Southern Highlands

The Southern Highlands has a number of large language groups. Most of the pastors came from the Wiru and Kewa language groups, which are closely related linguistically and culturally. The practices of these people show considerable similarity to the two previous groups. As the pastors discussed these issues, again and again they would say: "Are we talking about what we used to do, or what we do now?" Cultural practices are changing rapidly. Often another pastor would speak up and say: "Everything is changing. Some people still stick to the old ways and beliefs, while others have adopted Christian ways, and others follow a mixture of both old and new."

Before Death

People want to find out the cause of the illness, and so the following steps will be taken. First of all it is important to restore harmony in the family. All differences, angers and resentments must be confessed. Any outstanding debts will be paid back. If compensation needs to be made for any past grievances, then it is important that this is paid as quickly as possible. Sickness is not seen as primarily a physical problem, but as the result of literal "dis-ease" in the social order. People will call in a diviner to find out the cause of the sickness. If the sickness is caused by the spirit of someone who has died, then pigs will be killed and offered to the spirit of that person, so as to restore harmony and end the sickness.

People will pay close attention to dreams for clues as to what has gone wrong and is causing the sickness. Have ancestral spirits been upset? Who may have been upset and so put a spell upon the sick person? Much time and effort is given in trying to find the supernatural cause of the sickness.

The family stays close by if the sickness continues. They pay close attention to the last words of the dying person. These words may provide a clue to the problem causing the sickness. There is also the final blessing to the family, and the dividing up of land, trees and other possessions. There may be instructions concerning revenge and payback to some person who has offended the dying person in the past. Meanwhile, some family members may tell the dying person to be sure and send them word as to who caused the death so that they will take revenge upon the culprit.

These days, the pastor is also very involved in ministering to the family at this time. One mature pastor sees ministry to the sick and dying as a very important aspect of his ministry. He said that people have learned and believe that when they die, they go to be with the Lord. In earlier times, the usual final words of a person concerned the dividing up of his property. But this is changing: often the final words of a person are testimony regarding eternal destiny. These final words can be words of thanks or words of deep regret. Sometimes people say: *"Mi pilim pen na mi save nau mi go long hel."* (I am in agony and I am lost and on my way to hell). One dying man said: *"Mi amamas. Bikpela i wetim mi nau, na nau mi go i stap wantaim em."* (I am happy. The Lord is waiting for me and now I am going to be with him.) He opened his eyes and saw his two daughters-in-law standing beside his bed, crying. He asked: "Why are you crying? Go and be good wives and be obedient to your husbands. I am going to Papa God now," and with those words he died.

Often there are death bed confessions, as the dying person not only straightens the earthly relationships, but also relationships with God. Then the person can die in peace knowing that all is well between himself or herself and God. Yet despite the hope and certainty of heaven, it is easy for people to slip into the other ways of thinking, so that a few days later someone says: "I heard him outside the house last night."

At the Time of Death

When a person dies, there is immediate loud wailing to let people know of the death. The body is placed out in the open on a raised platform and a large makeshift tent is erected over the body to protect it and the mourners from the weather.

Once again the main concern is why the person died. Signs are sought, such as any body fluids coming from any body opening. It is very significant if this happens when a certain group of mourners approach. Likewise, any movement of the hands or legs when people approach is observed.

Sometimes bamboo divination is done. This is practiced in a number of areas in PNG, not just in the Southern Highlands. Some of the person's hair is tied to the middle of a two-metre length of bamboo, which is held by a number of men. The dead person is addressed and asked to lead the people to the person responsible for causing his death. This is used especially if it is thought that the death was caused by someone in the community. The bamboo becomes animated with the "spirit of the dead person" and pulls the people to the house of the guilty person. The guilty person is forced to confess, for in the minds of the people it is impossible for the bamboo to be wrong: it is led by the spirit of the dead person, who knows the truth.

203

Mourning Period

The family members show their grief by loud crying, and smearing themselves with mud. People show intense grief by cutting off a finger joint, cutting their ear lobes or by pulling out clumps of hair. The maternal tribe of the dead person come caked with mud, and cut down bananas and sugarcane. They destroy gardens, and fight anyone who gets in their way. They are angry that the clan and family allowed their relative to die. But after their initial outburst, they settle down to mourn. They also bring pigs and money, which they give to the grieving family. However, all this wealth must be returned twice over to them at the end of the mourning period, just as in Simbu.

During this time of grief, the normal orderly work of the village is suspended. People do no work and do not go to their gardens. The children sit still and the women stop making their *bilum*s.

If a man has died, then his widow and daughters-in-law wear black clothes and cover their faces with white clay; other people bring food to them. At times the wailing is very intense, especially when a new group of mourners arrive. At other times, the mourning dies down, except amongst the immediate family who are seated around the corpse. People sit in small groups and tell stories about the important things that the person did or said while alive.

In the house at night, people will sing chants. Some of these praise the dead person, while others express grief at their great loss. Sometimes chants will accuse people of having caused the death and will allude to threats of payback. Along with this will be times for *lotu* (church service). These services will be held each night in the large house where the body is kept, and often in the morning as well. Pastors find this an excellent opportunity to bring comfort to the people. They use this time to appeal for calm and pray for God's peace upon the people. They speak against payback and revenge, and urge people to leave revenge in the hands of God. They remind them that God is the righteous judge and that he will repay any wrongs that have been committed (Romans 12:17-19).

Burial

If a child dies, there is not usually a big gathering for the mourning period and the body may be buried the next day. However, if an important man dies, then burial may be delayed for three to four days until family members can gather. The body will be dressed for burial. Sometimes, when a person feels death is very near and he is at peace with dying, he may request the family to help him get dressed, so that he will be ready to go and be with God. Depending on the status of the person in the village, a coffin may be prepared or purchased. Otherwise the body is wrapped in a new blanket or bed sheet for burial.

If the death was caused by a fight or car accident, people return to the place of the death and reclaim the spirit of the dead person (just as the Simbu people do). A chicken may be killed and its feathers burnt in a fire or else a piece of pig meat may be roasted over a fire in order to entice the spirit. The dead person's name is called and a ritual specialist will strike the ground softly with special leaves. Each time he strikes the ground, he makes a short soft whistle. The people wait quietly in anticipation of an answering whistle which signals the presence of the spirit. They keep calling and whistling, trying to lure the spirit closer. It is anticipated that the whistle of the specialist and the whistle of the spirit will come closer together both in timing and in location. When the two whistles coincide, they gather together the dust of the ground from that particular location, wrap it up in the leaves and take it back to the village for burial.

Sometimes people put a bush knife, axe or arrow into the coffin with instructions that the spirit is to go and take revenge on the one who caused the death. Others argue that this is a very dangerous practice that can cause many deaths. Some people may put money into the coffin or grave to show their sorrow. Intimate belongings (such as a cup, plate or spoon) may be placed in the coffin. Some say that this is for the dead person's use, others that it is done because they are afraid that if others use them they may get sick. There is also the fear that the spirit may come back to the house to get them.

The family decides on a burial place. People are buried in a graveyard near the village, or they may have chosen a particular place before dying. People of importance are often buried near the roadside where the grave will be seen and the person will be remembered by all the people who travel along the road.

There will be a final funeral service for the burial of the dead. This is conducted by a pastor in the village. Many communities in the Southern Highlands have more than one church in the village and sometimes there is a bit of discussion and tension about who is given the responsibility of conducting the burial service. Sometimes the pastors and congregations cooperate and take various parts of the service. Few people are buried without any Christian ceremony at all.

A length of bamboo may be placed in the grave with one end near the head of the dead person. The other end extends above the ground. An appointment is made with the dead person: family members say that they will come back between seven or eight in the evening to receive any messages from the dead. It is believed that if they wait any later, then the spirit will have gone off somewhere else and not be around to give any messages. This may be done for a few days, until the family receives a message either from the bamboo or another method.

End of the Mourning Period

During the time of mourning and prior to burial, money is collected to buy food and a feast is prepared. This always includes pigs, but may also include frozen meat from trade stores. The area where everyone has been sitting during the mourning period is cleaned up.

Speeches are made in honour of the person who died, and speeches of appreciation are also made to those who have helped. The food is distributed, with special prominence being given to the clan of the dead person's mother. Money and pigs equal to twice what the mother's line contributed are now distributed to the mother's clan. After the distribution of the cooked food, people are free to leave and the official mourning period is now over.

Care of the Grave

A wooden cross will be placed on the grave, usually with the date and the name of the person who died. The grave may be planted with flowers and *tangkets* or limestone rocks to designate the area of the grave. A small house a little over a metre long with a metal roof may be built over the grave, as is done in other Highlands areas. If the fear of *sanguma* is strong, then a tent will be erected, a lamp will be lit each night, and people will camp out near the grave to protect it from *sanguma* people. Any visit of a dog, rat, bird or snake will be understood as a visit by some evil person disguised as an animal.

The Spirit of the Dead

Melanesians believe that the spirits of the dead are never far away and can make their presence felt whenever they choose to (Trompf 1979:134). They believe that if the spirit is not happy with the living, then the spirit will bring sickness, cause gardens to become dry and barren, or cause any variety of calamities upon the living. On the other hand, if the dead are happy, then they will ensure fertility and prosperity. The spirits may reveal themselves in a number of ways. They may appear as a bird, snake or rat living near the house. A wagtail bird that flies along the path people are walking is taken as a good omen that the spirit is walking with them. If a spirit wants to communicate, it will choose someone who was very close to him or her, and communicate with that person.

207

The dead are contacted for help and success in any number of areas: gardens, hunting, family problems, finding lost pigs, success in school exams, success in government elections etc. Some also contact the dead in order to get supernatural help in criminal activities (e.g. opening safes, stealing cars, protection from police, power to make themselves invisible to other people, etc.).

Traditionally, the bones of the dead were placed in a spirit house and sacrifices were made to them in these places. These spirit houses no longer exist. This practice was discouraged as much by government officials as by missionaries (Trompf 1991:42). This change in practice has led to a degree of uncertainty about where the spirit goes. Spirits may turn into, or appear as, a butterfly, bird, snake, rat or some other animal. Some think that the spirits follow the streams down to the main river and eventually to the sea. Some believe the spirit remains at the gravesite or even the place of death. It is thought that the spirit of a person who dies in a different province will eventually return to his or her own province.

Conference Evaluation

There were three stages to each conference.

- The pastors looked at their traditional practices.
- They studied Scripture passages related to death, burial, and the resurrection.
- They reviewed their traditional practices in the light of their understanding of Scripture. They discussed what was acceptable, and what areas needed to be changed.

There was widespread similarity of practices reported among the three groups. The evaluations done by the pastors were also very similar. Therefore, I will report the results of all three conferences together.

208

Before Death

The practice of the family gathering together to resolve differences, to clear up misunderstandings and confess any jealousy, resentment or anger is positive and should be retained. The pastors related this to James 5:13-16. They felt that pastors and church people need to be more active and provide leadership in this area. The practice of paying back all debts is also a good custom and should be encouraged. It gives the sick person peace and creates good will in the community.

Divination

Divination often takes place before death, because people are trying to find the cause of the sickness. Since the Bible forbids it, the pastors felt that divination needs to be discouraged, and that Christian prayer for the sick should be encouraged. They felt that some diviners were guessing as to the cause of the illness and others were seeking to get answers from the spirits. They did not believe that the spirits contacted were really the spirits of the dead, but deceiving spirits, and so their answers were not to be trusted. (We will look at their reasoning about this in more detail later.)

Divination also takes place after death, as people seek to find a cause for the death. The practice of looking for signs and trying to find the person responsible for the death goes along with divination and often leads to accusations, disagreements, arguments and fighting. It was admitted that this is a long-standing practice and that it will take time to change. People need to learn that just as there is a time to be born, there is also a time to die, and that vengeance must be left in God's hands (Ecclesiastes 3:2). It is a good thing to pray for God's peace to cover the people at the time of death. This will minimise a lot of the problems.

Last Words

They felt that last words and final blessings were very important. Jacob blessed his sons before he died (Genesis 49). There is a problem when a dying person instructs others to take revenge on

209

someone who has wronged them. It was felt that this needs to be discouraged and that Christians need to leave matters of revenge in the hands of God, rather than taking them into their own hands (Romans 12:18-19). If the pastor and/or other Christians work closely with a dying person, then this can be a very positive time: a person can die with a positive testimony of God's goodness and love, which will have a powerful impact on the rest of the family. When a person dies obviously at peace with God, then the talk of payback and compensation often fades away.

During the Time of Mourning

It was agreed that people need to demonstrate their grief visibly, through crying and ritual wailing. Chopping off finger joints was excessive, but smearing their bodies with mud was a culturally acceptable way of demonstrating grief and sorrow. Likewise, the new custom of wearing black clothes was also an acceptable way of showing one's sorrow.

In Kobon, it was felt that mourning should not be excessive or prolonged. When others see someone mourning excessively, they are tempted to say: "She is still greatly upset about her husband's death. Therefore we must find out who caused the death and take revenge so that life may return to normal again." Also in Kobon, the people agreed that the practice of the widow sitting underneath the corpse of her husband was unnecessary, very unpleasant and also unhealthy. Christians need to show comfort to those who are grieving, pray for God's peace upon them and not submit them to unnecessary, unpleasant experiences (Romans 12:13; 2 Corinthians 1:3-7).

Destruction by the Mother's Clan

It was felt that this behaviour causes a lot of fear and tension between clans. The immediate family have the grief of losing their loved one, as well as fearing the attack of the maternal clan. It was felt that Christians should not join in this destructive behaviour and should strongly discourage it. Jesus tells us to be merciful and also to be peacemakers (Matthew 5:7,9).

Compensation

Compensation is deeply ingrained in Melanesian cultures and is very complex. It was felt that if there was an obvious cause of death, as when someone is killed in a fight, then compensation is acceptable and helps to bring peace to the community. The practice of looking for all sorts of minute signs in order to find the killer, and then demanding compensation on the basis of questionable evidence, led to disputes and ill-feeling between the clans.

The custom of the maternal clan giving money and pigs and then expecting to receive double this amount in return is deeply ingrained, but it has become a burden. Instead of cementing relationships, this practice has now become a source of conflict. I am told by pastors from the Angugunak area in West Sepik, that the maternal clan sometimes came to the place of mourning totally naked and remained naked until they had received compensation. These feelings are so strong that sometimes they would tie the corpse to the bed and not allow it to be buried until compensation had been paid.

The concept of payback ensures that this custom continues. One clan thinks: "We had to pay them a lot of money last time, so now it is our chance to get some money back." To refuse to pay the money will only create conflict. The only way this custom will change is if the maternal clan introduces the change. If Christians discourage it and speak against it then change will come over time. If Christians go along with it, so as to get their share of the money, then things will never change.

Burial

Since the time of mourning extends for at least three days for an adult, there is ample time for a pastor and the church people to minister to people at this time. This is especially so at nights when people crowd into the largest house in the village. Their thoughts are on the shortness of life and on their relative who has just died, so they are looking for a message of comfort and hope.

Worship Services and the Funeral Service

The church has a lot to offer people in their time of grief. The pastors thought it was good that people spend time talking about the person who has died and also to sing songs in honour of the dead (as David did in 2 Samuel 1:20-27).

The time of death is not a time to worry about denominational differences, but to minister to all those who are grieving and distressed. During the time of mourning, all work stops and people have time to think and listen. They are open to receive expressions of sympathy, comfort and hope. Traditional religion has no hope to offer at the time of death, for the dead person has moved on to a rather shadowy existence and the relationship between the living and the dead is characterised by tension and fear.

The Christian however, has the assurance that the believer who has died has gone to be with Christ (Philippians 1:21-23; 2 Corinthians 5:6-8). Jesus promises that he has gone to prepare a place for us so that we may be where he is (John 14:1-3). There is the hope of the resurrection - the body that is lowered into the grave will one day be raised to life and will live again (1 Corinthians 15). For the Christian, death is not the end. A life that is even better than this present life is in store for all those who believe in Christ (John 11:25).

Caring for the Mourning

It is customary to take food to the people who are mourning. This is an area in which the church can excel and show love and compassion. Words of comfort will carry much more weight if they are backed up with deeds of kindness. Other areas of help are in preparing the body for burial, digging the grave and continuing to visit the family even after the official time of mourning is over and most people have returned to their homes. If the church wants to speak out against revenge and payback it must earn the right to be heard.

212

Recently, a group of twelve pastors met together for a week of Bible study. In a nearby village, a person died, accusations were made about the cause of death and a fight was brewing. There was a lot of tension and two clans were preparing to fight. The pastors decided to intervene. They all contributed money and bought a generous amount of rice and sugar. Then dressed up in their "Sunday best" and took their gift of food to the people who were mourning. The pastors cried with the people and presented their gifts. They slept in the village overnight. They read from the Scriptures, sang songs, prayed for the people and talked about peace and reconciliation instead of revenge. The village people had previously decided not to bury the body until they had taken revenge for the death. The visit of the pastors diffused the tense situation. God's peace settled on the village. The pastors helped the people in every possible way and conducted an impressive burial service. The next day they visited the other clan who were preparing to defend themselves against attack. The pastors were able to announce that there would be no attack. They brought the two clans together in reconciliation. It is in ways like this that changes will come to society as a whole.

Contacting the Spirits of the Dead

The pastors in the conferences were unanimous that this practice was not acceptable, whether by traditional methods such as through a medium, or by putting a bamboo tube down near the coffin (Deuteronomy 18:11-12).

The pastors indicated that the primary reason for seeking to contact the spirit of the dead person was to find out who had used sorcery or witchcraft, and so caused the death. They likewise did not approve of the practice of using a length of bamboo and asking the spirit of the dead to lead them to the killer. One of the pastors in Simbu said that before he became a Christian, he had participated in this practice. He said that a spirit certainly does energise the bamboo and causes it to move. He was one of six men holding onto the bamboo and the bamboo literally pulled the men through the village, causing them to jump ditches with far more agility than is normally

213

possible. There is no mercy shown to the person who is marked by the bamboo. They are either beaten up or killed on the spot. The end result of this activity is generally accusations, violence and usually more death. They said that it is significant that Satan is described in the Bible as being a liar, accuser and a murderer (John 8:44; Revelation 12:10).

Caring for the Grave
The pastors felt that caring for the grave by keeping it clean and tidy was one way in which Christians could show respect for the dead. They were very critical of some charismatic groups who have placed much emphasis on the spirit and have ignored the body.

House Over the Grave
Some felt that this practice was a harmless way of showing respect for the dead, and that it had a practical benefit in that it sheltered the coffin from the rain. Others felt that it could be taken to indicate that the spirits of the dead were in the graveyard, whereas Christians believe that the spirits of the dead have gone to be with the Lord. Some indicated that there was a lot of confusion in the minds of many Christians. At church they hear the pastor say that when people die they go to heaven. They also hear him say that when Jesus returns, the dead will be raised. This last statement indicates to many that the dead are still in the graveyard. These two statements seem to contradict each other, and confuse people.[62]

The people in the Kobon area said that it was not their custom to build a house over the grave, but they had seen people in the Wahgi Valley do it and so a few people had started to copy them. Most of the pastors saw no value in introducing it or encouraging it in the Kobon area.

Some of the pastors in Simbu and Southern Highlands felt that people should be encouraged to find some other way to indicate a person's importance in the community other than by building a fancy house over the grave. One grave near Mt Hagen has a very beautifully painted, neat looking house, almost three metres square with a front door and windows on each side. It is surrounded by a flower garden and finally by a strong wire fence. Located on the edge of the main road it proclaims loudly the status of the man who died. The pastors felt that Christians should focus their attention on the heavenly home which Jesus has gone to prepare, for both rich and poor alike, rather than on a house built over a grave.

Burial Problems

Sometimes burial can be a problem, especially if a man has indicated that he wants to be buried near the house but the family decides that he should be buried in the graveyard where the other clan members have been buried. One pastor told the following story.

An old man wanted to be buried near the family house so that he could be near the family and look after them. After he died, the rest of the family decided that he should be buried in the graveyard. When they picked up the coffin to transport it to the graveyard, they found the coffin to be extremely heavy. It was a terrible struggle for the four men to lift it onto their shoulders. A daughter then spoke to the coffin and said: "Papa, we are going to take you over to the gravesite where you can be near your brothers and sisters and where all the others are. It will be much better for you over there, so please do not give us any problems." Things seemed to change and it was no problem to take the coffin down the hill to the little stream before attempting to climb the other side of the gully to the graveyard. Once they tried to climb the slope at the other side, the coffin became extremely heavy. The young strong men struggled and sweated trying to carry the box up the hill to the other side. It should have taken only twenty minutes, but instead it took all afternoon as the carriers struggled with the box. They kept changing carriers but it still took hours to get the body to the graveyard. Once they got there, they found the grave was

215

too short, though it had been carefully measured, and so it had to be extended in order to get the coffin into the grave. The family did not listen to the old man's request and he did not want to go.

I have heard this type of story from a number of other people.

Another pastor tells of helping the people to dig a grave on what appeared to be a dry raised piece of ground near to where other people had been buried in the past. They had barely dug down one metre, however, when the ground became swampy and unsuitable for burial. This was very strange for the ground all around was quite dry. They wondered what to do and then someone said: "While she was alive she said that she did not want to be buried here, but back in her father's village." So they filled in the grave and went to the place the person had mentioned before she died, and had no problem digging the grave. Obviously the spirit was now happy.

A lady who had been teaching at a Christian college died. The college decided that they should fly the body back to her home province so that she could be buried in her home village. They had similar problems with the coffin being very heavy and difficult to move. Eventually it was loaded on the plane for the final leg of the journey. There was very bad turbulence on the flight and the plane was bumping around. The sister of the dead woman spoke out loud: "Sister we are sorry that we brought you all this way. We should have buried you back at the college as you requested." Once the apology was made, the plane turbulence stopped and the rest of the flight was smooth. The highly respected national church leader who told me this story said: "I cannot explain this. My Christian understanding says: 'Absent from the body - present with

216

*the Lord,' but how do we explain this situation? It appears
that she was still present."*

On the other hand, there are numerous testimonies of Christian
people who have died at peace with God, their family and friends.
When he or she breathed their last, people knew their loved one had
departed this world and had gone to be with the Lord. The transition
seemed to be instantaneous. But is the departure of the spirit of the
dead from this life to the next always instantaneous?

Some Christian writers talk of the "unquiet dead", which they define
as being the "spirits of the departed, who have been unable to find
their proper place of rest and seek to bring this to the notice of the
living" (Mitton and Parker 1991:107). One role of the funeral service
is to actually commit the departed to God. This world is no longer
their home, but we entrust them to the heavenly Father who
determines where they should go. The funeral service thus has a
ministry both to the living and to the dead. It offers comfort and
hope to the living and entrusts the dead into the hands of the heavenly
Father (Mitton and Parker 1991:124).[63]

Sanguma

As the pastors reflected on the events that occur before, during and
after the burial process, one thing became very evident: finding out
the cause of death was a priority. People born in PNG have a life
expectancy of 55.2 years.[64] In Melanesian thinking, a person seldom
dies from natural causes. Only a very old person who has lived a
full life, and who dies peacefully at home at a ripe old age with
children and grandchildren all around him or her, is considered to
have died from natural causes. People are not so interested in
learning about what caused the death, but rather, *who* caused the
death.

After burial, people stand guard over the grave to prevent witches,
in the form of animals, from coming and disturbing the grave.
Currently this is a great fear. People say: "Our greatest concern is

not the spirits of the dead, but *sanguma*. They can cause a person to die in the prime of life. After the burial, the *sanguma* return at night to exhume the body, and feast on the flesh of our loved one."

CHAPTER NINE

THE PROBLEM OF SANGUMA

Thirty years ago, I remember a doctor being very puzzled when people brought in a woman who allegedly had a cat inside her and asked for an x-ray to find the animal. He tried to convince them that such a thing was totally impossible. These days, people do not bother to bring the person with *sanguma* to the hospital, for they know that scientific medicine has no way of handling it.

General science has not brought about a reduction in the fear of *sanguma*. Bernard Narokobi, a former parliamentarian and keen Catholic, illustrates this when he writes about the death of his mother (1985:63). She was a strong leader in her church and community, and as she came to the end of her life she was convinced that someone had performed sorcery and had made her sick. Modernisation does not eliminate the fear of sorcery. If anything, beliefs and fears are more widespread and much stronger. An experienced pastor in the Southern Highlands says that he hears far more talk about *sanguma* now than he did five years ago. In the Western Highlands, a church leader named *sanguma* as a big concern, and called all the Nazarene pastors together to discuss how they should respond to it. Mantovani writes:

Today, practically no death is regarded as natural and one blames sorcery for it, and tries to discover the sorcerer by asking the dead to reveal his or her killer. No accident is only the result of human error: behind it there is always bad will and sorcery, which must be avenged. The witch hunt, its ordeals, and the occasional lynching leave a bloody trail in certain parts of PNG. (1998:104)

219

Sanguma raises big problems for the church and is a serious issue for society as a whole.[65] How do we stop *sanguma* people from killing others? How do people prove that someone is a *sanguma* person or has a *sanguma*? And if someone confesses to having *sanguma*, how should the community respond? I have asked groups of pastors what is the biggest fear in the lives of people today. Again and again they have replied: "*Sanguma*." One experienced pastor said: "Our greatest concern is not the spirits of the dead, but the fear of death and especially the fear of sorcery. People should die at an old age, but *sanguma* respects no one and cuts people down in the prime of life."

Sanguma creates a different set of problems for modern people who prefer a rational explanation for the things that happen. Harriet Hill writes in regards to Africa: "To convince a Westerner that witchcraft is a spiritual reality is nearly impossible. To convince an African that it does not exist is equally difficult" (1996:325).

As I have studied *sanguma* beliefs, I have found myself asking: "Where is the line between reality and fantasy? Where is the line between material and spiritual, or are they interchangeable? Is it possible for a person to change form so that he or she appears like an animal?" Initially my response was: "There is no way that these stories can be true. It is totally impossible for a person to change form into that of an animal." Later I modified my approach and said: "I am not sure about the reality of the stories, but the fear is certainly very real. We have to provide a Christian answer to that terrible fear." As I have researched this further, I have heard stories from people whom I highly respect as outstanding Christians with mature judgement, and read international reports of similar phenomena, I have decided the world is a lot more complex than I first thought. There is a lot more to "reality" than can be analysed by empirical methods. Not all of experience fits within the rational confines of time and space.

I had the opportunity to pursue the subject of *sanguma* with students at the Melanesian Nazarene Bible College. In May 2000, I taught a course at the college on Contextual Theology. During the first two weeks, we dealt with the relationship between gospel and culture. During the second intensive period, we focused on the issue of *sanguma* and how the church should respond.

Thomas Bruno, who had been at the pastors' conference in Simbu, came to speak to the class about his experience of the spirit world. Bruno inherited spiritual powers from his father, who was a priest associated with a large spirit house on the Sepik River. Bruno was taught many of the ways of his people and his spiritual powers increased. Then, through a friend at university, he was introduced to books on Satanism, and developed his powers further. He did not discern any noticeable difference between the spirit powers associated with Satanaism and those associated with the spirit house in Sepik. He acted as a medium and spirits spoke through him. He associated with *sanguma* doctors and sought to develop his occult powers. Christians prayed for his conversion and in 1995 he was converted, and eventually set free from the spirits who had controlled him. God called him to preach and he is now working as a Nazarene pastor.

The Melanesian Understanding of *Sanguma*

Marie Reay, who has worked as an anthropologist in the Wahgi Valley, defines witchcraft as "an innate psychic or supernatural power and propensity to harm others" (1987: 92). She describes *kumo* as a creature which might look like "the foetus of a tree kangaroo. Allegedly, it lodges in a person's abdomen and takes over the host's will, impelling him or her to harbour unnatural thoughts and perform unnatural actions" (ibid).

Paula Brown, writing about the Simbu people, explains: "The witch involuntarily has a small creature (most often a bat, but possibly a bird, lizard, rat, snake) which is the *kumo* inside his or her chest or

221

head. It can change into another animal, leave the witch's body, usually at night and return ... The creature goes out to take flesh from a victim and brings it back to the witch to eat. Then the victim dies" (Brown 1977:26).

Similar beliefs are reported among the Abelam people of the Sepik Province (Forge in Douglas 1970:268). These beliefs show similarity to a description of the werewolf. Werewolf beliefs were widespread across many parts of Europe and can be traced back to early Greek legends. They are also found among the Bangyang people of West Cameroon (Douglas 1970:335). Familiar spirits in England and Scotland were considered to be like small domestic animals capable of evil deeds including murder (Robbins 1959). And similar beliefs are found among the Chiapas of Southern Mexico (Douglas 1970:195).

From where do such beliefs come? Why do similar beliefs appear from countries so far apart? There is no human contact between these very different cultures which are separated, not only by physical distance, but by thousands of years.

To understand these phenomena we need to start with the village stories. There are thousands of them, told over and over again; in the process of telling they become more dramatic. I have sought to track down stories that will take us as close to the source as possible. Many of these stories were told to me by pastors. This is significant for two reasons. Firstly, by virtue of their work, they are familiar with the fears and problems of the villages in which they serve. Secondly, many of them were exposed to missionary teachers at Bible college who had a modern, rational world-view. They consequently left Bible college rather sceptical about the reality of *sanguma*. The people who told me these stories are not "wild-eyed fanatics", but sane and sober pastors whom I have known for years and who have become convinced of the reality of what they have experienced.

222

Sanguma Can Take the Appearance of an Animal

This story is told by a well-educated pastor:[66]

Recently, my wife's uncle died and we went to the village for the mourning period. After a couple of days of mourning, the family killed pigs and prepared food for the people who had come to mourn. The plan was to bury the body after the distribution of the food. The grave was dug, but the food distribution took longer than we expected, and so we decided to keep the body one more night in the men's house and bury it in the morning. In the middle of the night, we heard lots of dogs howling in the graveyard, we rushed out with our flashlights, spears, bows and arrows, and bush knives. There were about a dozen large dogs all gathered around the grave. These were not our village dogs, but big well fed dogs, unlike any in our village. We yelled, shouted, and chased them away. My people were convinced that these dogs were in fact sanguma *spirits who had come to feast on the corpse, but were upset because the body was not in the grave as they had expected.*

At daybreak, my uncle went to check on the grave, and there in the bottom of the grave was a dog. He shot the dog, and shortly after, from the other side of the river, came the sounds of wailing. A woman had suddenly dropped dead in her garden. The conclusion is that the dog was the woman's sanguma *spirit and when the dog was killed, the owner of the spirit died at the same time. It was obvious to everyone that the* sanguma *were wanting to eat the body of my wife's uncle.*

Out of respect for our uncle, we chose people to keep watch over the grave every night with instructions to shoot any dog, rat, possum, or snake that might appear. A few

223

*nights later, my father-in-law and some other men were
guarding the same grave in the middle of the night. They
had set up a large tarpaulin as a tent, and had a Coleman
light burning which cast a bright light over the grave
area. They were armed with one gun, plus bush knives,
bows, and arrows. In the middle of the night, they saw a
large dog approaching the grave. My father-in-law raised
his shotgun and fired at the dog. The dog leapt in the air.
Immediately the Coleman lamp went out and everything
was pitch black. The butt of the gun was wrenched from
my father-in-law's grasp and he was left holding only the
barrel. He reached for his flashlight and it would not
work either. Next morning the shattered remains of his
gun butt was found fifty metres away among the coffee
trees. The dog that approached the grave was without
doubt a powerful* sanguma.

Dog at the Grave

A Bible college student writes this story about his own experience:

*One night I was assigned to grave duty to keep watch
over the grave of a relative. A number of us were squatting
around a small fire trying to keep warm in the chilly night.
In the middle of the night, we saw a large dog approach
the grave and begin digging. A brother fired his shotgun
and we let fly with our bows and arrows. The dog leapt
into the air in fright and avoided the arrows. Its tail stood
out straight, and projectile diarrhoea shot out of its rear
end as the dog disappeared into the darkness. At the same
moment in a nearby house, where a number of men were
sleeping, a man leapt out of bed with a terrible scream.
He was immediately apologetic for his trousers and bed
sheets were flooded with diarrhoea. He bundled
everything up and went off to the river to get himself
cleaned up. No further proof was needed. It was obvious*

that this man was a sanguma *person, and his* sanguma *had taken the form of a dog which had been shot at.*

Pig Returns an Arrow

A pastor was working in the Kobon area in a place that was noted for sanguma *activity. He found that his garden was constantly being ravaged by pigs, and although he carefully fenced the garden, they kept breaking in. They even entered in places where no pig could possibly get in. The hoof prints of the pigs were plainly obvious, however, the pigs did not dig up the food with their snouts like pigs normally do, but rather, picked the corn cobs like humans would. The pastor believed that some of the local people were wanting to scare him and drive him away, and so were coming as* sanguma *pigs and stealing all his food. One night he kept watch with his bow and arrow, and as the pigs came past his house, he shot an arrow into one of the pigs. The pig squealed and disappeared into the night along with the others. Apa went back to bed glad that he had scared them off. Next morning when he went outside the door, there was the arrow he had shot into the pig the night before. It was not lying on the ground, but standing upright with the arrow head piercing the ground. Now, how can a pig that has an arrow sticking in its ribs run off into the darkness and return to stick the arrow into the ground? People are convinced that the "pig" was a* sanguma *spirit in the form of a pig, and the human host returned the arrow and placed it upright in the ground.*

Pig Turns into a Woman

Another pastor reports:

When I was seven or eight years old, I was walking down the road on my way to play with my friends. As I was

225

walking, I saw a big pig walking up the road towards me. A thought flashed through my mind, "This pig is no ordinary pig." Suddenly the pig stood up on its back legs and turned into an old dirty woman. I screamed, turned and ran as fast as I could back to my father. He came quickly with his bush knife, but the pig and the woman had both disappeared.

Girl Inherits Bat From Her Mother

This story was reported by a Bible college student about one of his clan sisters:

A thirteen year old girl was staying at home looking after her sick mother. The mother became increasingly ill and one afternoon she called for her daughter: "Please go outside and you will see a bat flying around. I want you to catch it for me." The girl went outside and sure enough, there was a big fruit bat flying around the house. The bat flew toward the girl and she tried to catch it, however, it hit her in the chest and disappeared inside her. She went into the house to tell her mother and was shocked to find her mother had died. She ran to tell her father, and also told him about the bat. The village explanation is that her mother had a sanguma *which took the form of a bat. The mother knew she was dying and the* sanguma *wanted a new host before the woman died, and so before she died, the mother gave it to her daughter.*

The daughter now complains that the bat gives her no peace. It drives her outside of the house at night and forces her to eat human waste. She wants to get rid of the bat, but does not know what to do.

Sanguma and Supernatural Travel

Some have presumed that with education, Papua New Guineans will realise that these stories have no factual reality and that the tales will die out. But such is not the case. A well educated woman tells this story:

> One afternoon I was outside my house in Mt Hagen when my dog began to howl.[67] The pups lifted up their heads and also began to howl. I wondered why they were howling. Then I saw high up in the sky a big black bird flying toward the house. As it came closer, the dogs ran and cowered under the house. The large black bird alighted on a tree and in front of my eyes turned into a woman. It was a woman I knew from Port Moresby and I had long suspected that she was involved in the occult. She spoke to me and gave me a message, then turned back into a bird and flew away. When she was gone, I felt like I had been in the presence of an incredibly evil power. I felt physically sick and totally drained of energy.

I have heard some coastal people say that people from their area are very skilled in the use of occult power and can use it to travel from place to place very quickly. In some cases, the body remains at home in a virtually comatose state while the spirit travels; in others, the entire person is said to travel and then return home. A friend tells me that when he was working in Port Moresby, he knew of people from Milne Bay Province who would travel supernaturally to Port Moresby on Fridays when government workers were paid. They would visit their relatives, collect money from them, and then return home again all in the same day. There are many stories along this line.

A *sanguma* woman told Jenny Hughes that she and her companions would assume the form of flying foxes and fly from village to village, sometimes as far as a neighbouring province, in search of dead

227

bodies to eat (1985:452). I asked the Bible college students if they had heard these sorts of stories and almost all of them nodded their heads. These stories are not normally talked about when expatriates are present, for they usually ridicule such beliefs. The Melanesians believe them to be true, and point to the story of Philip, who is taken away by the Spirit and reappears at a town many kilometres away (Acts 8:39-40). They say Satan tries to duplicate the power of God.

Lights That Travel

It is commonly reported that *sanguma* travel through the sky at night and that they emit a strong light as they travel. *Sanguma* are credited with having supernatural powers and the ability to travel long distances in a very short time. Similar stories are reported from the Philippines (Henry 1986:23), Africa (Burnett 1988:137) and many other countries in the world. This same idea is also very strong in the stories related to European witchcraft.

The strong light *sanguma* emit as they travel enables them to see where they are going. People on the ground can see the lights, but not see the *sanguma* person (Hughes 1985:452). Informants say they have seen lights arcing overhead coming from separate locations, but toward a single destination. Others have witnessed what looked like fireworks: a bright light shot up into the air, bursting into many little lights. These then recombined into one light, which subdivided into two lights. These two lights went in opposite directions, and then recombined. It was a interpreted as gathering of *sanguma* people.

A Bible college teacher gives this report:

In 1999 I was near the Nazarene Mission Station in the Jimi Valley. About eight o'clock one evening, I saw a strong light, like it was coming from a strong flashlight, travelling just above the tree tops and flying down into the valley. A number of other people from my village also

228

saw it. The consensus was that it was a sanguma. *It was not a shooting star or a fire fly, but a strong bright light at low altitude.*

I asked the Bible college class if any of them had ever seen anything like this. About half of them said that they had seen the lights from *sanguma*. One described the light he saw as very bright, like a Coleman lamp that kept going on and off.[68]

Body Stays Put - Spirit Travels

Spirit travel is another form of travel. The person's body remains in one place, but the spirit leaves the body and travels to another area. David Burnett describes this from Africa:

A man awoke in the night to find his wife in a very deep sleep. He was concerned and tried to awaken her, but she would not respond. In desperation, he cut her skin with a knife, but she remained asleep, and no blood flowed from the wound. Finally, he rubbed pepper in the wound, but still to no avail. When morning came, the woman suddenly awoke in great pain from the wound. Her husband was then convinced she was a witch. (1988:136)

I read the above story to my class in the Bible college, expecting some exclamation of surprise or laughter. Instead, people sat nodding their heads. I asked: "Have you heard this type of story before?" "Oh yes," they replied. "We haven't gone as far as cutting the skin, but the rest of the story is quite common."

One student told this story which he heard from his father:

When I was a young man, I was very keen on a young woman in a nearby village. One night I was in her house sleeping beside her and woke in the middle of the night to find her body extremely cold and totally unresponsive

229

to my touch. I tried to waken her, but she made no response. I was worried and wondered what had happened to her, and so I waited and watched. Some hours later I heard the fluttering of a fruit bat. I looked up to see a bat fly into the house and start to crawl down the wall toward the girl. I was petrified. Suddenly the girl stirred, reached up, and clasped the bat to her chest at which point it totally disappeared inside her. Needless to say I was fully awake and all my hair was standing up on end. I was not prepared to lie beside her again. I claimed I was cold. I sat up, put more firewood on the fire, and stayed awake until daybreak. I went home, never to return to the girl's house again. It was obvious that she was a sanguma.[69]

Insatiable Appetite for Meat

One of the common stories is that people with *sanguma* have an insatiable appetite for meat. People that are always hungry are suspect, and if people appear greedy at a feast, they are strongly suspected to be *sanguma*. They are reported to eat pigs as well as human organs, as the next stories show.

Pangia, Southern Highlands

One person had a big fat pig, but noticed that the pig was losing weight and getting thinner and thinner. He gave some medicine to the pig, but it made no difference. Eventually he killed and slaughtered the pig and the postmortem examination revealed that the pig's liver and other internal organs were missing. They concluded that a sanguma *had stolen the pig's liver.*

Kobon, Middle Ramu

A man bought a pig for a large sum of money. He killed the pig and butchered it with the owner watching, but

when they opened the pig's abdomen, the stomach, liver,
a lot of the fat, and other organs were missing.

Pastor Hosea, who reported this story to me, was there when they
butchered the pig and saw this himself. This was the first time he
had ever seen this sort of thing. The only explanation that makes
sense to him is that *sanguma* had stolen the pig's liver.

Pastor Mark was rather sceptical of the power or reality of *sanguma*
until he witnessed the following event:

He was in the Middle Ramu area, when a very strong
storm suddenly arose. During the storm, a tree crashed
to the ground, a branch from the tree flew through the
air, struck a large pig and killed it. After the storm, the
people butchered the pig. It appears that the people had
some doubts about what had killed the pig for it takes a
very hard blow, and often more than one blow, on the
head to kill a pig.

Mark was watching as they butchered the pig, when
suddenly the people became very excited. A large part of
the pig's liver was missing and the remainder of the pig's
liver was stabbed and cut. Mark had been watching the
whole process and there was no way one of the butchers
could have done this. The external skin of the pig showed
no injury at all. Mark and the others who were present
were convinced that the damage to the pig had been done
by sanguma *activity.*

Sanguma Power Demonstrated

Another student reports seeing a demonstration of a *sanguma*
woman's power when he was still a boy in school:
Two important people had died in his village just a few
months apart, and so the people were very concerned to
find out who had caused their deaths. They tried their

231

normal procedures, but did not come up with any solid conclusions. They had heard of an old woman from the Gumine area of Simbu who was reputed to be very powerful at finding out the cause of death. Some of the men brought her to the village in the Western Highlands Province to help them. The woman was asked to find out who was responsible for the two deaths. The boy was not there to see what she did in order to find out, but it involved her going into a trance and contacting the spirit world.

He arrived home from school to find that the old woman would be staying overnight at his father's house. His father asked the old woman if she was hungry. She replied: "It has been a very busy day, my spirit is hungry and would like a live chicken." The father gave the boy money and sent him to buy a chicken. He returned with the live chicken, and when the old woman saw it, she was very excited and began laughing and laughing like she was drunk. She told him to set the chicken down on the floor near the door. The old woman made no attempt to go near the chicken, but simply stared at the chicken. The chicken began to shrink before their eyes, and after a few minutes, the chicken collapsed into a little heap of feathers. The old woman laughed and told the father to take a close look at the chicken. He picked up the chicken and was shocked to find that all the meat and innards had disappeared. All that remained was a pile of feathers and a few bones. The student said: "I saw that with my eyes. It was real. I did not sleep much that night, for I was afraid her spirit might get hungry and I would be the next victim."[70]

When people believe that *sanguma* is making them sick, many of them give up hope, for modern medicine has no cure for *sanguma*. The thought of an invisible force that strikes someone down, causing him or her to waste away and die, is a source of great fear. The only alternative people see is to call on a *sanguma* doctor, who is a person with more *sanguma* power, and who can counteract the present *sanguma*.

Removal of Organs

In the Kobon area, the *sanguma* person allegedly removes the organs surgically and then closes the person up with no trace of any cut; the person goes home only to die some time later (cf. Riebe 1987:214).[71]

A pastor describes the activities of his cousin, who has two spirits which he describes as being a bird and a dog. By staring at people from a hidden position, he causes people to become unconscious. He then cuts them open and removes the organs that are demanded by the *sanguma* spirit. Using supernatural power, he closes up the victim so that no signs are left and announces the time when the victim will die. He says that he does not eat the body parts, but that it is the two spirits who eat the body parts. In reality, they go into his mouth, even though it is the spirit that is demanding them. He does not control the spirit, but the spirit controls him.

Hughes reports that a *sanguma* woman confided to her that it was the *sanguma* that was responsible for killing people, and that they were beyond her control. "She was not sorry for the evil deeds she had committed as she was not responsible" (1985:452).

Stone-Man Sorcery - Southern Highlands

This is a form of sorcery that has its origins in places such as Kikori and Kerema in the Gulf and Western Provinces, and has moved from there up into the southern parts of the Southern Highlands. The term "stone man" refers to a small stone image (20 – 25 cm long), like a small doll, with a human face on it. These men are not carved, but are found in the bush. They are believed to have magical

233

powers and can move without human assistance from one place in a house to another. People buy these and use them to kill enemies. In order to be effective, they require a ritual specialist who has the secret knowledge to activate the stone image.

The person who wants an enemy killed, hires both the owner of the stone and the specialist with the power to activate the stone. They will creep through the grass and shrubs toward the victim. The first person of the trio has a small stick in his or her hand which is waved so as to prevent others from seeing them. The last person in the group covers their tracks and rearranges the grass so that no one will see where they have been.

Once they have the victim in sight, the specialist activates the stone image by special incantations. From this point on, the image is highly dangerous, and no one dares go in front of it. The person holding it, holds it away from his or her body and points it toward the victim, keeping the arm as still as possible. When one arm becomes tired the object is very carefully transferred to the other hand, without moving or upsetting the aim of the stone-man. The stone-man withdraws the blood from the victim and they watch the stone, which somehow changes its appearance to indicate that the person's blood has been withdrawn. At this point, the victim falls unconscious. The attackers then cut the victim open and may remove organs. Then, using leaves, they seal up the cuts so that no scars are visible. The controller then announces how many days the victim has before death. The attackers disappear and sometime later the victim wakes up, unaware of anything that has happened. A couple of days later, he or she may develop a bad cough or back pain, and quickly dies. Within twelve to twenty-four hours, the marks of the attackers become visible in the victim's body. There are black lines that quickly become putrid, indicating where the attackers slashed the victim.

In the Highlands of PNG, the body of a dead person can be kept in the village for three days without much decomposition. But one informant reported that he saw his father's body begin to decompose within twenty-four hours. Black putrid marks appeared on the body and the face, and the jawbone quickly became detached from the skull. The village people were convinced that this was the result of an attack by someone practicing stone-man sorcery.

How a Person Becomes a *Sanguma*

In one of the earlier stories, a girl received the *sanguma* from her mother. This is very common. In fact, many of the Bible college students said that *sanguma* is an inherited power (cf. Hughes 1985:459). Also, men can receive it from their wives, or wives from husbands. There seems to be a strong link between a person being demonised and ancestral involvement in the occult or the demonic (Dickason 1987:162; Warner 1991:106).

Another way a person can become a *sanguma* is by going to a ritual specialist in order to obtain magical power for some other purpose, but ending up with a *sanguma* spirit instead (cf. Hughes 1985:459). A pastor told me of a ten year old boy who was hungry, and stopped by an old man's house to see if he had any food.

The old man said to him: "Would you like to receive a magical power that will enable you to get all the food you would like? You would have lots of meat to eat and you would never go hungry again." To the boy, this offer seemed too good an opportunity to miss. He quickly agreed and learned the magic spell that the old man taught him. He found, however, that he had been deceived. He had received a rat spirit which was constantly hungry and always driving him to eat more and more food. He struggled with this for a number of years until he confessed his problem to the pastor, who commanded the evil spirit to leave in the name of Jesus, and the boy was set free.

People's Reactions to *Sanguma*

The clan responds in varied ways to people who have or are suspected of having *sanguma*. It seems that people with *sanguma* are treated with fear and are often given anything they want. One student wrote that people try to isolate themselves from those known to be *sanguma*: if they see a suspected *sanguma* person, they try to avoid that person. On the other hand, if they cannot avoid the *sanguma* person, then they will give him or her whatever they have in their hands. If a *sanguma* person walks past their house while they are eating they will invite him or her in. This is not because they like the person or enjoy the company, but because they fear the power and do not want to do anything to upset him or her.

A school teacher reported to me that there was a young boy in his school who had sanguma powers. He claimed to be able to see into the teachers' houses, and also into their stomachs. To demonstrate his power, he was able to accurately tell each of the teachers what he or she had eaten the night before. This frightened the teachers and they were afraid to discipline the boy or upset him in any way. There was one exception. The deputy headmaster, who told me the story, was a very strong Christian. The boy said: "There is such a powerful light shining out from your house that I cannot see into it. Your power is far greater than mine."

Reay claims that people are wary of those suspected of witchcraft, and desperately afraid of convicted and confessed witches. Some witches seem to take pride in being singled out. Reay describes a scene in which a person was accused of being a witch and acknowledged the fact with no sign of shame or remorse. "He stood alone, the object of spectators' undivided attention and seemingly revelling in his power to make people afraid. The confession was the witch's finest hour" (1987:94). Yet other people have been burned alive for being suspected of having the same power.

236

Stephen reports that in the Mekeo area near Port Moresby, a sorcerer is held in high esteem in the community and can be one of the leading men in the village (1987a:43). His power gives him status and he is able to keep control in the village. Pastors from the coastal areas have told me that very powerful sorcerers are often church leaders in mainline churches. They have power in the community and no one will oppose them for fear of what they may do.

People in the Highlands who are believed to have *sanguma* are often ostracised by the rest of the community, for people are fearful of them. People are very reluctant to confess to being a *sanguma* for then they will be rejected, and if anything goes wrong in the village, they will be blamed.[72]

Treatment of the Accused

Witch hunts are common in the Highlands, especially when someone has died. Those declared guilty may be driven from the community or burnt to death, drowned or buried alive. Some accused people bargain with the community and are allowed to live on the basis that they will use their powers to protect the clan from other *sanguma* spirits (Hughes 1985:454). They may become *sanguma* doctors: they use their powers to detect other *sanguma* and sometimes to heal people who have been attacked by other *sanguma*.

One person who is widely regarded as a healer in one of the towns in PNG, charges large fees for his services and pays a proportion of his money to the mainline church to which he belongs. The practice of sorcery is against the law in PNG; however, this man has apparently demonstrated to the police that he is a bonafide healer.[73] He has letters from police and church leaders stating that he is allowed to practice. He confided to one of his friends that he uses the names of "God" and "Jesus" in his healing ceremonies as a cover up. "The spirits I am calling on are tribal spirits, but if people knew that, it would scare some of them away. So I call them 'God' and 'Jesus' and then people are happy." Syncretism is alive and well.

Witch hunts are often based on suspicion and false accusations and have become a big problem in many parts of Papua New Guinea. A person can be suspected of being a sorcerer or witch for any number of reasons. Any behaviour out of the ordinary near the time of death, or an apparent lack of concern or indifference over a death, makes a person suspect. People who walk about at night are likely to be accused. Widows, the weak and the vulnerable are also likely to be accused.

If accused, there is very little one can do to prove one's innocence. People are tortured with red hot wires poked into their skin in order to make them confess (Silas 1993:67). Sometimes people confess to save their lives. He or she will then be tortured until the names of the accomplices are revealed, for it is believed that *sanguma* 'people act in groups.

Some headmen have been accused of being *sanguma* and consequently were driven from their villages, leaving behind their families, land and gardens. Some people of influence have become drifters, deserted by family and clan. Some move to a wife's or mother's village. One pastor reported to me that many of the people in squatter settlements in Port Moresby are those who have run away from their Highlands village after being accused of being a *sanguma* person.

Some confess to witchcraft and then bargain with the tribe: "Allow me to live and I will protect you from other witches. With my power, I can reveal other *sanguma* people and cure those who have been attacked." Hughes reports an interview with a *sanguma* woman who was about to be hung, and in exchange for her life, volunteered to cure the headman of the village who was very ill (1985:454). The healing took place and she gained a respected place in the community. People were not convinced, however, that her powers were

238

always used for healing and never for evil. It is commonly believed that a witch with greater power can neutralise an attack caused by someone with lesser power.

Death of Accused Witches

A pastor reported the following:

In 1997, while he was pastoring a church near the town of Goroka, a woman died. Her death was sudden and took the community by surprise. Immediately the talk turned to the cause of death and sanguma. *A spirit medium was called in to talk to the dead woman's spirit to find out the hidden information. The medium spoke with the voice of the dead woman and described in detail how an older woman had committed the murder.*

The accused woman was called and confronted with the evidence. She admitted to the killing, but pleaded that she did not want to kill the woman, who was a friend, but was forced into it by the spirit who would give her no peace until the woman was killed. The crowd was enraged. People beat the woman, stuffed her into a large coffee sack, poured petrol over the bag, and burned her alive. Police were aware of the incident, but did nothing - after all, she was a witch and deserved to die. There is no payback or retaliation for killings like this.

Another pastor reports:

While he was pastoring in Simbu in 1987, the leader of a nearby village died. The people of the village accused a woman of being a sanguma *woman, and they tortured her by burning her with red hot steel. She confessed to being a sorcerer and also accused two other women. No further evidence was required. The women were attacked by the*

239

mob, beaten up, locked inside a house, and the house
was set on fire. The women screamed as they tried to
escape the flames. One woman managed to break through
the woven wall of the house, but she was immediately
struck down with a spear in her abdomen, and shoved
back into the burning house.

This was not done secretly, but was well known in the community. The police and the government were aware of this situation and took no action. As far as they were concerned, the women were guilty and justice had been done.

An Academic Understanding of *Sanguma*

How are we to interpret these stories? This is an important question, for how we interpret them will influence how we respond to them. These stories do not fit easily within a modern, scientific world-view. Some people, including missionaries, have dismissed stories of *sanguma* as being superstitious nonsense and totally impossible. After this initial response, people stopped telling stories about *sanguma* to missionaries. Whilst the missionaries may think that the problem is solved, stories remain around the fire in the village.

Anthropologists, too, have dismissed the stories as being impossible, and concluded that the real issue is not with the supposed witch, but rather with the role of the people who accuse others of being witches. In Africa there are beliefs similar to those I have outlined. Some of the actions attributed to witches seem to be objectively impossible, and consequently, some African anthropologists have decided that "the proper study of witchcraft is the accuser and his motives for imputing witchcraft to persons who are actually innocent" (Reay 1987:100). But are we to ignore the witchcraft activity and focus primarily on those who accuse others of being witches? The accusations and the witchcraft trials are certainly big problems, but they are only part of the problem. What causes these beliefs to

240

arise, and what role do these beliefs and practices play in the structure and functioning of Melanesian societies?

Sanguma and Social Factors

Sanguma beliefs do not exist in a social vacuum. Society influences beliefs and behaviour, and these beliefs and practices also influence society. A number of anthropologists have written about witchcraft and sorcery in Melanesia.[74]

Witchcraft beliefs fulfil some positive roles in society.

1. Witchcraft beliefs encourage people to conform. The fear of being labelled a witch encourages people to act according to the norms of society. People avoid unusual and antisocial behaviour – characteristics which are likely to lead to accusations of being a *sanguma*. In this way the *sanguma* helps to enforce group ethics: people are careful to share food, for instance, for if they do not then they fear being attacked by an angry *sanguma*.

2. *Sanguma* provides an explanation for death, and so provides an answer to the question "who caused X to die?". Melanesians believe that there is always some specific reason behind every death, and are always seeking an answer. The belief in *sanguma* provides answers to such questions.

3. Witchcraft may be a way in which weak and marginalised people gain access to power in society. Whether this is a positive or negative feature is ambiguous.

4. *Sanguma* provides society with a scapegoat on which they can vent their wrath. Having a "thing" to blame allows people to express frustration and thus relieve tension in the community. Again, however, this is ambiguous, as the person on the receiving end would certainly not consider it a positive experience.

Kauga, a young married man who was a keen Christian, often went to various houses during the week to lead

241

evening prayer meetings and Bible studies. A popular school teacher in the community was killed in a road accident and the people looked for someone to blame. Since it was known that Kauga was often out at night, he was accused. People stormed into his house early one morning, dragged him out, tied his hands with strong rope, and strung him up from a branch of a large tree. A fire was lit under his feet and he was commanded to confess to being a sanguma. *He continually denied it, but the people persisted. They beat his wife and ransacked his house. Someone poured kerosene on his leg and this was set ablaze. After several hours of torture from his fellow villagers they decided that he must be innocent and allowed him to go. He took his wife, along with what few belongings he had left, and went to stay in his wife's village. Kauga came to the Bible college class. He described his ordeal to the class and displayed the large burn scar on his leg. The burn scar has healed but the emotional scars still remain.*

Sanguma appear to have more negative than positive effects. When fears and accusations are rampant, it is a sure sign that all is not well within a community: the community itself is "sick".

1. People live in great fear. A Melanesian person said: "Living with witchcraft is like living in the midst of an unending hidden war" (Bercovitch 1989:140). There is the fear of oneself or a loved one being killed by a witch, and so one is always on the alert. There is also the fear of being falsely accused of being a witch. Funerals, instead of being a time of giving comfort to the grieving, are often dominated by distrust, suspicion and accusations, as people try to find the alleged killer. Funerals are reminders that once again evil has triumphed and life has been cut short, probably by witchcraft.
2. Innocent people have been brutally tortured, some have been driven out of their village, and others have been killed

because people have accused them of being witches. Funerals are times of intense emotion and once a person is accused of being a *sanguma*, it is very difficult to prove his or her innocence. Some confess to witchcraft in order to save their lives, and then live the rest of their lives under the shadow of their false confession. It is a situation in which it is impossible to win.

3. Hill argues that a witchcraft world-view "encourages spiritual reductionism, avoidance of responsibility for actions, or consideration of other factors" (1996:330). When there are a number of deaths one after another in the same village, the *sanguma* stories are rife, and fear and suspicion are rampant. *Sanguma* beliefs do provide an explanation for death in a community, but unfortunately they may provide a wrong answer and thus prevent people from taking appropriate action.

How many times have deaths, which were due to preventable diseases, been attributed to *sanguma*? Community Based Health Care teams report that health teaching decreases the amount of *sanguma* accusations in an area. When people clean up their drinking water supply, construct toilets, dig rubbish pits in the village, wash dishes and dry them in the sun, sickness declines dramatically - and the number of *sanguma* accusations die down. They have told the people in village meetings: "You talk about *sanguma*, blame people, and beat on people as being *sanguma*, but you are all *sanguma*. When you do not have a toilet, you pollute the water supply and you bring sickness to others. You are a *sanguma* and you help to bring death to your village."

The health teams believe that the practice of blaming sickness on *sanguma*, when probably due to typhoid, can prevent people from making the necessary changes to their behaviour. As a result, sickness continues unchecked, fear grips the community, and people continue to suffer unnecessarily from sickness and also from witchcraft accusations and torture.

243

4. The *sanguma* world-view also "blocks progress because success incurs envy which brings on attack" (Hill 1996:330). The Bible college students said that this works in two ways. Firstly, people who are successful may become the object of other people's envy and so be attacked and killed. Secondly, people may refrain from advancing themselves for fear of being attacked by those who would be jealous. In either case, the socioeconomic result is the same: the village does not progress economically or socially and people's lives remain static. As Tippett says: "Sorcery ... is hostile, individual and antisocial. It is used to satisfy anger, jealousy, or to gain ends for personal profit" (1967:14).

Explanations for *Sanguma*

There are several explanations that have been given for witchcraft beliefs and behaviour (Harriett Hill 1996:326):

1. *Stress on Society*
The belief that all sickness and death has a spiritual cause creates a climate in which *sanguma* beliefs can flourish. When this is combined with tension caused by rapid social change, the situation is compounded. Melanesian cultures have been undergoing dramatic changes in the past forty years. Clan boundaries are no longer so clearly defined. People move from place to place, picking up new ideas and customs and abandoning others. New diseases have entered society. A formal education system has been introduced; young people who educated outside of the village are frustrated, for there are few jobs available in the towns and similar opportunities are not offered in the villages. Education, health services and roads in rural areas are declining in quality and quantity. Lifestyles are more cash-dependent. Prices rise as the kina devalues. All of these factors create social tension. People feel vulnerable as society changes rapidly. In times like this, death is another indication of the triumph of evil.

244

2. Social Structure

There is no doubt that *sanguma* beliefs are stronger in some societies (e.g. Kobon and Simbu) than they are in other societies (Enga and Southern Highlands). It could be that there is a relationship between social structure and the incidence of sorcery and witchcraft. Yet Simbu and Enga are similar in social structure, both being controlled by "big men", whereas Kobon people are very scattered and there are no real "big men". Such an argument therefore is unconvincing.

3. Psychological Problems

Many feel that there is a strong psychological reason for witchcraft beliefs and practices. For example, Malinowski writes that: "Witchcraft is primarily rooted in the psychological reactions of those suffering from ill health, misfortunes, inability to control their destiny and fortunes" (1961:96).

Stephen concludes her study by saying: "The images of witch and sorcerer reflect the propensity of the human psyche to project onto the external world its own unconscious contents. The infinitely varied beliefs and practices associated with them reflect the ways in which specific cultures translate and transform what is unconscious into the actuality of social behaviour" (1987a:297). The researchers who have rejected the possibility of the existence of spirits have a very difficult job describing spiritual realities in abstract theoretical language.

I agree that psychological factors are involved in witchcraft, for humans are psychological beings, but social and psychological factors alone do not completely explain the phenomena of sorcery and witchcraft in Melanesia. It needs to be remembered that humans are also spiritual beings. Using scientific terms to describe a condition that the Melanesians regard as spirit possession does not mean that we have arrived at a more true or profound explanation, but only that we have translated from one idiom into another (Ferdinando 1999:374).

245

Sanguma: Witchcraft or Sorcery?

As noted earlier, some people classify *sanguma* as being a form of witchcraft, whereas others consider it a form of sorcery. MacDonald writes: "The terms 'sorcery' and 'witchcraft' tend to be used interchangeably in Melanesia, perhaps because neither of them quite fit the particular type of magic to which they are applied in this part of the world" (1982:170).

Evans-Pritchard, writing from a background of research in Africa, was one of the earliest anthropologists to distinguish between a witch and a sorcerer. He gives the following definition:

> To Azande themselves, the difference between a sorcerer and a witch is that the former uses the technique of magic and derives his power from medicines, while the latter acts without rites and spells and uses hereditary psycho-psychical powers to attain his ends. (1937:387)

Using this definition, *sanguma* would be classified as being witchcraft for usually there are no rites or spells of other physical items involved. Stephen gives a different definition. She argues witchcraft and sorcery in Melanesia have often been treated as a single phenomenon, yet she sees a great diversity of beliefs and practices spread across a wide spectrum:

> At one end, there are those who are believed to have "hidden powers" to harm others, who are blamed for death and illness in the community and, on this account, are socially despised and vulnerable to public accusation, exile and execution. At the opposite end are individuals believed to control "mystical means" to kill others, who are believed to use these powers on behalf of the community and, on this account, are socially powerful and rewarded for their services ... I have referred to the socially despised and condemned as "witch" and the socially powerful as "sorcerer". (1989:216)

This would clearly put *sanguma* under the category of witchcraft. What is the source of the power behind witchcraft? Evans-Pritchard, in the definition above, mentions "hereditary psycho-psychical power". Stephen mentions "hidden power" and "mystical means." What exactly does all this mean?

Psychic or Demonic?

Is the power behind witchcraft psychic or is it demonic? Hill says that it is possible to perceive witchcraft as "an evil spirit that has invaded an individual. In this model, witchcraft itself is inherently evil. The solution is simply to expel it" (1996:337). Unfortunately, Hill does not go on to discuss how to deal with demons or evil spirits. Perhaps she does not accept this as an explanation. Hill emphasises that witchcraft is a psychic power that can be used for either good or evil purposes. She uses the term "witchcraft" to refer to "the psychic, unconscious power", and sorcery to refer to "the conscious calling on spirit beings for help" (1996: 333). This definition is similar to that given by I. M. Lewis:

> Witchcraft is defined as the psychic power to harm, where the thought is father to the deed. Sorcery, in contrast, is taken to require the use of external and observable techniques – spells, potions, and other dark acts. Witchcraft exists only in the mind; it is known by its effects, whereas sorcery (like justice) must be seen to be done. (1971:13)

There are differing opinions as to whether sorcery and witchcraft are good or destructive.[75] I understand psychic ability to be the ability that some people have to see into the spirit realm and/or relate to spirit beings (other than God) within the spirit world. Some people are naturally gifted this way and other people, through training, have developed their capacity to do this. In this way, psychic ability is of itself a neutral ability that can be used for good or evil.

There are many spirits in the spirit world. Some are obedient to God, others rebel against God. People quickly come under bondage to rebellious, deceitful spirits. Witton and Parker suggest that when a person with psychic ability comes under the Lordship of Jesus Christ and the influence of the Holy Spirit, then "this ability becomes sanctified and they are the people who are more open to the more intuitive gifts of visions, pictures, words of knowledge, etc." (1991: 82). It should not be assumed that this is a simple transition. It means a radical break, usually involving deliverance from demonic spirits and a submission to the Lordship of Jesus Christ and the infilling of the Holy Spirit.

Pastor Thomas, who was once a sorcerer, now has a ministry in which visions, healings and words of knowledge are very important. However, he would emphasise that he has made a total break with the spirits he once dealt with, surrendered his life completely to Jesus Christ and now listens only to the voice of the Holy Spirit. The change did not come about through education or a retraining of his psychic powers, but through a total change of allegiance from demonic spirits to Jesus Christ.

In supporting her view that witchcraft is a psychic power, Hill quotes Mary Douglas: "In an enquiry into witchcraft as a principle of causation, no mysterious spiritual beings are postulated, only the mysterious powers of humans"(1970: xvi). It seems that Hill is basing her analysis upon the findings of social scientists who have ruled out the possibility of evil spirits and so are left to try and find some other explanation. The reason anthropologists and many missionaries have struggled to understand witchcraft is that they both share a very similar world-view. Both have been greatly influenced by the Enlightenment and the way it divides the world into "natural" and "supernatural" categories, and then concentrates primarily on the natural world. Consequently, although they have many differences in viewpoint, both have a struggle accepting that evil spirits really do exist.

Sigmund Freud, who has had an enormous influence in the twentieth century on how Westerners view the world, once wrote that: "spirits and demons were nothing, but the projection of primitive mans' emotional impulses" (Freud 1938:868). From a modern scientific perspective it is hard to believe evil spirits can live within people, can manifest themselves in various forms, including that of an animal, and coerce people to obey their commands. Tippett suggests that: "One reason Western theologians, medical men, and psychologists have trouble with the cross-cultural study of demon-possession is that they refuse to do their thinking outside their own scientific world-view" (1976:143). Spirits are not academically acceptable, and consequently many Christians are very unsure about what to do with Satan and demons.

For many people, "Belief in demons went out with a belief in dragons, elves, the tooth fairy, and the Easter Bunny" (Arnold 1997:24). Some people see the choice as having to choose between "a modern scientific world-view or devolving into a gullible uncritical acceptance of a primitive prescientific world-view" (ibid). Science deals with the empirical world, that which can be seen, touched, measured and critically analysed. Those things and theories that cannot be handled in a scientific way are disregarded.

Yet belief in spirits should not be dismissed as irrational. Ferdinando argues that "if one concedes the existence of at least one supernatural spirit being, God, there is no logical basis for denying the possibility that other spirits, albeit of a different order, may also exist" (1996:107). Spirits exist outside of that empirical dimension and, as part of the non-empirical world, cannot be evaluated by empirical means. But that does not mean they do not exist.

Modern scientists have concentrated their energies on exploring, understanding and manipulating the physical world. Some people in other cultures, especially shamans, have concentrated on exploring, understanding and manipulating the spirit realm. By creating partnerships with spirit beings through trances and spirit possession,

249

people have been able to travel back and forth between the realm of time and space and the spirit realm. To believe in the existence of spirits is not illogical.

Many theories concerning witchcraft, sorcery and spirit possession have been put forward by various anthropologists and sociologists. The problem is that the people who promote them do not believe in the reality of the spirit world, and although they genuinely wish to understand Melanesians, they have rejected the Melanesian explanation.

Melanesian Christians understand the phenomenon as being a form of demonisation. *Sanguma* is not a projection of a person's mind, but an unwelcome resident living within the person, who threatens violence to the person if the wishes of the *sanguma* are not carried out. Many of the stories are exaggerated and there are natural explanations that can explain some things – but there is a large amount of material that cannot be explained away. Often people are accused of being *sanguma* when they are innocent, but it does not mean there is no reality to the concept of *sanguma*. Many people have confessed to having *sanguma* spirits, and yet Western researchers do not want to acknowledge the reality of what Melanesians confess. As Tippett says: "The Western missionary ... is working in a Melanesian world, facing a Melanesian philosophy, and will have to learn to understand Melanesian thought forms, and fight for Christianity on Melanesian levels" (1967:101).

Sorcery has persisted as an explanation for death because Melanesians have been correct, at least some of the time: *sanguma* has been the cause of some people's deaths. *Sanguma* beliefs exist because people expect a supernatural cause for every death, and because there are *sanguma* spirits who have the power to kill people.

Sanguma as Demonisation

Most of the stories I have heard reveal that the *sanguma* is a spirit that urges the person to agree to its wishes, and threatens the host with destruction if he or she does not obey the spirit's commands. In Simbu, Wahgi and Kalam, the *sanguma* entity is not called a "spirit" as such, for that word is used only for a spirit that looks partially human or to refer to a ghost. *Sanguma* is not human, and yet has a will and can speak. Reay describes *sanguma* well: "The *kumo*, though only a thing (yap), is described as an invisible creature with appetites, volition and the ability to issue compelling and easily understood commands in the host's own language"(1987:111). This agrees with Hughes' description from Simbu (1985:452), and Riebe's description among the Kalam people (1987:214). Papua New Guineans speak of *sanguma* as being an evil entity separate to the person, which can go and come, but which seeks to control the person.

This concept of *sanguma* can be seen in the following story:

A young man, Kapi, was accused of being a sanguma *and was driven away from his village. He went to see his tribal sister Moni, a pastor's wife, who was sorry for him and took him in. Kapi had a tremendous appetite and Moni had to struggle to satisfy his hunger. One week when the pastor was away, Kapi finished his plate of food and then demanded Moni's plate of food. She refused to give it to him and rebuked him sharply. She put her baby down to sleep and went outside to wash the clothes. While she was outside, the* sanguma *(a possum) said to Kapi: "She was rude and nasty to you. Go ahead and kill her baby." Kapi replied: "No. He is my little cousin. I do not want to touch him."*

The sanguma *persisted: "Come on. Let's kill him." This led to a struggle of wills between the* sanguma *and Kapi. In the struggle, Kapi called out. Moni came in wondering what was wrong. Kapi reassured her that nothing was wrong.*

251

Moni went out of the house and the struggle between Kapi and the sanguma *started again. The* sanguma *was urging Kapi to let him kill the child. Kapi refused, but the* sanguma *said: "If you will not touch him, then I will." There was an internal struggle and in the midst of it, the baby woke up crying. Moni came in, picked up the baby, and comforted him. That night the baby became ill. In the morning, the baby would not drink milk and became worse. That afternoon two of Moni's brothers arrived. They saw the sick baby and guessed that Kapi was responsible. They were very angry. They threatened to chop Kapi into pieces with their axes if he did not confess. He confessed the story as outlined above. He also said he would stop the* sanguma *and that the baby would soon be alright. Sure enough, the next day the baby was well.*

The *sanguma* is a separate being with a will of its own and yet is somehow dependent upon the human host cooperating with it. This is consistent with *sanguma* being an evil spirit that is separate to the person in whom it lives. The evil spirit is driving the person to destroy other people, against the person's judgement. This is part of the reason for the fear. No one is safe. The *sanguma* respects no one and even attacks close family members. It is completely non-human and antisocial.

Evil spirits have different levels of strength and occupy different positions in the hierarchy of evil. They can also have differing levels of attachment to humans (Kraft 1990:12). It is possible, therefore, for a strong demon to be weakly attached, or for a weak demon to be strongly attached. The stories we have looked at show the *sanguma* demon having a strong degree of control over the person and largely compels the person to obey the *sanguma* spirit's wishes. Figure 16 shows the varying levels of control or influence that a demon may have on a person. The scale goes from low levels of influence at the left to almost total control at the right.

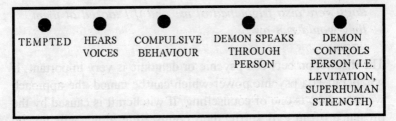

| TEMPTED | HEARS VOICES | COMPULSIVE BEHAVIOUR | DEMON SPEAKS THROUGH PERSON | DEMON CONTROLS PERSON (I.E. LEVITATION, SUPERHUMAN STRENGTH) |

Figure 16. Demonisation and Increasing Degrees
of Demonic Control

Pastor Thomas Bruno sees *sanguma* activity as a form of demonisation. Thomas was closely related to the head spirit of his village. This head spirit had considerably more power than the animal-type *sanguma* spirits, for all the spirits are arranged hierarchically. Thomas inherited this spirit at or soon after birth, and he received other spirits later through his own involvement in occult practices. The level of control he allowed the spirit to have varied from time to time. Thomas says there is a very strong association between demonic spirits and death.

Sometimes I would go up into the mountains in Simbu and collect bones from the burial limestone caves. I would bring them back and keep them in my house. Sometimes I would crunch them into powder with my teeth and swallow them in order to gain the power of the dead person and so add it to my supply of power. I would also collect blood stained clothing from people who had been killed in car accidents and call upon them in an effort to get more and more power. We were very conscious that there was power in blood. I loved to wear black clothes and was fascinated with death and graveyards.

Often I would get very strong feelings from the spirit to steal a child, kill it and eat it. This happened quite often, and whenever I came near babies, they would cry, and very young children would run to their mothers. Pigs and

253

*dogs were also frightened of me and if I looked at them,
they would run away.*

The distinction between psychic or demonic is very important. If witchcraft is a psychic power which can be tamed, the approach we must take is one of counselling. If witchcraft is caused by the presence of an evil spirit, then counselling alone will not be sufficient.[76] The evil spirit must be commanded to leave in the name of Jesus. Bruno says his father taught him one of the fundamental rules of the spirit world: "The weak must always give way to the powerful." According to Thomas, this is the basis of "psychic healing". If a disease is caused by one witch and his or her familiar spirit, then it can be healed by another witch who is in conjunction with a more powerful spirit. He gave a personal example:

*As a youth, Thomas had a long standing sore on his leg
that would not respond to any form of medication, either
Western or traditional. Various traditional healers tried
to heal him, but were unable to help. Eventually, his father
took him to a person who was reputed to have even more
power. The sore was diagnosed as being caused by a spell
from a sorcerer. Thomas was asked: "What would you
like me to do, remove the curse or kill the sorcerer?"
Thomas was young, impulsive, and frustrated from the
constant pain he had endured for three years. He said:
"Kill him." The healer then took a large leaf similar to a
banana leaf, and rolled it up so it formed a long green
tube. He then spoke into the tube and called the names of
the head spirits of all the villages from the head down to
the mouth of the Sepik River. He called on them to destroy
the curse and the sorcerer. He said to Thomas: "If there
is a large explosive noise, then my power is greater than
his power and he will die. If there is no large noise, then
he is more powerful." He then struck the leaf on the floor.
There was an explosive crack just like a gun shot. The
next day the opposing sorcerer was dead.*

254

Was this power good or evil? Was this witchcraft or sorcery? It varies according to perspective. This was not the result of innate psychic power belonging to the sorcerer: the power belonged to the spirits that he was in contact with. According to Thomas, there is constant rivalry in the world of the demonic. Each person seeks to increase his or her power in order to out do someone else. Christians can rejoice, for Jesus has defeated Satan and so has authority over all the powers of evil.

Before we get into practical ways of dealing with *sanguma*, we need relevant theology. Hiebert, Tienou and Shaw call this a "theology of the invisible". The invisible world includes the triune God and his ministering angels. It also includes Satan and his demons, who oppose God and seek to keep people from turning to God in repentance and faith (1999:371).

Biblical Understanding of the Spirit World

The accompanying diagram (Figure 17) is a model of the spirit world. It is biblical and enables us to understand such things as *sanguma*. The diagram is in three sections: the top section is God the creator, who is separate from creation but actively involved in creation. The next section is the realm of angels and spirits. The Bible shows us that although all angels, spiritual powers, rulers and authorities were created and given power by God, not all are operating in obedience to God (Colossians 1:16; Ephesians 2:2). The bottom section is the physical realm of people and things.

Arnold gives a clear definition of Satan: "The devil is an intelligent powerful spirit being that is thoroughly evil, and is directly involved in perpetrating evil in the lives of individuals as well as on a much larger scale … He is not an abstraction, either as a personification of the inner corrupt self, or in the sense of a symbolic representation of organised social evil" (1997:35). Satan likes people to believe that he is an alternative god, with equal power, authority, wisdom and strength. But in reality, he is simply a rebellious servant (Hiebert

255

et. al. 1999: 276-277). Subtle, cunning and more powerful than we are, but still a created being, he must ultimately submit to the authority of God.

Angels are God's staff for running the universe. They give guidance, protect from danger, provide for and assist God's people (Hebrews 1:14). They rejoice when people turn from sin and come back into fellowship with God (Luke 15:10). There is indication in Scripture that they can influence what we call the "forces of nature". This is seen in the various plagues on Egypt, the pillar of fire that led the people out of Egypt (Exodus 14:19), killing enemy soldiers (Isaiah 37:36). In the book of Revelation, they control the forces of nature when so directed by God.

By him all things were created: things in heaven and on earth, visible and invisible, whether thrones or powers or rulers or authorities; all things were created by him and for him (Colossians 1:16).

REALM of GOD

OBEDIENT

DISOBEDIENT

REALM of ANGELS

Cherubim
Seraphim
Archangels
Angels

Tribal deities
Deceiving spirits
Bush spirits
Sanguma spirits

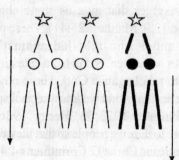

Obey God.
Worship God.
God's messengers.
Protect, assist, and give direction to people.

Seek to deceive, control, and tempt people to do evil. Work in people and cultures so that they do not reflect the image of God.

PHYSICAL REALM OF TIME AND SPACE

Figure 17. A Biblical View of the Cosmos

The terms "thrones or powers or rulers or authorities" indicate spiritual beings with differing levels of authority, but the Bible nowhere spells out a hierarchy of angelic beings, even though that was an important topic among Jewish writers in the inter-testamental period (Arnold 1992:98). Not all angels have stayed faithful to God. Though the Bible does not give us all the details, it is clear that there was a rebellion in the heavenly realms, and as a result a number of the angelic beings, led by Satan, are in revolt against God (Ephesians 6:12; Revelation 12).

The writers of the Old and New Testaments do not try to prove the existence of demons; they assume they exist. Although the Bible does not give us a detailed explanation for the origin of demons, there are biblical passages that give us some clues (i.e. Ezekiel 28:12,15; Revelation 12:9; Matthew 25:41). These passages portray Satan as a fallen angel who rebelled against God and was consequently cast out of heaven. Satan led a celestial revolt leading a myriad of angels to rebel against God. These other lesser angels who followed Satan became what we know as evil spirits or demons (Unger 1952:15; Philpott 1973:52; Henry 1986:57-74; Lewis 1976:353). They work to deceive people so that they worship anything or anyone other than Jesus Christ (2 Corinthians 4:4). They are evil, tempt people to do evil, and so distort and destroy people who were made in the image of God. Evil spirits seek to control people. As people give them access to their lives, the evil spirits quickly lead them until they become the very antithesis of all that is good and holy. Warner expresses it well:

> [These fallen angels] became like disgruntled employees who throw sand into the gears of the machines they operate in order to sabotage operations and to "get" the boss. The fallen angels now use their delegated power in the material realm to create alienation and to pervert God's good creation. Human suffering and the destructive forces of nature were not part of what God pronounced "very good". This is the work of an enemy. (1991:31)

258

The Holy Spirit is not part of the created order and so is not some super angel, but he is the dimension of the Triune Godhead who is at work in the world. He corrects, guides, teaches, encourages, rebukes and strengthens Christians. He works in the lives of Christians, transforming them so they will reflect more of the image of God. He works in the lives of non-Christians and seeks to lead them to God.

Humans are spiritual beings who have physical bodies and who live in a physical world. However, through prayer, worship, meditation and other various rituals, they also have access to the spiritual realm. Christians, along with supporting angels, are God's agents for extending God's rule and authority in this world. Unfortunately, Christians have not always done a very good job of being God's ambassadors and have sometimes reflected the ways of this world, rather than reflect the ways of God as revealed in Jesus Christ.

Because Jesus lives a sinless life, is completely obedient and gives himself as a sacrifice for sin through his death on the cross, God raises him from the dead. He is now seated at the right hand of the Father "far above all rule and authority, power and dominion, and every title that can be given" (Ephesians 1:21). This means that Jesus is supreme over all angelic beings and all evil spirits. This is good news for Christians, for those who are united to Christ through faith have "been raised up with Christ and seated ... with him in the heavenly realms in Christ Jesus" (Ephesians 2:6). This means that Christians have been given authority in the spiritual realm and do not need to live under demonic oppression. Christians can use this God given authority to release people from demonic bondage such as *sanguma*. This understanding is absolutely essential if we are to be effective in understanding the authority Christians have in relating to *sanguma*.

A Biblical Understanding of *Sanguma*

In seeking to develop a biblical understanding of *sanguma*, I have found John 8:44 very helpful. Here Jesus says very plainly that Satan is both a murderer and a liar. This tells us that Satan is powerful and does have the power to destroy people, and also that he is a liar and therefore exaggerates and boasts. Satan is like "a roaring lion seeking whom he may devour" (1 Peter 5:8) and seeks to intimidate others. Satan is also "the accuser" (Revelation 12:10), who delights in accusing people before both God and others. We should not be afraid, for the Scriptures plainly tell us that "the one who is in [us] is greater than the one who is in the world" (1 John 4:4).

Sanguma is an evil spirit which controls certain people and drives them to harm, destroy and cause death to other people. Although Satan has come to "steal, kill, and destroy", Jesus has come to give life in all its fullness (John 10:10). We are not to be controlled by fear of *sanguma,* but we should rejoice that Jesus is greater than all spiritual powers and he is able to set *sanguma* people free from their spiritual bondage.

If people think their sickness has been caused by a *sanguma* person, they often feel there is no hope for them. When I was teaching at Bible college, we discussed this.[77] "A person is sick and it is believed that the sickness is caused by *sanguma*. You are the pastor and they have requested your help. What would you do?"

1. *We need to build up the sick person's faith in the power of God.*
God has not given us a spirit of fear (2 Timothy 1:7). Scripture reading and Bible teaching can be very helpful to destroy fear and build up people's trust and confidence in the power of God. Psalm 91 is very reassuring for those who feel they have been attacked by witchcraft or sorcery.

- We can remind the sick person that Jesus casts out demons, and is more than able to defeat the power of sorcery.
- Jesus defeats Satan on the cross, and demonstrates this through his resurrection (Colossians 2:15).
- God's power is greater than that of evil spirits (1 John 4:4).

The prayer team should share experiences of deliverance. Christians can build up the patient's faith by sharing stories of God's miraculous help in other times and places.

2. *The family needs to confess any disharmony.*
The family needs to spend time confessing any ill feelings, jealousy, resentment or anger (James 5:14-18).

3. *The family needs to confess faith in Christ for healing.*
The leader of the prayer team can ask the family: "Do you believe that Jesus is able to heal this person and that Jesus is greater than *sanguma*?" They should sing songs which express their faith and so encourage the family to believe in God's power to heal.

4. *There should be prayer by the pastor or prayer team leader and others.*
The leader can ask the family: "Is there anything that you need to destroy? Do you have special leaves, tree bark or other charms that you have been relying on for healing power?" If such things are present, the family needs to destroy them, and then in the name of Jesus, the pastor needs to command the evil spirit to leave.

5. *There should be evaluation concerning what has happened.*
The leader asks the sick person:
- What did you experience while we were praying?
- When we spoke to the evil spirits, did you feel anything happen?
- If so, what?

If not completely released, evaluate the situation. Is there anything else that has come to mind, which you need to confess or dealt with? Is there still fear of *sanguma* and the power of evil? More songs and Scripture may be needed to increase faith, and more prayer, until the person is confident of Jesus' power to deliver and to heal.

6. *Consider the possibility of medical attention.*
The person may be suffering from a common disease such as malaria or typhoid, which has been compounded by the sick person fearing that he or she has been attacked by *sanguma*. Medicine can be given in addition to prayer and Christian counselling.

We have seen that Westerners have not known how to respond to *sanguma*, and as a result, the church has not given it the attention it deserves. Because no one speaks about it in church, people feel that the church cannot help. Included have been suggestions from Bible college students of how the church can be more involved in ministering to the victims of *sanguma*. The people with *sanguma* are victims, the people they attack are victims and the people who are falsely accused are also victims. All of these need the ministry of the church.

Most of the stories in this chapter have described *sanguma* in people's lives. There is, however, a greater reality which is the power of Jesus Christ. The following story demonstrates the power of Christ over the *sanguma*:

Pastor Kaula went to visit a church in the Maring language area in the Jimi Valley. He knew that some very powerful sanguma *people lived in this area. He visited people in the village and tried to talk to one old man, but the man was very sullen and withdrawn and even more so when he heard that Kaula was a pastor. Kaula suspected he was one of the* sanguma *men and invited him to attend the service in the church that evening, but the old man was not at all interested. It was a hot afternoon and Kaula went to a small nearby stream to wash. While washing, he had the uncanny feeling that someone was watching him. Trying to be as discrete as possible, he glanced around and spotted the old man staring at him from behind the tree. Kaula said to himself: "Okay old man, try your utmost. My God is greater than your power. You cannot do a thing to me." Kaula deliberately took a long time having a wash, giving the old man plenty of time to use his power. Then he walked back up the hill to the village.*

Later in the afternoon, he saw the old man and again invited him to the church, but the old man just grunted. That night as Kaula preached in the church, he spotted the old man in the congregation. He gave an altar call and invited those who would like to experience the peace and power of God's love and forgiveness of sins to come to the front. One of the first to come was the old man. Kaula talked to him, and he said: "I have three sanguma *spirits. This afternoon I tried all my powers against you and they could do nothing. I would like to give my life to God." The old man found freedom that night.*

It is important that the church understand this problem of *sanguma* theologically, and develop ways to deal with it.

Focusing attention on the power of evil can be dangerous, as it can take our attention away from the much greater power and reality of Jesus Christ. Marilyn Rowsome has good words of advice:

We need to think seriously about the spiritual powers expressed in the traditional beliefs. These powers are real and powerful ... but we need to turn the eyes of the people to Christ who rules supreme over the spiritual powers as Creator, Redeemer, Victor and Living Lord. Yes, be aware of the presence and power of spiritual powers, but know

and proclaim the greater power of God and the victory
every believer has in union with Christ in this present
age ... With this clear teaching firmly fixed in your thinking
and demonstrated in your life, meet the needs of both
unbelievers still bound by the spiritual powers and
Christians still living in fear of spirits. (Rowsome 1993:60)

Theology must be contextualised so that the church does not sit silent and helpless, ignoring the problems of *sanguma*. "Any theology that does not portray Jesus Christ as an all powerful Saviour who here and now can free people from all fear, especially the fear of witchcraft and sorcery, is inadequate" (Healey and Sybertz 1996:22).

CHAPTER TEN

THE CHRISTIAN RESPONSE TO THE SPIRITS OF THE DEAD AND TO *SANGUMA*

In Port Moresby in the middle of the night, Willie was woken up by a distinct rap at the door. He sat up, puzzled; he wondered who could be out there at this time of night. He went to the door and asked: "Who is there?" No one answered. But again, he heard someone knocking. He cautiously opened the door and peered outside. No one was there. "That's strange," he thought, and went back to bed, but could not get back to sleep. "What is happening back in the village? I wonder if everyone is alright." He had not been back to the village for almost a year. Some hours later, he was at his office in the government buildings and the phone rang. It was his cousin from the Highlands informing him that his favourite uncle had died in the middle of the night. Willie thought to himself: "That explains it. He must have been the one who came knocking at the door in the middle of the night."

Jesus is victorious over the powers of Satan. Because of his death and resurrection, he is now Lord of the living and of the dead. What are the implications of this for a theology of death and the spirits of the dead?

In the pastors' conferences, we examined the Scriptures to see how the patriarchs responded at times of death. We looked also at the Old Testament understanding of the place of the dead, and laws forbidding people to communicate with the spirits of the dead.

265

Death and Burial Among the Patriarchs

The pastors looked at the lives, and especially the deaths, of the patriarchs to see what burial practices were observed and how they responded to death. The following examples were looked at: Abraham (Genesis 23; Genesis 25:8-11), Rachel (Genesis 35:19-20), Isaac (Genesis 35:28-29), Jacob (Genesis 49:29-50:14), Joseph (Genesis 50:24-26; Exodus 13:19) and David and his response to the death of Saul and Jonathan (2 Samuel 1). The pastors noted the following points:

1. It is important to have a special place for burial. Abraham is content to move from place to place, but once his wife dies it is extremely important to him to buy a cave for her burial place. The pastors felt that this also demonstrated Abraham's faith that one day God would give all of this land to him.
2. Rachel dies while travelling from one place to another and she is buried with a special pillar to mark her grave. The dead are treated with respect.
3. It is a desired thing to die "old and full of years" (Genesis 35:29).
4. Jacob and Esau live very different lives separate from each other, but come together to bury their father. Funerals are a time of recalling a common heritage and unity.
5. Last words, blessing and instructions are very important (Genesis 49:29-33).
6. It is important to be buried along with the other members of one's family, e.g. Jacob is taken back to be buried with Abraham and Isaac (Genesis 49:29-33; 50:12-14), and Joseph requests that his body not be buried in Egypt, but taken back to Canaan at the time of the Exodus (Genesis 50:24-25).
7. People often fast when a person dies (2 Samuel 1:12). Sometimes mourning is both loud and long (Genesis 50:10). Songs of lament are sometimes composed in honour of the person who died (2 Samuel 1:19-27).

8. Care of the body after death is very important. The people of Jabesh Gilead venture into an enemy stronghold in the middle of the night to retrieve the bodies of Saul and his sons. They give them a proper burial and fast for seven days to show their grief (1 Samuel 31:8-13).

Melanesian people often assume that the "Christian" practice should be similar to the practices of the expatriate missionaries, according to which emotions are tightly controlled, even at time of death. This study showed the pastors that it is not wrong for people to express their emotions. The pastors found they had much in common with the tribal people of the Old Testament.

To the Hebrews it was very important to give proper treatment to the corpse and have an honourable burial. To leave the dead body unburied or to let the corpse be prey for birds and wild beasts, was thought of as the worst of all fates (1 Kings 14:11; Jeremiah 16:4; 22:19; Ezekiel 29:5). All of the above verses show how important it was to be buried with the ancestors.

Communicating with the Spirits of the Dead

The pastors noted that many of the practices associated with death and burial in the Old Testament are very similar to cultural practices in PNG. Having a special place for burial, loud wailing, fasting and lamenting are all important. If someone dies away from home territory, people want to bring the body back home, for it is important to be buried with one's forefathers. When an important person dies, normal village life stops for a week or more, and life does not recommence until the burial and mourning have ended.

There is one practice, however, that is very common in PNG, but which is expressly forbidden among the Hebrews: consulting mediums and talking with the dead. The following references were looked at and findings noted:

Leviticus 19:31	Do not turn to mediums or spiritists.
Leviticus 20:6	God is opposed to all who turn to mediums or spiritists.
Leviticus 20:27	Mediums and spiritists are to be stoned.
Deuteronomy 18:11	Divination, sorcery, witchcraft, the casting of spells, mediums, spiritists, the interpreting of omens and consulting the dead are all forbidden.
Isaiah 8:19	People should enquire of the Lord rather than turn to mediums and spiritists.
Isaiah 19:3	God will bring to nothing the plans of those who consult spirits of the dead, mediums and spiritists.

These passages very clearly prohibit people from consulting spirit mediums in order to contact the dead for advice, direction and help. Why does God put such a strong prohibition on this practice? The burial practices of the Israelites are similar to those of the people in their surrounding cultures, but this prohibition sets them apart from the others. God commands the Israelites to honour their parents (Exodus 20:12). They honour them with a respectful burial, but after they have died, they are not allowed to contact them. Why does God make such a law? Why doesn't God want people to converse with the spirits of the dead?

Before we reply to these questions, there are others that we must address. Where are the dead? Are they near us or far away? Is it possible to contact them and can they reply to us?

The Place of the Dead

What happens when a person dies? Where does the spirit go? What does the Bible say? These questions are very important if we are to deal intelligently with the issue of appeasing ancestors and contacting them for advice.

The pastors looked at a selection of verses from the Old Testament related to *sheol* (variously translated as the grave, or the pit):

Isaiah 38:18	It is a place of no hope, no praise and no singing.
Psalm 88:5, 11-12	It is a place of darkness, oblivion, cut off from God's care.
Psalm 31:17	It is a place of silence.
Job 7:9-10	It is a place of no return. The person who dies will never come to his house again.
Job 10:21-22	It is a land of gloom, deep shadow, and a place of no return.
Job 38:17	It is like a prison with strong gates.
Isaiah 5:14	It is like a monster that opens its mouth and swallows people.
Isaiah 14:15	It is like a deep pit.
Ezekiel 26:20-21	It is like a pit in the depths of the earth. People who go there will not return to the land of the living.

The picture is one of gloom, darkness and silence; without hope or joy. The pastors were far more familiar with the New Testament teaching that the spirits of the dead go to be with the Lord, and they were very surprised by the bleak Old Testament view. They were also surprised that the Bible should have two viewpoints that are so different.

The pastors mentioned that there is a conflict between the teaching of the Bible and traditional practice. People apparently succeed in communicating with the spirits of the dead, but these verses again and again show that the grave is a place of no return (Job 7:9-10; 10:21; Ezekiel 26:20). Such a place is in conflict with the traditional view of seeing ghosts, seeking to contact them and hearing from them. If the place of the dead is a place of silence, then who speaks to the mediums? If the dead are in a place of "no return", then who, or what, lives on in the graveyard? This led to the next question:

Do the Spirits of the Dead Ever Appear to the Living?

In Papua New Guinean thinking, the dead appear to the living. People see ghosts, and they seek to contact the dead to find out information from them. This practice is clearly forbidden in Scripture – and yet there are two occasions when spirits of the dead do appear to the living. The first is when King Saul asks a medium to contact Samuel (1 Samuel 28), and the second is the appearance of Moses and Elijah on the Mount of Transfiguration (Matthew 17:3; Mark 9:4; Luke 9:30).

Saul and the Witch of Endor
The pastors struggled with this passage (1 Samuel 28). They had read the verses forbidding anyone from consulting the dead, and those describing *sheol* as a place of no return, and then they came to this passage where the spirit of Samuel comes back and talks with Saul. They discussed this in groups and then we had a full discussion of this story.

They felt that it was significant that the woman cries out when she sees the spirit of Samuel. Her cry indicates that what she sees is quite different to what she normally saw, for her "apparent success was a quite exceptional event and one that terrified even her" (Ferdinando 1996:123). In this story, the words of Samuel seem very authentic, as if they really are his words. The message that is brought to Saul is a message of judgement; it brings no hope. Samuel says that the kingdom had been taken out of Saul's hands and given to David, and on the next day Saul and his sons will be with Samuel in the place of the dead. "Samuel speaks as a prophet, not as a ghost, and the seance became the occasion of a sermon" (Gordon 1986:196). This story does not open up the way for people to contact the dead, for this event quickly brings God's judgement. Saul dies because he consults a medium for guidance (1 Chronicles 10:13).

Moses and Elijah
In the New Testament, Moses and Elijah, who had both died many years before, appear to Jesus on the Mount of Transfiguration. This event is different to the story of Samuel for this is not a seance, nor is it initiated by a medium. These two godly men both had extraordinary deaths: Elijah did not die but was caught up in a chariot of fire, and Moses died up on Mount Nebo overlooking the promised land. God took care of his burial for "no one knows where he was buried" (Deuteronomy 34:6). J. Sidlow Baxter suggests that this transfiguration scene tells us much about life after death: Moses represents those who die believing in God; Elijah represents those who are alive and are caught up to meet the Lord in the air (1 Thessalonians 4.17). Both are with the Lord whose "humanity is iridescent with his divinity" (Baxter 1959:80). In this way they give us a preview of all that God is preparing for his people.

The transfiguration shows that there is human survival beyond the grave; that there is personal individuality, and people know and recognise each other. It also demonstrates that the "departed are still actuated by keen concern in the things which happen on this earth. But supremely we see that the eyes of that other world are upon our Lord Jesus" (Baxter 1959:81). Moses and Elijah talk with Jesus about "his departure", which he will accomplish in Jerusalem (Luke 9:31). The Greek word is used to refer to this departure: "the exodus". Just as Moses had led the people out of bondage in Egypt, Jesus is to "accomplish the exodus of all of His redeemed people from bondage to sin and death and Satan" (Baxter 1959:81). This incident is not just a chance happening, but a tremendous encouragement and confirmation for Jesus, and an unforgettable teaching event for the disciples. Peter refers to it in connection with the power and glory of the second coming (2 Peter 1:16-18). Also in reference to the second coming, John says: We will be like him, because we will see him as he truly is (1 John 3:2 CEV).

271

These are the only two instances in the Bible where the spirits of the dead appear to the living. They show us that, although it is possible for the dead to appear, it is not normal and only happens with God's permission. It should also be noted that, "Nowhere in the Old or New Testaments are the dead represented as themselves taking the initiative to make contact with their living descendants, neither to communicate, nor to harm, nor to bless" (Ferdinando 1996:123). The fact remains however, that in PNG spirits are seen in the graveyard. If they are not the spirits of the dead, then who are they?

The Rich Man and Lazarus

Jesus tells a story that gives us insights into the place of the dead (Luke 16:19-31). In traditional European theological interpretation, a story such as this is less important for teaching truth than a chapter devoted to the future life (such as 1 Corinthians 15). Melanesians, however, enjoy stories and like to seek out their hidden meanings. I found that this story generated much more discussion among the pastors than did 1 Corinthians 15. The class members raised the following points:

- Contrary to common belief, prosperity does not indicate God's blessing, and poverty does not indicate God's curse. In this story, the rich man, who is a "big man" in society, does not have a name. In contrast, it is the poor, weak, "nobody" - the man of no importance - who has a name. Jesus thus shows that God's perspective is very different to ours.
- The rich man dies and is buried. No doubt there would have been a big party, lots of speeches and an impressive grave, but he finds himself in torment. Lazarus dies, and there is no mention that he was buried for he was a person of no reputation. He is however, known to God, and the angels come and take him to "Abraham's side", the place of the righteous dead.

272

•There are only two possible places one can go to after death. There is a great gulf fixed between the two sides, and it is not possible to cross from one to the other.

•The pastors felt that the events indicate that the story took place in a contemporary setting. This story is not after the great resurrection, because the rich man's brothers are still alive and going about their normal business.

•There is no indication that there is a second chance or some other opportunity to repent. There is no indication that the rich man has repented of his arrogance and self-centredness. He expects Lazarus to be like a servant for him, to fetch water and take messages to his brothers.

•Although it does not say that it is impossible for the dead to return to the living, the story indicates that it will not happen. The rich man is certainly not free to go and warn his brothers, or to pass messages to them.

Absent From the Body - Present With the Lord

Jesus' death and resurrection bring transformation to the whole human experience of death. In the Old Testament, the concept of *sheol* is one of deep gloom, but now death loses its sting and is "swallowed up in victory" (1 Corinthians 15:54). We see this in the death of Stephen. As the rocks pelt down on him, he has a vision of heaven. He sees heaven open "and Jesus standing at the right hand of God" ready to welcome him (Acts 7:55-56).

Paul does not fear death. He says: "To live is Christ and to die is gain ... I desire to depart and be with Christ" (Philippians 1:22-23). At another time, he says he will "prefer to be away from the body and at home with the Lord" (2 Corinthians 5:8). Instead of something to be feared, death is seen as sleeping (1 Corinthians 15:18-20; 1 Thessalonians 4:13-15). In the book of Revelation, a voice from heaven declares: "Blessed are the dead who die in the Lord from now on" (Revelation 14:13). Death is referred to as sleep because it is temporary. Although body and spirit are separated at the time of

273

death, there is a time coming when the body will be resurrected and the body and spirit reunited, not to be separated again. This gives hope to Christians.

Between Death and the Second Coming

We noticed earlier that there was confusion in the minds of many Melanesian people concerning the question, "Do we go to heaven when we die, or when Jesus returns?" Some interpret the resurrection to mean that the dead are in the graveyard waiting for the resurrection. This goes along with the traditional understanding, that the spirits of the dead are nearby and watching over the living.

In traditional religious beliefs, the spirit lives on in a nebulous shadowy existence. The relationship between the living and the dead is rather ambiguous: although people want the dead near, they do not want them too near. Ghosts can be unpredictable and violent at times. Mbiti says: "The food and libation given to the living dead are paradoxically acts of hospitality and welcome and yet of informing the living dead to move away. The living dead are wanted and yet not wanted" (1969:84). The same situation applies in PNG; the presence of a ghost is a cause of great concern.

We discussed this in the conferences. There is good news in the gospel. When we die, the spirits of the righteous go to be with the Lord even though the body goes to the grave. But that is not all: when Jesus returns, the spirits of the righteous dead will return with him (1 Thessalonians 4:13-14). The bodies of the dead will be raised and transformed so that they become incorruptible. God will change our old physical bodies so that they will be like Jesus' resurrected body.

The spirits of the righteous dead are with Christ now in heaven and when Jesus returns, he does not return alone. "When God brings Jesus back again, he will bring with him all who had faith in Jesus before they died ... The Lord will return from heaven. Then those

274

who had faith in Christ before they died will be raised to life" (1 Thessalonians 4:14,16 CEV; cf. I Corinthians 15:51-53). This means that the separation of spirit and body that took place at the time of death will be reversed. The spirits of the righteous dead will be reunited with their bodies, and the bodies transformed to live eternally in the glorious presence of God in a renewed and transformed universe.

The Spirits of the Dead

The person who believes in Jesus does not fear death. Hebrews 2:15 says that Jesus comes to destroy the devil and "free those who all their lives were held in slavery by their fear of death". Jesus, by his death and resurrection, defeats death. Jesus has eternal life and gives eternal life to all who believe in him.

All this is good news, but it raises other questions. If the dead are with Christ and are not free to go and come without the direct permission of the Lord, then how do we explain the spirits who appear as the recent dead, and bring messages from the departed? What sort of spirits are those who appear to people in graveyards? Who are these spirits that speak through mediums? If they are not the spirits of the dead, then who are they?

The pastors all thought that people really do see spirits in the graveyard, and that mediums really do hear voices. Some had witnessed these things for themselves. Yet in view of this Bible study, the pastors felt that the spirits experienced were not really the spirits of the dead, but other spirits pretending to so. The following verses were noted in support:

1. Satan is a liar and the father of lies (John 8:44).
2. Satan has a kingdom and is the ruler of demons (Matthew 12:24-26).

3. Satan "blinds the minds of unbelievers so that they cannot see the light of the Gospel of the glory of Christ, who is the image of God" (2 Corinthians 4:4). Satan blinds people by causing them to believe that their parents and grandparents care for them more than God does. Satan wants people to think that God is distant and far away, but the ancestors are close by and they care for the living.

4. Satan can masquerade as an angel of light for he is very deceitful (2 Corinthians 11:14). Paul talks about false apostles and deceitful workmen (2 Corinthians 11:13). Jesus warns against false prophets (Matthew 7:15). If Satan can produce false prophets and apostles, it is also likely that he will produce false ancestors. In other words, spirits that pretend to be spirits of deceased relatives are in fact demons who lead people astray so that they do not worship God.

The pastors agreed that the spirits who appear to people and talk through mediums are not really the spirits of the dead, but deceitful spirits who pretend to be the spirits of the dead and so draw people away from faith in God. This would account for the huge majority of cases. There may, however, be a few exceptions. The key point is that the spirits of the dead are not free to do what they like. Jesus is Lord of the living and dead: all are under his control (Romans 14:9).[78]

Christian Melanesian Response

One of the pastors who took part in the Simbu conference, Thomas Bruno, has talked face to face with the spirits. He described one encounter to me. This took place in the house of a person who was a healer. Bruno was shown into a small room that was kept specifically for talking with the spirits. He describes what happened:

There was no light except for a little kerosene lamp that was turned down low. I sat there in the dark and the silence. Then the glass in the partly open window began to rattle. As I watched, a misty smoke came sliding through the window. It curled up in the air, then slowly turned into the shape of a man, sat down in a chair opposite me, and we talked face to face.

Thomas often went to the graveyard; he was fascinated with death and felt it was a place to obtain more spiritual power. I asked him about the spirits in the graveyard. He said:

Some people think the spirits in the graveyard are the spirits of dead people. But they are really evil spirits who pretend to be the spirits of the dead in order to deceive people. People who would not think of talking to an evil spirit are very happy to talk to a spirit which they think belongs to an uncle or aunt or grandfather. All of these spirits are under the control of Satan and they deceive people by pretending to be ancestral spirits.

Jesus: Lord of the Living and of the Dead

The Bible tells us that the dead are no longer here with us, but are with God our heavenly Father. They are at home with him, he cares for them, and protects them. They do not require gifts of food, and do not sleep in the little house in the graveyard. They have gone to be with the Lord, for he is Lord of both "the living and the dead". This phrase is crucial in understanding the realm of the dead. Jesus dies, rises again and is alive forever more. He holds the "keys of death and the world of the dead" (Revelation 1:18 CEV). The dead are "alive" and under the authority of Jesus Christ. We will now apply this to three stories.

A Widow's Story
My father was a very hard worker and had many pigs, but other people were jealous of him and, according to my mother, they killed him with sorcery. He died when I was very young; my mother was left to raise five young children. My mother continued to live in her husband's

277

village, but she was not happy. She was not treated kindly and some of the people were saying unkind things about her. She wondered what to do. One day she took all of us kids into a coffee garden where we would be out of sight from everyone. We sat down, and mother cried for she did not know what to do. My mother says that while she was sitting there, she heard a noise, looked up and saw a person standing some distance away. She thought it was the spirit of my father; he beckoned her to come. She was frightened and held us children close. The figure was motioning to her and as she watched, she got the impression that he was pointing in the direction of her home village. She looked again and he had disappeared. She believed that it was the spirit of her husband who had appeared to indicate to her that she should return to her home village. The next day, she took all of her children and returned to her parent's village. My uncles and my grandparents took good care of us and everything went very smoothly. It was obviously the right decision.

An Attack by a Spirit

A young coastal man, Koki, woke up in the middle of the night and heard two people talking. One was deep and gruff, and the other was the calm voice of his father saying: "Calm down. Calm down." Koki came out of his room to see his mother sitting on the floor shaking all over. Her eyes had turned until only the whites of her eyes were showing, and she was speaking with a man's voice. When he saw this, he knew it was the spirit of his dead cousin. Often the spirit would take possession of his mother. When the cousin had died a few years before, Koki's mother had kept a shirt and a pair of shorts that belonged to him. From time to time, the spirit would take control of her, she would tremble all over, and the spirit would speak through her. The gruff voice coming from his mother was saying that evil sorcerers were trying to

278

break into the house and were wanting to kill Koki's father. The father was very fearful, but tried to keep calm. He thanked the spirit for the information, and respectfully requested the spirit to come out of his wife, leave her alone and let her return to her senses, but the spirit refused. All this time, Koki was standing, watching and listening to everything that was happening.

The spirit was quiet for a while, but Koki's mother was still shaking and her eyes were still white. Then the spirit said: "If you want me to leave, tell Koki to pray and I will leave." The father looked up at Koki and said: "Son, can you do that?" Koki was shocked. He looked at his worried father and his mother who was still shaking. Koki knelt beside his mother and prayed. He commanded the spirit saying: "In the name of Jesus who died and rose again, I command you evil spirit to leave my mother."

Instantly his mother stopped shaking, and her eyes and speech became normal. They made her a cup of tea and gave her some biscuits to eat. She drank and ate, and everything was normal. They all went back to bed and nothing disturbed them for the rest of the night. Koki says: "I know that there is power in the name of Jesus, and that Jesus has power and authority over all evil spirits."

Confronting Deceiving Spirits

Bill and Lusi are a young couple living near a large PNG town. Lusi's father had died the previous week. One night, a few days after his burial, his spirit was heard outside the house, calling for Lusi. She replied: "Go away, I don't want to see you." She was frightened for she believed it was an evil spirit outside. The spirit said: "Come out here, I have something to give you," but Lusi refused to go outside. This exchange went on for a while, but she would

279

not move. He said he would come back the next night as he had something to give her.

The next night more people gathered at the house, including her husband Bill. They prayed that God would show them what to do. Later in the evening, they could hear the spirit outside. He called for Lusi to come out, but Bill answered. The spirit replied: "No. I don't want Bill. I want Lusi and only Lusi. No one else is to come out." He was loud and insistent and eventually they opened the door and Bill and Lusi stepped outside. Lusi said: "You are not my father, for my father is in heaven. You are an evil deceptive spirit and I do not want to receive anything that you may want to give me. So now, in the name of Jesus I command you to go and never come back here again."

There was a whoosh and a roar and something flew off through the garden and into the night. Next morning they looked outside and the corn and bananas in their garden were all smashed down and pulverised. They were shaken but glad that they had taken their stand against the evil spirits. Lusi knew her real father would never have acted like that.

How are we to understand and interpret what is happening in these last three stories? Such tales need to be addressed thoughtfully and carefully, and not simply dismissed.

The class of Bible college students discussed the story of the widow seeking direction. They thought that most likely it was either an angel, or perhaps God allowed the spirit of her husband to appear to her. Genesis 21:17-19 tells of Hagar who had been turned out of her house and wandered in the desert with a child, until they were at the point of death. An angel comes to them with words of hope and leads them to water. Psalm 146:8-9 says: "The Lord loves good

280

people and looks after strangers. He defends the rights of orphans and widows." Angels are "ministering spirits sent to serve those who will inherit salvation" (Hebrews 1:14). It is therefore possible that God sent an angel to help the woman, but that the woman who knew little or nothing about angels interpreted it as being the spirit of her husband. Some would say it is possible that Jesus, who is Lord of the living and of the dead, allows in his mercy the spirit of her husband to return to help her (Mitton and Parker 1991:80). Scripture does indicate that this is not the normal way in which God works.

In the second story, it appears that an evil spirit is pretending to be the spirit of the cousin. The spirit then disappeared when commanded in the name of Jesus. In the third story, the people involved concluded that this spirit was not the father but a deceitful spirit.

As a general rule, the spirits who come to visit as ghosts are not the spirits of the dead, but deceitful spirits who come to confuse, frighten and so entangle us in bondage and fear. They frighten people with fear of danger and calamity if they are not continually satisfied with food etc. They threaten to bring sickness, destruction and evil upon the living if people do not satisfy their every wish. It is for this reason that God does not want us to talk to, seek advice from or to have anything to do with demons. Christians should not be involved in communicating with the spirits of the dead, for when they do so they come under Satan's control. Isaiah asks: "Why consult the dead on behalf of the living?" Instead of asking the dead, people should "inquire of their God". Those who turn to the spirits of the dead and reject God will "see only distress and darkness and fearful gloom, and they will be thrust into utter darkness" (Isaiah 8:20, 22).

The Spirits of the Dead at Times of Sudden Death

When a person is killed in a sudden or violent manner (such as a car accident or a tribal fight), Melanesian people go to the place of death and entice the spirit of the dead person to return to the village. Mitton and Parker talk about the special needs of people who die

281

"unprepared deaths": people who die suddenly, with "little or no opportunity to prepare their souls for death, and leaving their family and friends" (1991:106).

When a person is killed suddenly, it is appropriate for Christians to go with the immediate family to the place of the accident. The pastor can read appropriate Scripture passages, and have a special prayer committing the spirit of the person to the care of the Lord. The pastor can pray for God's peace upon the family and all who are grieving in this time of loss. In this way, the church is meeting this felt need in a Christian way. If we do nothing, there is a large vacuum which people will continue to fill with traditional non-Christian rituals. "The reason spiritualism has thrived is because the church has had very little to offer the bereaved" (Mitton and Parker 1991:115).

Honouring the Dead

While our parents are alive, we are to honour, respect, assist, care for and demonstrate our love and appreciation to them. Surely this relationship of love, honour, and respect should not end at death, but keep on going. But in what ways should Christians honour their parents after they have died?

Funerals

As people's view of death changes, so the practices and rituals that they follow at the time of burial will also change. Very few people in PNG will be buried without some form of Christian service. Paul wrote: "We do not want you to be ignorant about those who fall asleep, or to grieve like the rest of men, who have no hope" (1 Thessalonians 4:13). Papua New Guineans have found that there is hope and they do not grieve like they once did. The practice of cutting off finger joints at time of death, which was once quite common in the Highlands, is now rare. The amount of mud that mourners apply to their bodies at time of death has also decreased, but it remains a significant sign of mourning for both Christians and non-Christians.

282

A young woman, the mother of three young children, died suddenly from a brain haemorrhage. A Christian, every Sunday she would bring flowers to decorate the church and always had a testimony to share of God's goodness and grace in her life. I walked into the church before the funeral, and found women from the church busily decorating the church with armloads of flowers. The pastor's wife was organising some young people as they decorated the sanctuary with balloons and streamers. I talked with the women and we cried together, for all of us were saddened and surprised at the sudden death. I then commented on the decorations. I said: "This looks more like a party than a funeral." They said: "We are celebrating in the midst of our grief. She is in heaven with the Saviour whom she loved and served. We are celebrating her radiant life and we know where she is. There is a party going on in heaven today and so we celebrate with her." As the funeral service progressed, I noticed the choice of songs that were sung: they all focused on the theme of life. Jesus is alive and Jesus gives us life.

In another town, a young boy died and a funeral service was held in a large church. The parents were both committed Christians and they had a real peace that their boy was now with the Lord. Often women in mourning will dress in black, but I noticed that this family chose to wear white meri blouses with black laplaps. This was their way of symbolising the hope and peace they felt, even in the midst of their grief.

The church in Melanesia is growing and maturing. People continue to look for ways to express both the grief they feel for the loss of a loved one, and the peace they feel knowing that their loved one is with the Lord. They also look for ways to express honour and respect for the loved one who has died.

Prayers for Goodbye at a Funeral
Relationships are very important to people in Papua New Guinea, especially relationships between the living and the dead. Mitton and Parker argue that funerals need to provide people with an opportunity to express their love, forgiveness or apologies to the one who has died. I believe that this would be very meaningful in Melanesia. Mitton and Parker recommend the following prayer:

> Loving Father
> If only I had known that N_____ was going to die so soon. There are some personal words I would have shared with him, and some things we had yet to do together. But I missed the opportunity. Yet Lord, I do rejoice that you are the God of the living and of the dead.
> Therefore in your presence I share with N_____ my unsaid words and my unfulfilled deeds. N_____, through Jesus Christ I speak my words and offer the things I would have done for you.
>
> (In a time of silence share your own thoughts with N____.)
>
> Father, I thank you for this opportunity to share my heart with N_____ through Jesus Christ your Son. I now say farewell and release N_____ to you. Keep him in the knowledge of your love; bring him joy and peace and the assurance of our love for him, through Jesus Christ, the Resurrection and the Life. Amen. (Mitton and Parker 1991:128-129)

Care of the Graveyard
The pastors felt that one practical way of showing respect is by keeping the graveyard clean and free from weeds. Others were concerned about this, for in the past some groups have had a

graveyard cult: people cleaned the graveyard, planted flowers there and said prayers hoping that the ancestors would repay them with money and fertility for their families, pigs and gardens. People were reluctant to spend too much time in the graveyard, for they did not want to be misunderstood. Others, however, felt that this was no reason to neglect the graveyard.

The practice of building little houses over the grave also involves the concept of honour. Many felt that the main reason for building a house was to show a person's status in society. The more important a person was, the more impressive is the house that is built. Others felt that they should find some other way to show honour because a house indicates that someone lives there - but no one does. Jesus says: "There are many rooms in my Father's house ... I am going there to prepare a place for each of you" (John 14:2). Christians honour and respect the dead, but do not need to provide them with houses or food. The spirits of the righteous dead are living with Christ, and Jesus has promised that he will protect and care for them; consequently, there is no need for Christians to build a house over the grave.

Communion of Saints
One important scriptural truth is that "Christ died and returned to life so that he might be the Lord of both the dead and the living" (Romans 14:9). Those who believe in Christ go to be with him. The implications of this have not been spelled out adequately. This concept has been expressed in the term the "communion of saints" which became part of the Apostle's Creed from the fifth century onwards. The traditional interpretation of the phrase refers to the "union of all believers, living or dead, in Christ, stressing their common life in Christ and their sharing of all the blessings of God" (Gouvea 1984:257). This means that all believers, both the living and the dead, are in Christ and enjoy fellowship with him and therefore with each other. This thought has been expressed in some of the hymns of the church.[79]

285

The thought of unity between believers on earth and believers in heaven is expressed in a hymn by Charles Wesley, "Happy the Souls to Jesus Joined".

> The church triumphant in thy love,
> Their mighty joys we know;
> *They sing the Lamb in hymns above,*
> *And we in hymns below.*
>
> Thee in thy glorious realm they praise,
> And bow before thy throne;
> We in the kingdom of thy grace:
> *The kingdoms are but one.*
> (C. Wesley 1966:535. Emphasis added)

This hymn emphasises the unity and oneness between believers on earth and the redeemed in heaven. They sing above and we sing below. Likewise, they praise and bow before the throne and we do the same on earth, for "the kingdoms are but one". This concept is very important. It has not been emphasised in PNG, and not in evangelical churches. I do not know of any songs in Pidgin that express this concept. It takes the traditional belief (and also Christian belief) that the grave is not the end, that life continues after death, and ties it to the Christian belief that those who have died are with the Lord, and thus gives a sense of unity. When they are worshipping the Lord, people can feel that their loved ones are rejoicing in heaven and praising the Lord there.

Jesus is Lord both of the living and the dead. The church of Jesus Christ consists of all believers, whether alive or dead, and Jesus is the centre where the dead and the living can meet. The communion service reminds us of Jesus' death, his resurrection and his coming again at which time all will be united with him. The Anglican Church in Kenya has included reference to the ancestors in the communion service. This prayer is included:

286

Gracious Father we heartily thank you for our faithful ancestors and all who have passed through death to the new life of joy in our heavenly home. We pray that surrounded by so great a cloud of witnesses, we may walk in their footsteps and be fully united with them in your everlasting kingdom. (Bediako 1995:229)

Later in the service, there are these words: "Therefore with angels, archangels, faithful ancestors and all in heaven, we proclaim your great and glorious name" (ibid). Mitton and Parker say: "There is a tendency in the Western church, once the eulogies and the funeral services are over, to forget those who have died. We need to cherish our dead and make acts of remembrance and thank God for them at proper times and seasons" (1991:45). Unfortunately, Western missionaries have exported this problem of ignoring the dead to many other cultures.

Setting People Free from *Sanguma*

In the chapter "The Problem of *Sanguma*", it was concluded that the *sanguma* is an evil spirit who lives within a person and coerces the person into doing things that a normal person would never want to do. This includes such things as eating human waste, killing people and eating the bodies of the dead. We also saw that when the spirits have been confronted and commanded to leave in the name of Jesus, people have been transformed. Jesus defeats Satan through his obedience, humility and self-sacrificing death. It is very important to be totally convinced of this when we come to face evil spirits, for we are not confronting them in our power, but in the name and power of Jesus.

287

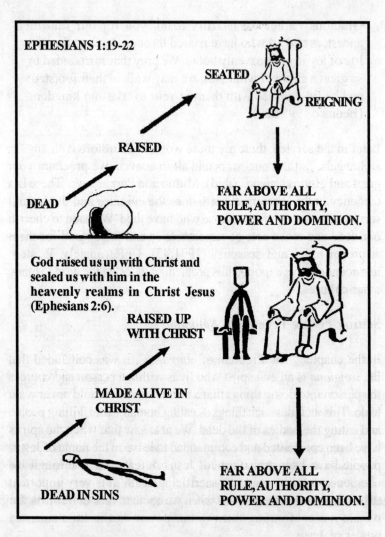

EPHESIANS 1:19-22

SEATED

REIGNING

RAISED

DEAD

FAR ABOVE ALL
RULE, AUTHORITY,
POWER AND DOMINION.

God raised us up with Christ and
sealed us with him in the
heavenly realms in Christ Jesus
(Ephesians 2:6).

RAISED UP
WITH CHRIST

MADE ALIVE IN
CHRIST

DEAD IN SINS

FAR ABOVE ALL
RULE, AUTHORITY,
POWER AND DOMINION.

Figure 18. The Believer's Position in Christ

Jesus is Lord of all, and He is supreme over all spiritual forces. This means that not only is Jesus far above "all rule and authority, power and dominion", but by virtue of our being raised with Christ, we are seated with Him, and therefore we also are over "all rule and authority, power and dominion" (Ephesians 2:1-6).

We are no longer victims at the mercy of capricious vengeful spirits, but we have victory over all the powers of evil through Christ. This is the good news of the gospel.

The upper part of Figure 18 shows what happened when Jesus died and rose again. He was raised up and seated at the right hand of God in heaven. The lower part of the diagram shows the change in us that occurs when we believe in Christ and are united to him. We were dead in our sins but we have been made "alive with Christ", and have also been raised up and seated with him in heavenly places.

If Jesus is above all spiritual powers then it is logical that we are also in a place of authority and therefore need not be afraid of evil spirits. When we are in union with Jesus, we are in a place of authority and they must obey.

As we looked at this diagram, one Bible college student said: "That is helpful. We do not need to be intimidated by Satan or evil spirits, for we are seated with Christ. We do not think of them as evil spirits who are big and powerful looming over us. Instead, Christ has won the victory and he is in the highest place and we are united with him. We share in his victory and so we can speak with authority." Another student compared it to the difference between a policeman and a big semi-trailer truck on the Highlands Highway. The truck is big and powerful, much more powerful than the policeman. But the policeman has authority and can step out on the road and wave down the truck; the truck will stop because it recognises the authority of the policeman. In the same way, we have authority over the spirit world because we belong to Christ and we are entitled to speak in his name.

Steps to Freedom
After studying our position with Christ in the spirit world, we discussed the issue of helping people to become free from *sanguma* spirits. The Bible college students spent time discussing the seven steps to freedom outlined by Neil Anderson (1990a:199-252):

289

1. Renounce previous or current involvement with occult practices and false religions.
2. Reject falsehood and accept the truth. Doctrinal affirmation.
3. Reject bitterness and anger, and forgive others.
4. Reject rebellion against authority figures and instead pray for them.
5. Renounce pride and accept humility.
6. Renounce and confess all sinful habits and choose freedom in Christ.
7. Renounce the sins of our ancestors and any curses that may have been placed upon us.

The first item on this list generated considerable discussion. Anderson suggests that Christians need to make a complete break from all non-Christian religious practices and organisations (1995:280). However, this does not relate to the Melanesian situation. After praying for guidance to know how to handle these cultural issues, the Lord brought my attention to Acts 19:17-20. Here the believers in Ephesus become very aware of the power of evil spirits; past practitioners of sorcery bring out their sorcery paraphernalia, confess their deeds and burn their sorcery materials. I asked the class: If this story were to take place in PNG, what things would the people confess and what items would they destroy? They listed the following:

Practices to be renounced. If a person has been involved in any of the following activities, then these should be confessed. Scripture verses that relate to this are 2 Corinthians 6:14 – 7:1.

- Sought out a diviner for advice.
- Prayed to spirits in graveyard.
- Called on the spirits of the dead for help.
- Gone to a sorcerer for healing from sickness.
- Participated in killing pigs, or making other offerings to the spirits.

- Gone to a sorcerer for magic to help in business, exams, gardening, sickness, love magic or any other reason.
- Prayed to Satan or used things like ouija boards or cards that have been dedicated to Satan.
- Been present when people have tried to call on the spirits of the dead.

Things to be removed or destroyed. The students said some people dedicate plants or parts of plants to the spirits. Some of these (such as *tangkets* or ginger roots) are grown near homes or pig houses to give protection. Others (such as sacred leaves or small pieces of tree bark) are kept in wallets, *bilums* or hidden in houses. They felt that these things needed to be destroyed.

Things belonging to the dead. Bones of dead people, their hair, clothes or *bilums* that are kept in order to get in contact with the spirits of the dead, should all be destroyed.

Things dedicated to the spirits. Feathers, flutes, masks, carvings, pig's teeth, stones and spears that have been dedicated to the spirits of the dead should likewise be destroyed.

Things to be re-dedicated. Sometimes things that were used in evil ways can be dedicated to God and used for his service.

A dramatic example of this from the South Pacific is the killing stone that was used by Ratu Cakobau, the leading chief of Fiji and a notorious cannibal at the time of missionary contact. It had been used for the killing of hundreds of people before they were cooked and eaten. After the conversion of Cakobau, the stone was cleansed and dedicated to God and used as the baptismal font in the Methodist Church. What had been a symbol of death now became a symbol of new life and a witness to the transforming power of God (Tippett 1977:97).

291

One woman mentioned that she used to go to a certain house to conduct a Bible study and prayer meeting. Every time she visited that house, she found it hard to pray, and people were restless and inattentive. She talked with some of her Christian friends who had noticed the same thing. They decided to pray and ask God to show them the cause of the hindrance. As they prayed, God impressed upon the mind of one of them the picture of an old arrow. The next time they went to that house, they asked the old man - the owner - if he had an arrow that was of special significance to him. He replied: "Yes I have a special arrow. It is one that my father made and he used it to kill an enemy. I have kept it all these years to guard this house. It is dedicated to my father and it will keep this house safe from the enemies." They asked him: "Where do you keep it?" He replied: "It is up there in the roof of the house watching over us."

The women realised that this weapon, which had been used to kill a person and had been dedicated to the spirits, was right up there in the roof of the house blocking their prayers. Over the next few months, they made it a special matter of prayer that God would speak to the old man's heart, and that he would be willing to surrender the arrow and trust God for protection. They also talked to him about the need to let go of this arrow and trust in God to be his security from the enemies (Psalm 91:1-2). After a few months, the old man said that he was ready to trust in God, and took down a bundle of arrows from the roof of the house. The old man proclaimed his trust in God alone, and they took the arrows outside and burned them. The change of atmosphere in the house was very noticeable, and from then on, there was much greater freedom in prayer and Bible study.

We discussed this in the class at the Bible college. Then there was time set aside for the students to think, pray and make a personal list of things that they needed to confess, renounce or destroy. This was a very serious and solemn time. We spent about thirty minutes in silent prayer as the students prayed through their list. Then I suggested that they go home and go through this exercise with their spouses and children, and get rid of anything they had in their house that needed to be removed or confessed.

We concluded the two week intensive course with a communion service. Before taking the communion elements, I gave the students opportunity to share what God had shown them, taught or done in their hearts during the two week course.

One student said that as a teenager he had been part of a raskol gang in Port Moresby. They used sorcery to cover themselves with a shield of darkness so that people or police would not be able to see them. They used a variety of sorcery and magic techniques to help them pick locks, protect them from bullets and to give them success over other gangs. He eventually gave up being a gang member and gave his heart to the Lord. Although he had confessed his sins in a general way, he had not specifically confessed the sorcery he had practiced. He said: "This week I took time, and I thought back over my life. I confessed my involvement in sorcery, and got rid of anything I had kept for protection. When I did this, I experienced a dramatic change in my life. I have a wonderful new freedom in my prayer life and in my relationship to Jesus."

Another student said that he became a Christian three years ago, and a year after his conversion, he came to Bible college. The whole time he had been in college he had been plagued with stomach pains, terrible headaches and constant illness. He had been to the Bible college clinic, but they had not been able to find out the cause of

*the illness. He had been to see the missionary doctors
and they had done all sorts of tests, and given him bottles
of medicine, but nothing had really helped. He said: "This
week, however, as I prayed through the list, I realised
that although I had confessed my sins in general, I had
not confessed them one by one. I also thought about what
I had in my house, and I realised that I still had things in
my house which I had stolen from others." He had also
made tape recordings of the old tribal fight stories of who
killed who and the names of those whose deaths still
needed to be avenged. He realised that these all needed
to be removed from his house, for there is no place for
hatred and payback in the lives of Christians. He removed
all these things from his house and disposed of them. Since
then he had felt a huge change. He said: "Before, I would
always get headaches when I tried to read my Bible or to
study. Now all that is changed. All of my stomach pain
and headaches stopped instantly. I have a new joy and
peace in my life that I never had before. My Christian
life feels completely renewed."*

As long as we hold onto wrong things in our lives, we provide access
for Satan to enter our homes and to weaken our Christian lives.
Satan will use these things to keep us in bondage and stop us from
experiencing the freedom that Christ wants to give us. In the story
from Acts 19, we read that after the people had burnt the items
associated with spirits and sorcery, "The Lord's message spread
and became even more powerful" (Acts 19:20).

Breaking the Curse

One student pastor told me the following story, which came from
his pastoral experience:

*One day, back in his home province of Milne Bay, he
preached that Jesus was greater than Satan and that he
could set us free from Satan's power. After the service, a*

man named Tom said to him: "My family is under a curse. My father died, and six months later my mother died. Six months later my eldest brother died. I am worried for soon it could be my turn."

The pastor assured Tom that God was greater than any curse. Tom prayed and asked God to forgive his sin and make him a child of God. The pastor prayed that God would protect Tom with his blood and break the power of the curse. The pastor said: "We need to go to your house and get rid of anything and everything connected with spirits, Satan, magic or sorcery." When they went to his house, Tom said he had been given a human bone which was supposed to keep his family safe. The pastor asked Tom: "Who do you believe is the greater: Jesus who died and rose again and can never ever die, or this human who died and is still dead?" Tom said: "I believe that Jesus is all powerful and I will depend on him for my protection."

They went through every room in Tom's house and took out everything they thought could have associations with evil. They prayed and asked God to cleanse every room from evil. After they left each room, they put some oil on the door and declared that the room was sealed with the blood of Jesus against any evil spirit.

Tom and the pastor then took the stuff outside and burned it. When it burned, there was a terrible smell of rotting flesh and they heard screams coming from the flames like there were dozens of people screaming.

They then decided to walk all around the property and claim the area in the name of Jesus. The other people present were feeling a bit shaken and so everyone held hands and walked around the property. They prayed that

295

God would cleanse it and commanded all evil spirits to leave in the name of Jesus.

Since then, there has been no more sickness. Tom has started a business which is going well. He says there is a totally different atmosphere in the house since it was cleansed.

Release From *Sanguma*

One of the students raised this question in class: "A person in the community admits to having a *sanguma* spirit. How will you go about setting that person free?" The class spent time discussing this question and came up with the following steps:

1. **Assemble a team of committed Christians**. These are people who have faith that Jesus is greater than all the powers of evil. Their main task is to provide support in prayer. They should work closely with the team leader and share any thoughts or ideas with the team leader.

2. **Start from a position of authority**. The leaders should state that Jesus has defeated all the powers of evil and all evil spirits must submit to the name of Jesus. Command all other evil spirits to leave the area and forbid them to create any interruption or disturbance. The *sanguma* spirit must do what we command and is not to cause any wild or disturbing activity.

3. **Claim God's protection**. The leader should ask a team member to claim God's protection on all the people who are present, and also on their families and those that they love.

4. **Overcome lies by proclaiming truth**. Satan keeps people in bondage and fear through his lies and convinces them that there is no hope for them. We can break this bondage through proclaiming the truth of Christ's victory. Jesus has won the

296

victory over Satan through his death and resurrection, therefore, all evil spirits must submit to the name of Jesus. Tell people that evil spirits must submit to the name of Jesus. The truth of God's Word helps build up faith that Jesus is able to help them and set them free.

5. **Elicit a personal history from the person**. The team leader can ask the following questions:

• How did you get this spirit?
• Was it passed down from a relative, or did it come as a result of requesting magical powers?
• Have you been involved in sorcery or magic? What do you need to confess?
• Do you have any special objects or plants that are connected with this power, e.g. tree bark, ginger, ancestral bones etc.?
• How is your own spiritual life? Have you asked Jesus to forgive your sins?
• If the person is not sure of salvation, then lead him or her in steps of repentance and faith in Christ as Saviour.

6. **Break ancestral ties**. If this spirit was received from some relative or passed down through the family, ask the person to renounce this family linkage in the name of Jesus. "In the powerful name of Jesus I renounce this evil spirit that came to me from _____ and I do not want to be in bondage to it any more. I claim the blood of Jesus to break this evil connection with _____." You can tell the person: "By faith in Christ you have become part of the family of God and have turned from Satan to God. You have been washed in the blood of Jesus and this is greater than any linkage caused by some human blood line."

7. **Break any ties to occult rituals**. If *sanguma* entered due to a person's request for magical powers, then the person should renounce all involvement in sorcery and confess all occult involvement. The person should confess and renounce

297

all leaves, sacred words, tree bark, bones or other objects connected with spiritual powers. The person should also confess all bitterness, anger and jealousy that would give space to Satan.

8. In Jesus' name, command the evil spirits to leave. Send them to Satan and forbid them to return.

9. Evaluate what has happened. The team leader should inquire, "Do you feel completely free?" The person will need support with prayer, counselling, Christian fellowship and encouragement. Tell him or her that if the demons try to return, they are to be sent away in the name of Jesus.

A Story of Deliverance

One of the components of the House Model for contextualising theology is Christian experience. The following story was told to me by a Papua New Guinean pastor:

A few years ago (1993), I was asked to speak at a camp meeting near a small town. I was a young pastor and this responsibility was very great so I felt a real need to spend time in prayer and fasting in preparation for the services.

The first night I preached about the broad way and the narrow way. I emphasised that Christ is the only way to God, and that true and genuine repentance is necessary. On the second night, I again stressed Jesus as being the only way of salvation. I gave an altar call; a number of people came forward, and I tried to counsel with each one. One woman said to me: "Please could you come to our house? My husband and I have some problems and we need your help."

298

I went to the house and met her husband. He was a Lutheran pastor and had been a pastor in that town for fifteen years. The woman said: "We have a big problem. We live regular lives during the day, but at night we change and we eat dead people." I was shocked. I was not expecting that sort of problem, certainly not from a pastor.

I asked the husband about this, but he glared at me and replied in a very deep voice: "I will kill you!" The woman said: "We need help. I came to the church and thought that you would lay your hand on my head and cast out the evil spirit, but you have come and talked to us. Can you help us?" I realised then that the deep voice coming from the man was actually the evil spirit within him threatening me.

I was not expecting a confrontation with an evil spirit and had never been in a confrontation with a demon before. I quickly prayed for God's protection and help. I rebuked the evil spirit and commanded it to be silent. I spoke to the man about his need to believe in Jesus and in Jesus' power to set him free from this evil spirit. I told him that Jesus had won the victory over Satan through his death on the cross, and that the blood of Jesus has power to set him free. It was difficult to talk, for the evil spirit kept butting in and interrupting. Again and again I had to rebuke the spirit and command it to be silent, but the evil spirit, speaking through the man, would continually make threats to kill or destroy me. I emphasised that there was victory in Christ and that Jesus could set him free from the evil power within him. I prayed again asking God to protect us from any attack by the evil spirits and to cover us with the blood of Jesus.

I asked him: "Do you want to repent and give your life to Jesus and ask for forgiveness?" The man struggled to get words out of his mouth, for the demon was gagging him and preventing him to talk. With great effort he said: "Yes."

I led him phrase by phrase in a prayer of repentance. I prayed with my eyes open, for the evil spirit continued to make threats against me. Again and again I had to silence the evil spirit. This pastor, who every Sunday led the prayers in church, now struggled with all his might to make a simple prayer of confession and repentance. Every word was a struggle for the man to say. He concluded the simple prayer and then I gave a command to the spirit: "In the name of Jesus, I command you, evil spirit of sanguma to leave this man and never return. He does not belong to you, but has been purchased and washed with the powerful blood of Jesus. I therefore command you to leave." The man struggled and his body became tense and rigid. I watched his eyes and they were glaring at me, and I could sense the hatred and evil pouring out of them. Then he slowly fell over and lay on the floor, shaking. He lay there shaking for about fifteen minutes. Saliva ran from his mouth and there was a terrible smell of sulphur. I said to the others: "Don't be afraid. Keep praying, God is working." God really helped me, for I had never experienced anything like this before in my life.

Then the man started to vomit, but nothing came out, except a terrible smell of sulphur. We kept praying and commanding the spirit to leave. He stopped retching, and lay limp on the floor as if he were dead. After thirty minutes, he started to wake up. He opened his eyes. He saw me and gave me a beautiful smile. He sat up and said: "Praise God, I am free." Now he could speak with

300

a normal voice. We hugged each other and praised the Lord. It was then that he told me his story. This time there were no interruptions from the evil spirits: they had left. He said:

When I was eight or nine, I went through a tribal initiation. Much of what I learned was good. We were told to respect our elders, to be generous and give to those in need. We were told to maintain harmony in the tribe and help others. We were to respect women and not to steal other people's wives. But the climax of the initiation was the special ceremony to receive supernatural power. In the first part of this ceremony, a small incision was made in my wrist and a small piece of ancestral bone was inserted. The incision was closed supernaturally by rubbing a special tooth, which they said was the tooth of a spirit, over the incision. The skin closed together and healed instantly, leaving no mark. This procedure was to give me power in hunting.

When I went hunting, I could shoot an arrow at a pig and the arrow would go with such force that it would go right through the pig and come out the other side. If I was in a fight, I could strike a person a blow with my fist, and if I said a certain magic phrase then he would be unconscious until I told him he could wake up. But if I said a different phrase, then he would not wake up and would die.

In the second part of the initiation, we were taken out into the forest and one of the old sorcerers took a knife and sliced my abdomen open. I didn't feel much pain at all. They placed something inside me, a piece of ancestral bone, and then closed me up.

301

Again they took this tooth, rubbed it over the incision, and the wound came together and sealed up just like someone was closing a zipper. They said this would give me power and that I would be protected from my enemies, for I would have more power than they had. They told me that I would have power to remove spells, curses and sicknesses from others. I was told that if I was cut or injured in time of war, then all I needed to do was to take this tooth and by rubbing it on the wound I could heal myself.

There was a negative side to this power about which they did not tell me. I quickly developed a terrible appetite for meat. I did not use my power to kill people, but when people died, then I had a terrible compulsion to eat them. We did not take a spade and dig them up, but went to the grave and by supernatural power, caused the meat of the person to materialise and then we would take it home to eat. Sometimes I would smoke it over the fire. We would catch possums for the children, but my wife and I would eat human flesh. I had given this same power to my wife and she would join with me in eating human flesh, but her power was never as strong as mine.

When I was initiated, I was told that from time to time I would need to renew my power. To do this, I would need to go to the forest and take my sacred tooth and a knife with me. I was to be very quiet and lie down on the ground and operate on myself. Taking the knife, I would cut my abdomen open and remove my liver and lay it aside on the grass. Then as I lay there, snakes, including big pythons, would come out of the forest and would slither over me and would drink my blood. When they were satisfied, they would go away. Then and only then was I free to move. I would replace my liver and seal up the cut using the sacred tooth. When I did this, my supernatural power would be renewed. This was an act of complete trust and submission to the powers as I made myself available to them as a living sacrifice. I did not see any conflict between doing this and being a pastor.

I continued this double life for many years and felt no problem. However, one time I told my wife: "You stay here. I am going to town to get some frozen meat." She knew what I meant. I was going to the morgue at the town hospital to get some meat from a corpse. The town is five hours by truck, but I went by supernatural spiritual travel. I went into the morgue, and while there, the electricity went off. I became very frightened and the spirits in the morgue began to chase me. I ran all the way back, but I had a body. The other spirits appeared to be the spirits of the dead and they were free of their bodies so they could go faster than I could. My wife, sensing that I was in danger, had opened the door for me. The Coleman lamp was burning, I rushed into the house, slammed the door and collapsed on the floor. The light was too bright and the other spirits did not follow me inside. I decided that I needed to stop this practice, or else I would soon be dead. Since then I have been searching for freedom. Now Jesus has set me free."

The pastor who related this story said: "I told him that it was essential that he get rid of the tooth and never touch it again. I counselled him and helped him to get established in his Christian faith. At the end of the week I left the area. However, I did meet up with the Lutheran

303

pastor five years later and received a big hug. It was good to see the man still enjoying the presence of God in his life."

It amazes me that a pastor who had been leading a church for many years, had preached, baptised and served communion, and yet there seemed to be no conflict with the evil spirit. I wonder how much of the Spirit of God was involved in services, or if the pastor merely read words out of a book. There seemed to be a peaceful coexistence. Yet when the pastor wanted to become completely free, there was much interference and he struggled to even speak a few words. When the demonic is not confronted and dealt with, then evil goes underground and the result is split-level Christianity or syncretism.

Dealing with *Sanguma* in the Community

We brought in a church leader to tell his story to the Bible college class. He had been accused of *sanguma*.

> *He had been strung up from a branch of a tree, with his hands tied over his head, and suspended over a fire for a number of hours as his own clan brothers tried to force him to confess to being a* sanguma. *He maintained his innocence and eventually they released him, but he still has burn marks on his leg. He left his own birth place and went to live in his wife's village.*[80]

The students in the class were very touched by his story. Almost every person in the class had seen people being tortured, or knew of someone who had been tortured in order to force him to confess to being a *sanguma* person. They discussed these problems and came up with the following suggestions of how such situations could be approached:

1. Education must take place in the church and community. These are some of the points they felt needed to be emphasised:

- *Sanguma* is the activity of Satan.
- *Sanguma* is a spiritual problem and must have a spiritual solution.
- People cannot remove spiritual forces by physical beatings.
- Jesus can drive out demons and set people free.
- Satan and all evil spirits will eventually be destroyed.
- Christ can protect us from the power of *sanguma* (Psalm 91).
- Christians have authority over evil spirits.

2. The church must be prepared to deal with *sanguma*. For the church to deal with this problem in the community, some important factors are necessary:
- Pastors and Christians must be respected. They must live what they say they believe.
- Pastors and Christians should be spiritually prepared to deal with *sanguma* problems.
- Christians must be involved with the mourning and helping the family of the deceased. If they are not involved when people are mourning, the pastor and church people have not earned the right to be listened to.
- Much of the torture is done by young people who are bored, frustrated and who have little or no status. Torture gives excitement and a sense of power (Silas 1993:63). To counteract this, the churches must have a ministry to youth.

3. Prayer makes a difference in a community. Prayer walks may be made through a community proclaiming the Lordship of Jesus Christ over the village and insisting that Satan's power be driven out. Christians should pray at the time of death and ask God's peace to surround the mourners.

If, at a person's death, a sorcerer is brought in to determine the culprit, then Christians could pray that his divination will fail. One pastor said that he had done this. The diviner tried for three days to obtain answers from the spirits but received no reply. He announced that his power would not work in that village and left the area. The pastor and a group of committed Christians were also praying for

305

God's peace to rest on the people. People forgot about the witchcraft accusations and the village life soon returned to normal.

4. Leaders in the community must unite to defeat *sanguma*. The pastor must have good relationships with the other church leaders and leaders of other organisations in the community. They must discuss what they, as leaders, should do to break down the incidence of *sanguma* in the community. One way of working together is to introduce the concepts of community based health care, where the community works with the health training team and together they decide how to go about meeting the needs of the community. This gives people confidence in what they themselves as village people can do to improve their life style. In many communities, it has brought transformation to the village.

The question was raised: "If a person is accused of being a *sanguma* and torture is about to take place or has already started, what should the church people do?" Here are the answers that were put forward by the Bible college students:

• The pastors and Christians should surround the area and pray.
• The pastors and church leaders should speak to the headmen of the village. "If this woman has *sanguma* then this is a spiritual problem and we will deal with it, for physical force will never solve a spiritual problem." Hopefully the leaders will be glad to get the person off their hands and will turn him or her over to the church leaders. They should then deal with the situation prayerfully, using the guidelines set out earlier in this chapter.

Dealing with a Confessed *Sanguma*

The following story shows a person's experience of demonisation and deliverance from *sanguma* through the power of Christ:

A young boy, belonging to a Christian family, died very suddenly in Kundiawa. His body was taken back home to the village for burial. Immediately there were

306

suggestions that the death had been caused by sanguma. *The boy's father, who was a strong Christian, said: "My son was a keen Christian and I know that he has gone to be with the Lord. I do not want to hear any talk about* sanguma *and finding witches." However, the boy's uncles were very upset about the boy's death and started trying to find out who had caused the death. Various people were accused and some were beaten, but all denied it. Then one of the leaders of the village was attacked. The leader was told: "You are the* sanguma. *You were down in the town and you were at the house shortly before the boy died. You must be responsible." Surrounded by an angry mob, the leader reluctantly admitted that he was responsible. A big fight would have erupted, but a policeman who was there and who was also a good friend of the boy's father, came to the man's rescue. He used his authority to calm the crowd and said: "I will take him down to the town." He took him in his police car to the town, but instead of taking him to the police station, he took him to the church. Three pastors were at the church at the time, and the policeman delivered the* sanguma *man to the pastors and told them to sort things out. The man told his story to the pastors.*

"I am a village leader and have three wives. I recently discovered that my third wife has sanguma *and she has passed the* sanguma *spirit on to me. Recently I became a Christian in the Foursquare Church, but the evil spirit has not left me. When I go to church, the spirit will leave me as soon as I get near to the church. Consequently, while I am in church, I feel free and I praise and worship the Lord, but when I leave the church, the spirit is waiting for me. Sometimes I am able to stay free for a few days, but often my wife will do something to*

307

make me angry and then the spirit comes back into my life.

"The spirit pushes me to attack people. Five weeks ago, I was in town and the spirit pushed me to attack Junior (the boy who had died), but he was surrounded by a strong shield and I could not touch him. This last week, I was there and visited their house and again the sanguma *said to attack him. I refused: 'He is like my grandson and I cannot harm him.' The* sanguma *insisted that I attack him, but I kept on refusing. The* sanguma *spirit became very angry and insisted that I must. The spirit insisted that if I did not kill the boy, then he would kill me instead. This struggle continued inside me and the spirit became very angry. Eventually I gave in, and the spirit attacked. All I did was to turn and look at the boy, and the boy fell down and quickly died. They took him to the hospital and the autopsy showed a perforated bowel, but there was no history of the boy being sick before his sudden death, nor any explanation about what could have caused the sudden perforation of the bowel."*

The man confessed this story and said that he desperately wanted to be free from these evil spirits. The pastors prayed for him and commanded the *sanguma* spirit to leave. The man testified that God had indeed set him free. He did not want to return to his village for he would not be welcome, but went to another area to stay with his married daughter.

Authority

At the conclusion of the classes, a number of students shared what they had learned. They felt bolder, for they realised that because Jesus had won the victory over Satan, they had also been given authority to deal with the spirit world. The following story was told by Gabriel Kaula, a person who has learned through personal experience that Christians need to use their God-given authority to deal with the demonic:

Gabriel was appointed as District Superintendent Supervising over twenty Nazarene Churches in the Jimi Valley in the Western Highlands Province. He moved his family into the area, and into the pastor's house that was allocated to them. He had not been there long, when one evening his house started shaking as if it was in an earthquake. He ran outside and was surprised to find that nothing else was shaking. He asked other people: "Did you feel the earthquake?" But no one else had felt anything. This happened more than once.

Other strange things happened. There would be sounds of people knocking at the door, but when he opened the door, no one was there. This happened at all times of the day or night. His little boy became very sick with a very high fever, and they were very concerned. They drove three hours to the hospital, but the doctors could find no cause of the fever. He quickly improved, but when they returned to the Jimi, he became sick again. This happened numerous times.

One time his wife was in the house with the children, and there was a strange noise. A whirling flame came in through the window and appeared in the room. His wife was frightened, held the children close to her and called on Jesus' help until the fire disappeared. Every pane of glass in the window was broken, but the fine screen wire on the outside of the window showed no marks at all. These happenings were very bizarre and Gabriel felt that there was something demonic behind them.

Gabriel called the pastors together and discussed it with them. Some said that he needed to leave the Jimi and go to another place to live. One pastor suggested that since there used to be a graveyard in that area, he must have done something to upset the spirits, and they must be causing the problems. Gabriel was not too impressed with their spiritual insights. They prayed together and walked around the house claiming the protection of the blood of Christ, but nothing much changed and strange things continued to happen.

One night, a friend who was staying with them went outside and noticed a person hiding in the shadows near the house. Gabriel made some inquiries in the village and found that this person was suspected in the village as being a sanguma person. Gabriel went to his house the next morning and said to him: "If you want some money or food, come down in the daylight and ask me and I will help you. But you are not to come and stand outside my house at night!" The man was rather surprised at Kaula's boldness and seemed very subdued. But weird things continued to happen in the house.

Gabriel came to the conclusion that Satan was trying to scare him off so that he would leave the community. Gabriel wrote out the verse: "Greater is he that is in you than he that is in the world" (1 John 4:4). He pinned it onto the shirts of his children and put it in his own pocket and they all memorised it. The family was united in the belief that God had called them to the Jimi Valley, and they would not surrender to Satan's scare tactics.

After several months, Gabriel decided he had suffered enough of this harassment. He sent his wife and children to bed and said: "I mean business and I am going to have this out with the devil tonight and I am not going to bed until it is settled. If Satan is mad at me or upset at me then he has to come and talk to me and we will have it out face to face." At 9 pm., Gabriel opened the back door of

310

the house and propped open the screen door. He stood on the back porch, and called out: "Okay Satan, I have had enough of you harassing my family. If you are mad about something, or you have anything you want to discuss with me, then come and say it. I have my Bible. I am ready and waiting for you. The door is open. Come in and we will talk about it face to face."

He went inside, sat down at the table with his Bible open so that he was facing the open door and waited and waited. Ten o'clock and then eleven o'clock came and went and nothing happened. At 12 o'clock, he went out on the porch and stood there looking out into the darkness. He listened for any sound that might indicate that Satan or demons were near. He heard nothing so he renewed his challenge: "If you have anything to discuss with me, then come and we will talk. I am the head of the house, and you deal with me. You leave my wife and children alone. I am here waiting to talk." Nothing happened. One o'clock came and went and so did two o'clock. At two o'clock, he went out on the back porch and looked out into the darkness. He listened, but again he heard nothing. He said: "You have had your chance, but you did not come. On the authority of the Word of God, I command you Satan, and all of your demons to get out of here and in the powerful name of Jesus I command you to go and never to come back again."

He said that was the end of the trouble. No more knocking or mysterious sicknesses or shaking of the house. Satan was defeated. Gabriel told this story to a meeting of 250 pastors. He said to them: "We are on the victory side. Jesus defeated Satan at Calvary. Satan is a liar and like a roaring lion, will do everything he can to scare us, defeat us, and run us out of the village. But, my brothers, do not give in. Do not run away. Stand firm and stand strong.

311

*You have authority that was given you by Jesus Christ.
The Holy Spirit lives within. He is greater than all the
forces of hell. 'Greater is he that is in you than he that is
in the world.' Use the power of the Holy Spirit and the
authority of Jesus Christ to defeat the enemy and give
the glory to Jesus. He has won the victory and we must
live and walk and work in the knowledge of that victory."
The audience broke into spontaneous applause with
shouts of "Amen" and "Hallelujah".*

This story and others in this chapter demonstrate the importance of
Christian experience in developing a theology that is relevant to
people's lives.

CHAPTER ELEVEN

LIFE AND DEATH IN THE VILLAGE

Changing the Agenda

The little MAF plane took off from Mt Hagen airport and turned north, climbing high to cross over the Jimi-Wahgi divide on the way to Dusin in the Kobon area. I looked out the window and marvelled at the changes that had taken place in the Highlands since the first Europeans had come into the Mt Hagen area less than seventy years before. Now Mt Hagen is the third largest town in PNG. Such rapid change in such a short time.

I also thought about Dusin, where I was going. I had first visited the area in 1969. There were no missionaries living in the area. In fact, many of these people had never seen a European before. They were still using stone axes and bamboo knives. We traded with salt in order to buy vegetables. Nazarene missionaries were assigned to the area. They began churches and schools, and a health clinic was established. An airstrip had been dug by hand into the side of a mountain ridge. Kobon people had gone to Bible school and trained as pastors. Since then, many positive changes had taken place. For the past five years, I had been visiting the area to conduct pastors' conferences and give oversight to the work of the church.

I was going to meet with the missionary and the church leaders of the almost thirty Nazarene Churches in that area. We would be reviewing the growth and development of the church, discussing the annual budget and whatever other items the board members might want to bring up.

The little airstrip looked so small perched there on the mountain ridge. The pilot carefully lined up for his approach, and avoiding the numerous clouds, he skilfully manoeuvred the plane, bringing it down neatly at the bottom end of the airstrip. The plane bounced slightly as it taxied up the grass strip to the turning bay. Disembarking, I shook hands with James and Philip, two of the church leaders. They remembered when the first planes flew over their valley and they had hidden in terror from the flying monsters. Now they lived near the Dusin airstrip and called up on the mission radio to book chartered aircraft to fly out bags of coffee, and bring in goods for their trade stores. Truly they had seen 10,000 years in one life time (Kiki 1968).

A few hours later, three leading pastors, three laymen, a missionary and I sat around a table and convened the meeting. As normal, I asked for special prayer needs on the district. One pastor told about a problem in his village. The wife of the councillor had died the previous week, and the people thought that someone had performed witchcraft. An old village woman was suspected as being responsible. They beat her up and she confessed to having killed fourteen people in the past four years. She also gave the names of two other women who were involved. They had all been beaten, and locked up in a house. The village people are very angry, and are discussing what to do. The village headman had a shotgun and some were saying: "Shoot them." Others said: "Lock them in a house, and burn them to death." Others threaten to cut them into pieces with their axes. The feeling in the village was: "These are evil wicked women and they do not deserve to live. The sooner we kill them the better."

This is PNG. It has become Christian rapidly, and many of the village people would consider themselves Christian. This village was divided fairly evenly between Nazarenes and Anglicans, as well as a number who had not made any move toward Christianity. But the fear of witchcraft is very strong among all of them. And the desire for payback and revenge is also very strong. These are real issues that the church must address. Theology in Melanesia must grapple with situations like this. These are the prayer requests that Christians bring to their heavenly Father. What do we do? The wife of the headman of the village has died, and another woman has confessed that she is guilty of causing the death through witchcraft. The village wants justice to be done. The pastor says: "Help! What do I do?"

Theology must deal with the issues of life. There are issues in Melanesia that Western theologians have hardly heard of, let alone grappled with. Many missionaries in PNG have not known how to handle these issues. They have tried to ignore them, hoping that in time they would disappear. But these are the issues the church in Melanesia must address. It must do so quickly for as this story shows, the time is short for some people, and answers are needed now.

As District Superintendent, I was chairman of the meeting, and I looked at the items on the agenda: finance report, pastoral appointments, youth camp, annual budget, among other items. Now I wrote on my agenda "Three witches." I felt we needed to do more than just pray about it and then carry on with business as usual. We needed to deal with this issue.

I asked the missionary: "How long will it take to get to the village?" He said: "It is a good three hour hike to get there, and then it will take three hours to get back home. It will be a lot of climbing. We start at 2000 metres, descend to about 1300 metres, hike up the valley for an hour or more, and then climb back up to almost 2,000 metres. On the return trip, we will reverse the process." I was not planning on six hours hiking up and down rugged

315

mountains when I came in for the meeting, but I had
learned that, as a missionary, one has to be flexible and
do whatever is needed.

I said: "We need to go and visit these women. We will
deal with as many of these items as possible today. The
rest we will leave. If the church does not meet the needs
of hurting people, it has no right to exist. The budget can
wait. People must take precedence." The others were in
full agreement. We prayed and asked God for wisdom
and guidance, and for his peace on the people in the
village. We thought of the story of the woman taken in
adultery and the people wanting to stone her, and Jesus'
response that the person without sin should be the first to
throw a stone (John 8:7).

One of the emphases of contextual theology is that often the local
issues need to set the agenda for theology. The local situation raises
the issues. It is not enough for the church to teach the answers to
questions which people from another culture and another era have
asked in the past. The Bible colleges and seminaries must listen to
the churches and village pastors. They must hear the cries of the
people, and respond to them. If we do not deal with local problems
and cultural issues, then God appears as foreign. He is the "white
man's God". The people are asking: "Is God greater than
witchcraft?", "Can he save us and protect us?" The pastor doesn't
know what to do, and is asking: "Is there a Christian way to deal
with this problem?"

We left early in the morning and after three hours of hard
walking, we arrived at the village. I was not sure what to
expect in this encounter with a witch who had confessed
to killing fourteen people with her occult powers. I
followed the pastor, and stooped down to enter a little
hut. There, crouching in the cold ashes of an almost
extinguished fire, was the most pathetic, shrivelled up

woman I had ever seen. She squatted there in the dust and ashes, naked except for a tiny scrap of a loin cloth. Her face was swollen and her lips were puffy and cracked. She tried to speak, but no words would come out. The pastor explained that she had been beaten up on Thursday and Friday, and had not been given anything to eat or drink since then. It was now Tuesday. The missionary pulled out his water bottle, held it to her lips so she could drink some water. He touched her and quickly saw that she had a terrible fever. She held up her arms. We saw that her hands and forearms were terribly swollen. The missionary felt them gently and it was obvious that the bones in her hands and both arms had been smashed in the beating which she had received. It appeared she had some broken ribs and most likely had internal injuries as well. The missionary looked through his medical bag which he carries when hiking from church to church, and pulled out some pain killers. He gave her some to help relieve the pain. As he attended to her, I thought this must have been the first expression of compassion that she had experienced in a long time. But where are the Christians in this village?

Were they among her accusers and her attackers? Why did they not do something? Now I realised that they were as fearful of the sanguma as those who had made no move toward Christianity. I saw how inadequate our teaching and instruction had been. Yes, we had taught about baptism and communion, singing and giving offerings. The church had grown and changes had come. There were clear testimonies of people receiving new life in Christ. But there were some areas of village life that our Christianity had failed to reach. The fear of spirits, witchcraft, and sorcery were still very strong. Revenge and payback were extremely potent forces. Witches were seen as non-human, totally evil, and deserving of nothing other than death.

Jesus came to save the lost. If ever there was a poor lost soul, it was this shrivelled, beaten up woman. Our hearts ached for her, and also for the families who were grieving the loss of loved ones whom she had allegedly killed through witchcraft.

Two younger women were also there. They had been identified as her accomplices and they had also confessed to having sanguma. They, too, had been roughed up, but not to the same extent as the older woman. Using the pastor as a tok ples interpreter, we got the details of the story from the women. Apparently, the older woman and her accomplices would sneak up on a person working in a garden and stare until the person became faint and eventually unconscious. Then they would operate, remove organs, seal up the incision using their occult powers and slip away to feast on the organs they had obtained. The person would eventually regain consciousness and return home unaware of what had been done to him or her. After a few days, the victim would become seriously ill and quickly die.

Some weeks before, there had been a dispute in the village and this woman felt that she had been wronged. She had little power physically or socially, but she had taken revenge with witchcraft. Now the wife of the village headman was dead. She had confessed to a total of fourteen murders, some in her village and some in other villages up and down the valley.

We talked to the woman. She admitted having two sanguma spirits that she described as possums. We talked with her, prayed for her, and asked if there was any change. To my

318

dismay, she replied that the sanguma *possums were fast asleep. She was in great pain and struggled to talk. I wondered how much she had been able to understand in the midst of so much pain and suffering, so we gave her some more water to drink and turned our attention to the other two women. Their stories went along with what we had heard. These women had rarely attended church. They said that they wanted to be free of these evil spirits which were within them. I asked the pastor to explain to them that all people have sinned against God and all people are deserving of death. We explained that Jesus, who never sinned, has taken the punishment of our sin so that we could be forgiven. We explained that Jesus has died, risen from the dead and is greater than all evil spirits. Jesus has power to command the* sanguma *spirits to leave. The women said they wanted to be free. The pastor led the women in a sentence by sentence prayer of confession and repentance. They asked for forgiveness and expressed their desire to be set free from all evil powers. We laid hands first on one and then on the other. We prayed fervently for God to forgive their sins, cleanse their hearts and transform their lives. We spoke directly to the* sanguma *and commanded the spirits to leave and never to return. After prayer, we asked each one if anything had changed while we were praying. Both said the spirits had left.*

We now turned our attention back to the old woman. I asked: "Are the sanguma *still sleeping or have they woken up?" She replied through cracked and swollen lips that while we were praying for the other two women, the* sanguma *not only woke up, but had left. "They are not with me any more. They are gone." While we were talking with her, pus started to drain from a cut in one of her swollen hands. Pus poured out and formed a puddle in the ashes. It was obvious that she was riddled with an infection and had little time to live. We told her that*

319

although she had committed many evil deeds, there was forgiveness and salvation through faith in Christ. Death was not the end, for Jesus had prepared a place for her, a place of peace where there was no evil. We prayed that the blood of Jesus Christ would cleanse her heart from all the powers of darkness and wickedness. We prayed that her sins, though many, would be forgiven, and she would experience God's peace and forgiveness. We prayed that when she died, God in his mercy would accept her as one of his children and take her to heaven.

We counselled with the pastor. "These women are a part of your congregation. They are your responsibility. Feed them. Give them water. Care for them. Pray with them, talk to them. Encourage them to grow in their Christian life. You do not need to be afraid of sanguma. *The Holy Spirit who is in you is far greater than all the powers of* sanguma. *" As we stood up to leave the hut, the little old woman looked up and smiled at us. There was a peace on her face that was not there when we entered. The power and love of God had triumphed in her heart and defeated the forces of darkness.*

We talked with some of the village men. We said: "Sanguma is a spiritual problem. You cannot chase out an evil spirit by beating a person up. God is greater than sanguma *and he can command the spirits to go. He can set people free and change them so that they will never be involved in* sanguma *again. Burning these people to death will not solve the problems of this community. There is a better way. These women need forgiveness, but it seems that most people in this village have their hearts full of bitterness and anger. All of you need to repent of the anger and violence, and ask God to transform this village."*

*It was a long hike back to the mission station. I shared
my thoughts with the others. "This is what mission is about.
We must meet with people where they are, and deal with
the issues that are important in their lives. Their needs
have to take precedence over our agendas. God must be
seen as the one who is greater than all the powers of
darkness and able to meet the deep needs of their lives."*

*Later I heard that the old woman had died the next day.
The pastor gave her a Christian burial. There were no
further beatings, and as far as I know, the other two
women continue to live in the village.*

I wonder how many other people have been beaten up and sentenced
to death in similar manner. How many times have Christians joined
in the accusations and the torturing? How many times have
Christians stood by silent, helpless and fearful? Did anyone come
alongside to show love or compassion? Did any pastor stand up and
say: "Jesus Christ is greater than all the powers of *sanguma* and he
can set people free?" So many times violence, hatred and fear have
dominated villages; evil has triumphed again and again. There must
be a better way.

The Drama of Redemption

This book is a modest attempt to correct this situation. We have
needed a theology which takes the spirit world seriously and shows
that Jesus has triumphed over sin, death, the devil, and all the powers
of evil. Only as the church has a clear understanding of the death
and resurrection of Jesus and his authority over all spiritual powers,
can the church respond effectively to the issues of death, the spirits
of the dead and witchcraft.

Death and the Spirits of the Dead

The burial practices of the Hebrews, such as burial alongside other
clan members, loud wailing, fasting and lamenting, are very similar

321

to those practiced by Melanesians today. The big difference is that the Hebrews were forbidden to consult mediums or diviners in order to communicate with the dead, whereas this is commonly practiced in Melanesia.

The Old Testament portrays *sheol* (the place of the dead) as being a place of silence, darkness, inactivity and a place of no return. The New Testament shows that following Jesus death and resurrection death has been transformed. Jesus is Lord of both the living and the dead. Therefore Christians no longer have a great fear of death, for to be absent from the body is to be present with the Lord (2 Corinthians 5:8). The spirits of the dead are not free to wander around the village, nor do they sleep in the graveyard. It was the consensus of the participants in the pastors' conferences that the spirits which do appear in the village, or who speak through mediums are not the spirits of the dead, but rather deceptive spirits who pretend to be the spirits of the dead, and so keep people from faith and trust in Jesus Christ. On the other hand there is nothing in Scripture which says definitely that God cannot or will not allow the spirit of a dead person to appear to the living. The Bible clearly shows that this is rare.

When a person is killed suddenly, the traditional practice is to go to the place of death to capture the spirit and bring it back to the village. A Christian ritual could be substituted for this: Christians could gather together at the place of the death, and after appropriate Scripture readings, commit the spirit of the dead person to the Lord in prayer.

It is the belief of the church that all believers, both the living and the dead, are in Christ. Therefore, those Christians who have died and those who are still alive enjoy fellowship with Christ. In times of worship both the living and those who have died believing in Christ, join together in exalting and worshipping Jesus as Saviour. This is referred to as the communion of the saints. This Christian belief has not been adequately addressed in Melanesia and the church is poorer as a result.

322

Funeral services are important events that provide a Christian response to death. They provide comfort to the grieving, and formally commit the body of the deceased to the grave, and the spirit of the dead person to the grace and care of God.

A Christian Response to *Sanguma*

Jesus is Lord of all, and he is supreme over all spiritual forces. Consequently we are no longer at the mercy of capricious, vengeful spirits, but we have victory over all the powers of evil through Christ. Christians need not be intimidated for they have the armour of God, and the assurance that the Holy Spirit is greater than *sanguma* (1 John 4:4). People who have *sanguma* spirits need to be set free. Church leaders should be prepared to take the lead in this deliverance ministry. A number of practical steps were outlined by the pastors.

Many people are accused of being *sanguma* people and are tortured until they confess. Often they are innocent, but their lives are ruined through this violent and torturous process. The church must respond to this issue through education, prayer, united action by church and community leaders and community based health care projects.

Evaluation of the Contextual Theology Model

I began by aiming to develop a theology that was contextualised for Melanesian culture and which dealt with death and the spirits of the dead. The model for contextualisation has seven main components. Each is necessary in developing a dynamic contextual theology. The validity of the model was tested by using it with three groups of indigenous pastors.

Scripture becomes the foundation and the base on which everything stands. The participants looked at a wide variety of scriptural passages as they sought to understand the Old Testament practices and beliefs concerning death. They also looked at the biblical story of Jesus' death and resurrection to see how this has impacted the

323

Christian understanding of death. (See the chapters "The Drama of Redemption" and "The Christian Response to the Spirits of the Dead and to Sanguma".) The participants discussed traditional beliefs and practices related to death and dying. They also looked at traditional myths, and the hopes and questions the myths raised. The myths also provided points of contact between the traditional beliefs and the gospel.

The importance of culture in developing theology has often been ignored. A people's world-view is the filter through which they read the Scriptures. They also bring to the Scriptures the hopes, fears and questions of their particular culture and social situation. A contextual theology must answer the questions that are raised within the cultural context. We looked at the beliefs concerning death, the spirits of the dead, the causes of death, and also witchcraft, for death is often blamed on witchcraft.

The church is universal and has a long tradition of two thousand years. This is important to remember when doing contextual theology. If we neglect the rich resources of the history of the church, we impoverish ourselves. A missionary theologian or biblical scholar can make an important contribution if he or she can bring a historical perspective to the topic being considered. In looking at dying and the world of the dead, we draw on the insights of the church fathers and their understanding of Jesus' descent to the world of the dead. This is a doctrine that was very significant in the church for hundreds of years, but in the past 150 years has been increasingly neglected in the Western church.

Since the church is universal, we can receive help from Christians in other cultures who have faced similar problems in other times and places. Theology needs to be seen as the activity of the church as a whole, rather than the private domain of scholars. People must own their theology. Because of this, dialogue is an important component in theologising. This dialogue takes place between missionary and national, and between laity and clergy. The theologian brings his or her knowledge of the Scriptures and church tradition, and the lay person and village pastor bring the questions and social problems of the local people. Theologising takes place as these people interact and converse together.

In the pastors' conferences, there was much discussion and group interaction as village pastors discussed these issues together. Hopefully, these discussions encouraged them to go back home and continue discussions in Bible studies in their village churches.

Theology must relate to people's experience with God. In this book, I have given examples of people who have found deliverance and freedom from evil spirits through the power of Jesus Christ. Theology must deal with issues that are important to people, and it must also treat their stories and life experiences with respect. Too often, Western missionaries have dismissed Melanesians' stories relating to the spirit world, as being mere superstition and, therefore, of no value. Consequently, people often presumed that God was not capable of dealing with these cultural issues, and so continue to live in the fear of sorcery and demonic spirits. When people understand the victory that Jesus won on the cross, and his authority over the spirit world, then they are able to experience God's power in their own lives.

In the House Model, the centre post of the house is the cross of Jesus, symbolising that Jesus' life, death, and resurrection is the centre of our theology. In the conferences I conducted as part of this research, the pastors sought to develop a theology of death and dying. The incarnation of Jesus, his death, his descent to the place of the dead, and his subsequent resurrection and ascension, are all essential elements in understanding death and the after life. Jesus died and rose again from the grave and he is now Lord of both the living and the dead. Jesus was totally obedient to his heavenly Father even though it led to death, and is now risen from the dead and exalted far above all spiritual powers.

The Holy Spirit is the spirit of truth (John 14:17) who will guide people into all truth (John 16:13). Of all the factors involved in developing a contextual theology, this is no doubt one of the most important and yet the hardest to measure. Prayer for God's wisdom and guidance was a constant part of conferences and classes at the Bible college. When we came to the study of witchcraft, I sent a letter to a large number of people and asked them to support us in prayer as we studied this very controversial and uncharted topic. I was conscious of God's leadership, direction and special insights, both for myself personally, and for the members of the class.

Areas for Application

A theology is of little use unless it is applied to everyday life. We saw in the chapter on "The Melanesian Spirit World" the importance of rituals in Melanesia. Rituals are bridges linking the sources of power to the events of daily life. Traditionally, people have looked to the spirits of the ancestors to provide blessing, protection and fertility. Although Christianity has proclaimed God as being the one who will provide these assets, the church has provided little in the way of rituals to visually link God to the events of daily life.

This book has stresses that Melanesians are story tellers, and the Bible is God's story book. Consequently, it argues that narrative theology which emphasises the story of God's interaction and intervention in human history is the most appropriate way to teach the great truths of the Bible in Melanesia, and many other countries as well. Most Bible colleges, however, follow a Western model and teach systematic theology, emphasising individual doctrines, rather than presenting the Bible as one complete interdependent revelation of God (McIlwain 1991:5). As a result, it is possible for a person to complete Bible college and still not understand the overall story of redemption. How much better if Bible college students could learn the overall story of the Bible at the beginning of their training and let the Drama of Redemption provide the framework from which they could then study individual doctrines.

Areas for Further Study

I have offered a model which I believe will give people a workable example of developing a contextual theology. I have used this to deal with one area of theology, namely death and the spirits of the dead. There are many other areas which need to be dealt with in a similar way, such as payback, compensation and tribal fighting.

Another area that the church needs to address at the village level is the structure of the Christian family. The central "men's house" is an important part of Melanesian village life. Missionaries have often presented the nuclear family as being the Christian model. But is this a biblical model or merely a Western preference? The Bible says: "a man will leave his father and mother and be united to his wife", but how is this to be lived out in a patrilineal society where men and women have traditionally lived apart (Genesis 2:24)? Although polygamy has been forbidden by churches, it still exists. The Melanesian Institute conducted a major study on marriage in Melanesia dealing with the implications of being a Christian family in a Melanesian culture (Mantovani 1987; 1992; Conway and Mantovani 1990; Ingebritson 1990). However, the outcomes of this academic study need to be implemented at the grass roots level.

The importance of the clan, the *wantok* system of giving preferential treatment to clan members, and the implications of this for living in a cash economy are also areas that need much thought and research.

In the past, initiation ceremonies provided a rite of passage for youths as they passed from childhood to manhood. Today there is no such rite of passage and young people are not sure of their place in life. Many of the acts of violence, rape and robbery may be attempts by young men to prove their manhood by a display of bravado, often with tragic consequences. This is another area that the church must address as it seeks to bring all areas of life under the Lordship of Jesus Christ.

327

These are not easy questions, but often they are simply left hanging by the church. There is a reticence to pursue these issues further.

> The churches, whether in Costa Rica or Taiwan or Uganda, not only fear but often refuse to think through the faith again for themselves. And when it occurs to a church that it should be doing this, no one knows how to go about doing it. Year after year goes by. The Bible is not brought to bear upon local problems, the meaning of conversion for all of life is not explored, the means for spiritual growth are not utilised ...
> An honest fear of heresy surrounds any rethinking of this kind, not because of mistrust of the Word, but because of the long arm of mission history. (Gilliland 1989:13)

Gilliland highlights two problems: a lack of knowledge about how to contextualise and a fear of heresy. I believe the model of contextualising I have outlined can give Melanesians more confidence in dealing with social and theological issues. Melanesians also need to be encouraged to speak out and deal with these problems. Often national Christians, who are used to overseas leadership dominating the church, are afraid to tackle these issues. Often missionaries fear that the church is not ready to deal with these issues, and are fearful that perhaps the national church may come up with answers which are not totally orthodox. Such attitudes, however, indicate a lack of trust in the Holy Spirit to guide all believers into a knowledge of the truth. Western missionaries need to encourage true theologising to take place. They cannot give the answers to these questions. They can, however, be catalysts to help Melanesians identify the issues, study the Scriptures, and wrestle long and hard with applying the gospel to these and other areas of Melanesian life.

Summary

It is important that we contextualise the content of our theology and our methods of communicating that theology. I believe that this

Melanesian House Model of contextualisation is ideally suited for visual learners and oral based cultures, and is of value far beyond the borders of Melanesia.

It gives a solid biblical base to theology, and balances church tradition with the questions and perspectives of cultural context. The emphasis on dialogue ensures that there is participation by the people of the church, and the stress that it must relate to people's life experiences keeps it relevant. Finally it is centred on the central events of Jesus' life, death and resurrection. All of this is done in an atmosphere of prayer and dependence upon the Holy Spirit. Contextualising theology so that the good news of the gospel relates to the questions and fears of the people is an immense challenge, but it must be done.

Earlier, I referred to a teenage girl who had inherited a *sanguma* spirit from her mother. One of the Bible college students, who is from her village, decided to help her become free from this evil spirit.

With a fellow student, he went to the village and talked with the girl. She agreed that she wanted to be free from this evil spirit. They prayed for her, and in the name of Jesus commanded the spirit to leave. Following prayer, the girl said that the spirit had left her. The student returned to college thankful that the girl had been delivered from the sanguma. *When he returned to the village some weeks later however, he was disappointed to see that she had reverted back to her old way of living. It appears that although she was glad to get rid of the* sanguma *spirit, she was not ready to commit herself completely to God. Also, she may not have had the support and spiritual guidance that was needed. Just as rats are attracted to rubbish, so demons are attracted to sin in people's lives. Jesus says that if an evil spirit is cast out, but the heart remains empty, then the evil spirit will wander around and come back and reclaim the house, and may even bring*

other evil spirits with it (Matthew 12:43-45). Although
sanguma *and evil spirits are a big problem, they must not
become our primary focus. Instead, we should focus on
people being set free from sin, and for Jesus to become
Lord of their lives. Once Jesus has forgiven their sins we
can lead them on to complete deliverance from all evil
spirits, and help them grow in their Christian lives.*

Sanguma and other social problems will not disappear overnight,
but as churches unite in prayer and work together, they can see the
power of God defeat the powers of witchcraft and sorcery. They
can see these problems disappear from their villages and become
things of the past.

The church must speak to the felt needs of the people. Jesus is able
to set people free from sin and from the power of witchcraft. Through
the power of the Holy Spirit, they can live victorious Christian lives.
Christians must be confident that "nothing can separate [them] from
God's love - not life or death, not angels or spirits, not the present or
the future, and not powers above or powers below. Nothing in all
creation can separate [them] from God's love for us in Christ Jesus
our Lord!" (Romans 8:38-39).

Making the gospel relevant in Melanesian cultures is the challenge
that faces the church in Melanesia today. The House Model of
contextualisation is workable and practical. It can help Melanesian
church leaders respond more adequately, and with more confidence,
to this vitally important task. Jesus is the resurrection and the life,
and he wants to transform life and death in the village. When the
gospel is presented in such a way that it relates to the fears and
needs of the people, it has the potential of transforming both church
and culture.

ENDNOTES

1 The Church of the Nazarene is an evangelical holiness church that has been working in Papua New Guinea since 1955. The church operates a hospital and College of Nursing at Kudjip and a Bible College near Mt Hagen, Western Highlands Province. There are 400 local churches throughout PNG located mainly in the Highlands, with a smaller number in the coastal areas of PNG.

2 Pidgin is the Papua New Guinea form of Pidgin English and is the most widely used language in the Highlands and along the north coast of Papua New Guinea. With so many languages in Papua New Guinea, its primary value is to enable Papua New Guineans to communicate with each other. As people from different tribal groups intermarry, Pidgin is becoming for many people, especially young people in the towns, their primary language. Most missionaries, other than those working in Scripture translation, never learn any language other than Pidgin. Most of the words are derived from English but the grammar follows a Melanesian form. There is a weekly newspaper - *Wantok* - produced in Pidgin and a number of Provincial radio stations operate primarily in Pidgin. The entire Bible is available in Pidgin and is extremely popular.

3 The Summer Institute of Linguistics reports 826 languages for Papua New Guinea, of which 9 are extinct, 257 in Irian Jaya, 71 in the Solomon Islands, 109 in Vanuatu, 38 in New Caledonia and 10 in Fiji, giving a total of 1291 languages in Melanesia. This is approximately 20 percent of the world's languages (http://www.SIL.org/ethnologue/countries/Papua New Guinea/html).

4 All Bible references unless otherwise noted will be from the New International Version.

5 This historic journey is well described in the documentary and book *First Contact*, where both the European explorers and the Papua New Guinea highlanders are interviewed, and the two sides of the contact experience are explored (Connolly and Anderson 1987).

6 Histories are now being written that put the reports of the Australian patrol officers side by side with the recollections of the villagers (i.e. See Brown 1995).

331

7 *"Singsing"* is a Pidgin term for a clan festival. A *singsing* is more than a dance, for it also includes such themes as tribal strength, solidarity, body decoration, drumming, chanting and usually feasting. It is a time of celebration by the entire clan.

8 The Pidgin term *"wantok"* literally means "one talk". In a land of over 800 languages, a *wantok* is a fellow clan member who speaks the same language and to whom one is therefore obligated. Reciprocity exists between *wantoks*. With urbanisation the term has broadened, and now includes people from the same province, or even nearby provinces but different languages. The obligation to help a *wantok* takes precedence over all other obligations and so leads to all sorts of problems in a court system that is supposed to be impartial. A statement that is heard a lot these days is: "It is not what you know that counts, it is who you know that matters."

9 Mbiti describes a similar understanding of time in Africa. He says: "Time is simply a composition of events which have occurred, those which are taking place now and those which are inevitably or immediately to take place ... time is a two dimensional phenomenon, with a long past, a present and virtually no future. The linear concept of time in Western thought, with an indefinite past, present and infinite future is practically foreign to African thinking. The future is virtually absent because events which lie in it have not taken place." (Mbiti 1969:16-17)

10 In this respect, Melanesians are like the "Jews who demand miraculous signs" (1 Corinthians 1:22).

11 Lawrence and Meggitt generalise this observation to religion throughout Melanesia. "Everywhere religion is regarded as a means to or guarantee of material welfare", they write (Lawrence and Meggitt 1965:22).

12 In the cases of *sanguma* I have followed, there is definitely spirit involvement and some people have been greatly helped through exorcism. This is an area that Melanesian Christianity must address.

13 Cannibalism was not generally practiced by the people of the Highlands. According to this old man of Maina village, some groups that were located on the fringe between the Highlands and the coastal plains, such as the

332

Karimui area of Simbu Province did occasionally practice cannibalism. This may have been around 1950.

14 A radio.

15 A book written about the early missionary work done among the Dani of Irian Jaya and the role of aviation was entitled *An Hour to the Stone Age* (Horne 1973). The geographical distance was shortened, but the technological and cultural gulf was immense.

16 This letter is cited in Bede's *Ecclesiastical History of the English People*. Colgrave and Mynors 1969:108-109.

17 In Port Moresby, Harvest Ministries is a video and literature ministry of the Assemblies of God, and provides video tapes of various "televangelists" from around the world. These are watched in many corners of the country as a Honda generator and a VCR brings Benny Hinn, Morris Cerulo, Jimmy Swaggart and numerous other evangelists to the eyes and ears of Papua New Guineans. Consequently such experiences as the "Toronto Blessing" do not take long to cross from one side of the world to the other. Papua New Guinea is not exempt from the impact of globalisation.

18 "Historical Mainline Churches" are the Anglican, Roman Catholic, Lutheran and the United Church.

19 See reports by Strelan and Steinbauer.

20 Flannery ed. 1983a, 1983b, 1984.

21 The United Church was formed by the joining together in 1968 of the Methodist Synod and the churches formed by the London Missionary Society (Aerts 1991:81). On descriptions of activities in revival movements, Barr 1983a:9.

22 These two stages in conversion – repentance and a turn away from sin – are also described by Tippett in relation to the revival movements in Tonga and Fiji a hundred years before (1971).

23 A tendency to attribute all voices or impulses to being the "Word of the Lord" has likewise led to problems. But this is not a problem unique to

333

Melanesia. The gift of prophecy has at times operated along the lines of traditional diviners, and consequently degenerated into Christian fortune telling, and as a result has caused disharmony and division within the church rather than building up the church.

24 I have seen this personally in the growth of the Church of the Nazarene.

25 Revelation 22:24 speaks of the kings bringing their glory into the New Jerusalem, which speaks of the cultural treasures of the nations being brought into the service of the King of Kings.

26 It could be argued that culture could be seen as communal experience and so is included already in the Wesleyan quadrilateral. There is an advantage in separating it out as a distinctive category, for each culture has questions that are unique and which must be addressed.

27 Theologising needs to be ongoing: see also Thorsen (1990:236); Taber (1978a:76); Bevans (1992:13).

28 I found in teaching this model that it was best to follow the outline used in this chapter, and develop the model section by section, just as if one were constructing a house. If one presents only the final house model it can appear to be too complex, but when presented one component at a time, people more readily understand the process and essential elements for constructing a contextual theology.

29 The Melanesian Nazarene Bible College is located near Mt Hagen. The school offers a certificate program that is taught in Pidgin, and a Diploma and Bachelor of Theology that is taught in English. The college prepares students for ministry in the Church of the Nazarene in Papua New Guinea and the Solomon Islands.

30 This story is told by a Nazarene pastor who is from the Wahgi Valley which is culturally very similar to that of the Simbu Province.

31 This is a complex issue and will be dealt with in Chapter Nine.

32 Political parties in Papua New Guinea tend not to be formed around policies or ideology, but around the personality of political "big men" who have been able to attract a following.

33 The most outstanding Simbu politician was Sir Iambakey Okuk, who was the Deputy Prime Minister and also Leader of the Opposition at various times. His grave is enshrined in a large, specially built memorial on the main street of Kundiawa.

34 2000 census figures; National Statistics Office.

35 A Papua New Guinean might say that the spirit of the dead man whistled. Some Christians might say that it was not the spirit of the dead man, but a deceiving spirit that whistled to convince people that the spirit of the dead person was really there. The question of the source of the whistle is an analytical response, not a Melanesian one. A Western observer might say that the ritual specialist whistled, or that it existed in the minds of the people who longed to hear it.

36 The Catholic Church has tried to Christianise this event by placing a large cross at the centre of the ceremonial ground next to the phallic symbol (Schaefer 1981:213-223). How successful this has been is debatable. In some places, it appears that the cross has replaced the pole, but in other places, the crucifix may even be mounted on the phallic pole itself, thus bringing about a synthesis of the two belief systems (Hughes 1985:433).

37 Perhaps an explanation for birth defects or lack of proper growth and development.

38 Wesley Duewel, a veteran missionary, describes a similar belief in India: "The witch receives from the devil or another witch, an attendant demon, called a 'familiar' and usually having the shape of a toad, cat, dog, sheep, or rabbit. The witch is said in old books to use the 'familiar' to harm enemies or kill when necessary" (Duewel n.d.:29; also Paulsen 1970:158). According to *An Encyclopedia of Occultism*, the witch often becomes the slave of the "familiar" demon (qtd. in Duewel: 29; Spence 1960:440).

39 This type of behaviour will be discussed in more detail in the later chapter, "The Problem of *Sanguma*".

40 The Maring people are described by Roy Rappaport in *Pigs for the Ancestors* (1968).

41 See also Job 40:9; Psalms 77:18; 104.7; 144:6; Isaiah 29:6.

335

42 Jackson does not mention *Rumualye*. All of my information comes from pastors who had largely grown up in the church. No doubt some of what I heard is a modified story, as traditional beliefs are being reinterpreted in the light of Christian teaching. It is interesting to note that the Enga belief in *Aitawe* did not come to the attention of the Lutheran missionaries in Enga until they had been there for quite a number of years and the church was established. This is an area that would be interesting to study further.

43 The following list of references was put together from a computer search: gods (271), idols/idolatry (182), demons (82), evil spirits (28), Satan (48), Devil (34), Beelzebub (Prince of demons) (7), Baal (123), Asherah (39), Molech (20), Chemosh (8), Dagon (7). Various practitioners: spiritists (9), mediums (10), sorcery/sorcerers (14), diviners/divination (25), witchcraft (6), astrologers (9), magic/magicians (21), prophets of Baal/pagan priests (9).

44 Maria Dlugosz (1998) saw that myths were so important to the Enga people that she made Enga myths the focus of her PhD dissertation.

45 For examples of this type of myth, in relation to the Enga, see Weisnner and Tumu 1998:22-24. For examples related to the Simbu, see Brown 1995:18-19.

46 Some examples can be found in Burridge (1960:150-164). Mantovani (1984c:74); Whiteman (1984a:106).

47 Story told by Pastor Lukas, Church of the Nazarene, Dusin, Middle Ramu.

48 A *cuscus* is a large marsupial, like a possum, bigger than a racoon and which lives in trees. It is hunted for food and for its colourful pelt.

49 Story told by Pastor Vincent Puringi, Church of the Nazarene, Muli Village, near Ialibu, Southern Highlands Province.

50 This image of a fine thread attached from one person to another is an image that occurs quite often in myths and symbolises the importance of relationships in Melanesian cultures.

51 Other versions of this myth from the Enga Province are found in *Mae Enga Myths and Christ's Message*, by Maria Dlugosz (1998:152-160). Joe told this story at a pastors' conference and he described it as being *"gutnius bilong tumbuna"* (gospel according to our ancestors).

52 This miraculous birth, as a result of a woman swallowing a person who has turned into a mosquito, seems to be a mythological theme that is quite wide spread. It is found in myths from the Daribi in the Karimui District of the Simbu Province (Wagner 1972:109), and also in Enga (Dlugosz 1998:152-160). I also heard it in a myth that was from Tari in the Southern Highlands Province.

53 The dividing of the river with a stick does not appear to be an addition derived from Christianity. Although that is a possibility, the same symbolism occurs in a story with a similar theme from the Enga Province (Dlugosz 1998:153). Therefore I feel that it is safe to consider it as a part of the original story.

54 The significance of Jesus' descent to the place of the dead will be further discussed in the chapter "The Drama of Redemption".

55 "With Africa's rich storytelling tradition, the theology of story is a natural focus for African theologians" (Healey and Sybertz 1996:22).

56 I was unable to conduct a conference with pastors from Enga. However, the Southern Highlands Province shares a common boundary with Enga, and although there are differences in language, Enga has more in common with the Southern Highlands than with any other province.

57 These questions were discussed in groups. Each group then shared these ideas with the entire group and the results were written up on large sheets of paper. The result was a composite document that outlined the main points of the group. This process was followed with each of these four questions.

58 A *glasman* is, strictly speaking, a diviner, one who sees through a glass. Technically a *posin man* is a potion man or a healer. He or she may be male or female for it varies somewhat from culture to culture. They may or may not use special leaves. In reality, the same person generally performs both functions and the terms are often used interchangeably.

59 See full description on page 167.

60 An example is the late Sir Iambakey Okuk. Okuk was a very aggressive Simbu politician who aspired to become prime minister. He died suddenly of liver cancer, and was buried with great grief and mourning in the centre of Kundiawa, the capital of Simbu Province. Over his grave was built (at government expense) a large memorial shelter. It is rumoured that for a year after his burial, family members slept under the shelter beside the cement crypt.

61 This will be discussed in more detail in the chapter, "The Problem of Sanguma".

62 This matter will be addressed in the later chapter, "The Christian Response to the Spirits of the Dead and to Sanguma".

63 We will discuss this more in "The Christian Response to the Spirits of the Dead and to Sanguma".

64 See Papua New Guinea Yearbook 2005.

65 The Encyclopedia of Papua New Guinea has a combined article on "Sorcery and Witchcraft." The article makes a technical distinction between the two, saying that a sorcerer's capacity to harm depends on the "employment of harmful substances or objects", whereas a witch can inflict "sickness or death on others simply by staring at them or willing evil on them" (Glick 1973:182). However, it says that: "the two are closely linked and in some cultures, inseparable" (ibid). Mary Patterson says since there is widespread variation between cultures, that "whether we translate indigenous terms as sorcery or witchcraft is largely irrelevant." I have preferred to use the Pidgin term sanguma. I find most writers translate it as witchcraft (Brown 1977:26; Hughes 1988:66), but some classify sanguma as a form of "assault sorcery" (Glick 1973:182).

66 Westerners have assumed that beliefs in witches and sorcery will disappear when people are educated and/or are Christians. This is not the case.

67 Some people report that dogs may be sensitive to the presence of evil spirits (see Green 1981: 134).

68 The same type of activity is reported from Africa (Burnett 1988:137).

69 "Witches are widely believed to have great power, which they can use against others ... They enter a person and 'eat' inner organs causing illness and even death. Spirits often leave their bodies and take the form of a bird, bat, or other animal commonly associated with the night" (Hiebert, Tienou, and Shaw 1999:149).

70 "Witches prey on others, sucking the victims blood or eating their livers, hearts, or other vital organs, thereby causing a 'wasting away' disease" (Hiebert et. al. 1999:148).

71 This ability to operate without anaesthetic, remove organs, and then seal up the body without leaving any scars has been reported in other parts of the world. Sometimes this "psychic surgery" is used to heal people. It is described in detail by Michaelson in the book, *The Beautiful Side of Evil* (1982). The author assisted in 200 operations in Mexico in which the person performing the operation was an old woman whose body was taken over by a male spirit. She performed complex surgery with no anaesthetic, using only a kitchen knife and a pair of scissors. After surgery, the bodies were sealed up again with no stitches and they left no scar. These surgery sessions were observed by American surgeons who were impressed at the healing that occurred. The author later became convinced that the healing that occurred was not from God.

72 Michele Stephen defines a sorcerer as one who uses his power to heal or to punish those who do not conform. He is therefore held in high regard. She defines a witch as one who uses her power in evil ways and therefore is despised and ostracised by society (1989:216).

73 The PNG Government, in 1976, introduced a new law against acts of sorcery and provided penalties for these acts.

74 The main study is *Sorcerer and Witch in Melanesia* (Stephen 1987). Other articles have been written by Patterson (1974); Steadman (1975); Brown (1977); MacDonald (1982); Reay (1987); Riebe (1987); Stephen and Herdt (1989); Bercovitch (1989); Silas (1993); and Mantovani (1998). Jenny Hughes (1985) describes witchcraft beliefs and practices among the Simbu people.

75 Hill describes witchcraft as a power "that can be used for evil as well as good", but this is very similar to what Stephen calls "sorcery". The practitioner who is always evil and destructive is what Stephen calls a witch (1989:216). Other people reserve this definition for a sorcerer, and Patterson (1970:140) says that whether we translate indigenous terms as sorcerer or witchcraft is largely irrelevant.

76 Sanguma is very complex and counselling is important in dealing with the problem. The fear of sanguma often destroys the social cohesion of a village. Often innocent people are accused of sanguma and beaten, driven out of the village or even killed. Other people have sanguma spirits and need help but are afraid to admit it for fear of being killed or ostracised from the community.

77 I gave the class a question, asked them to discuss it in groups, work out their answers, and then share with the whole class.

78 This understanding of deceitful spirits masquerading as "false ancestors" is not unique to PNG. Allan Anderson did research in Africa among Pentecostal churches and Pentecostal-type African Independent Churches regarding their response to the ancestor cult. Anderson sums up by saying: "Ancestors do appear to Christians, but their response as believers is usually to reject the 'visitation.' The 'ancestors' they believe, are not ancestors at all, but demon spirits which need to be confronted and exorcised or idols which need to be spurned - for they only lead to further misery and bondage" (Anderson 1993:37). One person interviewed said: "Ancestors are evil spirits. Satan is able to change these spirits so that they resemble your parents who have died." Another said: "Ancestors are evil spirits that come in the form of our grandparents. This is the devil's trick so that we can worship them instead of worshipping God" (Anderson 1993:32).

The emphasis of the Pentecostal churches on the power and presence of the Holy Spirit is one of the things that gave the people boldness and confidence to reject the so called "ancestors". Anderson says: "They [spirits] have no power over Christians, because Christians have the greater power of the Holy Spirit within them, which overcomes all of Satan's power" (1993:37).

Merrill Unger has studied this phenomenon of communicating with the spirits of the dead. He says that the spirits involved are really "deceiving impersonating demons" (1952:158). Robert Peterson, a former missionary to Indonesia, has confronted spirits who claimed to be spirits of the dead and commanded them in the name of Jesus to reveal their true identity. They were forced to admit that they were not spirits of the dead at all but deceiving spirits (1976:122).

79 For example:
    For all the saints, who from their labours rest,
    Who thee by faith before the world confessed,
    Thy name of Jesus be forever blest. Alleluia
    O blest communion, fellowship divine!
    We feebly struggle, they in glory shine;
    Yet all are one in thee, for all are thine. Alleluia
    (How 1966:536. Emphasis added)

80 See the fuller account of this man's story in Chapter Nine.

BIBLIOGRAPHY

Bible verses marked (CEV) are taken from the Contemporary English Version, 1995, American Bible Society, New York.

Aerts, Theo. 1991. "Romans and Anglicans in Papua New Guinea." *Melanesian Journal of Theology* 7 (1) August 1991:1-123.

—. 1998. *Christianity in Melanesia*. Port Moresby, PNG: University of Papua New Guinea.

Ahrens, Theodor. 1977. "Concepts of Power in a Melanesian and Biblical Perspective." *Missiology* 5 (2):141-173.

Anderson, Allan. 1993. "African Pentecostalism and the Ancestor Cult: Confrontation or Compromise." *Missionalia* 21 (1):26-39.

Anderson, Neil. 1990a. *Victory over the Darkness*. Ventura: Regal.

—. 1990b. *Bondage Breaker*. Eugene: Harvest House.

—. 1995. *Helping Others to Find Freedom In Christ*. Ventura: Regal.

Ambrose, Vic. 1987. *Balus Bilong Mipela*. Melbourne: Missionary Aviation Fellowship.

Apea, Simon. 1985. "Footprints of God in Ialibu." In *Living Theology in Melanesia*. Point Series No.8. Goroka, PNG: Melanesian Institute. Pp. 216-253.

Arbuckle, Gerald A. 1985. "Inculturation and Evangelisation: Realism or Romanticism." In *Missionaries, Anthropologists and Cultural Change*. Darrell Whiteman, ed. Williamsburg, Virginia: Department of Anthropology, College of William and Mary. Pp. 171-214.

Arnold, Clinton. 1992. *Powers of Darkness*. Leicester: InterVarsity Press.

342

—. 1997. *Three Crucial Questions About Spiritual Warfare*. Grand Rapids: Baker.

Aulen, Gustaf. 1950. *Christus Victor*. London: SPCK.

—. 1960. *The Faith of the Christian Church*. Philadelphia: Muhlenberg Press.

Baal, Jan van. 1966. *Dema: Description and Analysis of Marind-Anim Culture*. The Hague, Holland: Martinus Nijhoff.

Barr, John. 1983a. "Spiritistic Tendencies in Melanesia." In *Religious Movements in Melanesia Today (2)*. Wendy Flannery, ed. Point Series No. 3. Goroka, PNG: Melanesian Institute. Pp. 1-34.

—. 1983b. "Spirit Movements in the Highlands United Church." In *Religious Movements in Melanesia Today (2)*. Wendy Flannery, ed. Point Series No. 3. Goroka, PNG: Melanesian Institute. Pp. 144-154.

Bartle, Neville. 1992. *Jesus Has Defeated Satan*. Wewak, PNG: CBM.

—. 1994. *Jisas Bai i Kambek*. Mt Hagen, PNG: Victory Books.

—. 1996. *Wok Bilong Holi Spirit*. Mt Hagen, PNG: Victory Books.

—. 1997. *Pasin Holi Bilong Bikpela*. Mt Hagen, PNG: Victory Books.

—. 1998. *Revival*. Mt Hagen, PNG: Victory Books.

—. 1998. *Diwai Kros Bilong Jisas*. Mt Hagen, PNG: Victory Books.

—. 1999. *Skulim Mipela Long Prea*. Mt Hagen, PNG: Victory Books.

—. 1999. *Wok Bilong Pasto*. Mt Hagen, PNG: Victory Books.

—. 2000. *Basic Themes of Melanesia World View*. Mt Hagen, PNG: Victory Books.

—. 2002. *Gutpela Lida tru*. Mt Hagen, PNG: Victory Books.

—. 2002. *Jisas i Winim Sanguma Na ol Kainkain Pawa*. Mt Hagen, PNG: Victory Books.

—. 2002. *Jisas I Winim Dai*. Mt Hagen, PNG: Victory Books.

Baxter, J. Sidlow. 1959. *Awake My Heart*. Edinburgh: Marshall, Morgan and Scott.

Bellwood, Peter. 1978. *Man's Conquest of the Pacific*. New York: Oxford University Press.

Bercovitch, Eytan. 1989. "Mortal Insights: Victim and Witch in the Nalumin Imagination." In *The Religious Imagination in Papua New Guinea*. Michele Stephen and Gilbert Herdt, eds. New Brunswick: Rutgers University Press. Pp. 122-159.

Bevans, Stephen B. 1992. *Models of Contextual Theology*. Maryknoll: Orbis Books.

Bloesch, D. G. 1984. "Descent into Hell (Hades)." In *Evangelical Dictionary of Theology*. Walter A. Elwell, ed. Grand Rapids: Baker. Pp. 313-315.

Blowers, Bruce. 1984. *My Personal Journey*. Mimeographed paper. Mt Hagen, PNG: Nazarene Mission.

Bowen, Earle and Dorothy Bowen. 1989. "Contextualising Teaching Methods in Africa." *Evangelical Missions Quarterly* 25 (3):270-277.

Boyd, Gregory A. 1997. *God at War: The Bible and Spiritual Conflict*. Downers Grove: InterVarsity Press.

Brennan, Paul. Ed. 1970. *Exploring Enga Culture*. Wapenamanda, PNG: New Guinea Lutheran Mission.

—.1977. *Let Sleeping Snakes Lie: Central Enga Religious Belief and Rituals*. Adelaide: Australian Association for the Study of Religions.

Brown, Paula. 1972. *The Chimbu: A Study of Change in the New Guinea Highlands*. Cambridge: Schenkman.

—. 1977. "*Kumo* Witchcraft at Mintima, Chimbu Province, Papua New Guinea." *Oceania* 48 (1):26-29.

—. 1978. *Highlands People of New Guinea*. Cambridge: Cambridge University Press.

—. 1995. *Beyond a Mountain Valley*. Honolulu: University of Hawaii Press.

Bruno, Thomas and Neville Bartle. 2000. *Set Free From the Spirits*. Mt Hagen, PNG: Victory Books.

Bubeck, Mark I. 1975. *The Adversary*. Chicago: Moody Press.

Bulatao, Jaime. 1966. *Split-Level Christianity*. Quezon City, Philippines: Ateneo de Manila University.

Bultmann, Rudolf. 1964. "New Testament and Mythology." In *Kerygma and Myth: A Theological Debate*, Vol. 1. London: SPCK.

Bulmer, R. 1965. "The Kyaka Enga of the Western Highlands." In *Gods, Ghosts and Men in Melanesia*. P. Lawrence and M.J. Meggitt, eds. Melbourne: Oxford University Press. Pp. 132-161.

Burnett, David. 1988. *Unearthly Powers: A Christian's Handbook on Primal and Folk Religions*. Nashville: Thomas Nelson.

Butler, Carolyn. 1993. "Applying God's Grace to an Animistic Society." *Evangelical Missions Quarterly* 29:382-389.

Burridge, Kenelm. 1960. *Mambu: A Study of Melanesian Cargo Movements and Their Social and Ideological Background*. New York: Harper and Row.

Campbell, I.C. 1989. *A History of the Pacific Islands*. Los Angeles: University of California Press.

Chao, Sr. M. John Paul. 1984. "Leadership." In *An Introduction to Melanesian Cultures*. D. Whiteman, ed. Point Series No. 5. Goroka, PNG: Melanesian Institute. Pp. 127-148.

345

Clowney, E.P. 1992. "The Biblical Doctrine of Justification by Faith." In *Right with God: Justification in the Bible and in the World*. D.A. Carson, ed. Carlisle: Paternoster Press. Pp. 19-37.

Codrington, Robert H. 1891. *The Melanesians: Studies in Their Anthropology and Folklore*. Oxford: Clarendon Press.

Colgrave, Bertram and R.A.B. Mynors. 1969. *Bede: Ecclesiastical History of the English People*. Oxford: Clarendon Press.

Connolly, Bob and Robin Anderson. 1987. *First Contact: New Guinea Highlanders Encounter the Outside World*. London: Viking Press.

Conway, Jeanette and Ennio Mantovani. 1990. *Marriage in Melanesia: A Sociological Perspective*. Point Series No.15. Goroka, PNG: Melanesian Institute.

Cramp, Geoff and Mapusiya Kolo. 1983. "Revival Among Western Highlands and Enga Baptists." In *Religious Movements in Melanesia Today (2)*. Wendy Flannery, ed. Point Series No.3. Goroka, PNG: Melanesian Institute. Pp. 93-106.

Crockett, Patricia J. 1979. "Conception and Birth: Belief and Rituals of the Makru-Mansuka." In *Powers, Plumes and Piglets*. Norman Habel, ed. Adelaide: Australian Association for the Study of Religions. Pp. 54-67.

Crocombe, Ron, and Marjorie Crocombe. 1982. *Polynesian Missions in Melanesia*. Suva: Institute of Pacific Studies, University of the South Pacific.

Curnock, Nehemiah. Ed. 1938. *The Journal of the Reverend John Wesley*. London: Epworth.

Cyril of Jerusalem. 1995. "Catechetical Lectures." In *Nicene and Post Nicene Fathers*. Second series, vol. 7. Philip Schaff and Henry Wace, eds. Peabody: Hendrickson. Pp. 6-157.

Dickason, C. Fred. 1987. *Demon Possession and the Christian*. Wheaton: Crossway Books.

Dlugosz, Maria. 1998. *Mae Enga Myths and Christ's Message: Fullness of Life in Mae Enga Mythology and Christ the Life (Jn 10:10)*. Nettetal, Germany: Steyer Verlag.

Dorum, Thomas. N.d. *Animism*. Photocopied term paper. Mt Hagen, PNG: Melanesian Nazarene Bible College.

Douglas, Mary. 1970. *Witchcraft Confessions and Accusations*. London: Tavistock.

Duewel, Wesley L. N.d. *Challenging Demonism and Occultism Through the Holy Spirit*. Greenwood: OMS International.

Dye, T. Wayne. 1984. "A Theology of Power for Melanesia." *Catalyst* 14 (1):57-75.

Dyrness, William A. 1983. *Let the Earth Rejoice!* Westchester: Crossway Books.

—. 1990. *Learning About Theology From the Third World*. Grand Rapids: Academie Books.

—. 1992. *Invitation to Cross-Cultural Theology*. Grand Rapids: Zondervan.

Ebhomielen, Paul. 1982. *Gustaf Aulen's Christus Victor View of the Atonement as it Relates to the Demonic in Africa*. PhD. dissertation. Waco, Texas: Baylor University.

Encyclopedia Britannica. 1990. *Encyclopedia Britannica*. Chicago: Encyclopedia Britannica.

Erikson, Millard. 1983. *Christian Theology*. Grand Rapids: Baker.

Evans-Pritchard, E. E. 1937. *Witchcraft, Oracles and Magic Among the Azande*. London: Oxford University Press.

Ferdinando, Keith. 1996. "Screwtape Revisited: Demonology Western, African and Biblical." In *The Unseen World*. Anthony N. S. Lane, ed. Carlisle: Paternoster. Pp. 103-132.

347

—. 1999. *The Triumph of Christ in African Perspectives*. Carlisle: Paternoster.

Flannery, Wendy. Ed. 1983a. *Religious Movements in Melanesia Today (1)*. Point Series No.2. Goroka, PNG: Melanesian Institute.

—. Ed. 1983b. *Religious Movements in Melanesia Today (2)*. Point Series No.3. Goroka, PNG: Melanesian Institute.

—. 1984a. "Mediation of the Sacred." In *Religious Movements in Melanesia Today (3)*. Wendy Flannery, ed. Point Series No.4. Goroka, PNG: Melanesian Institute. Pp. 117-157.

—. Ed. 1984b. *Religious Movements in Melanesia Today (3)*. Point Series No.4. Goroka, PNG: Melanesian Institute.

Forman, Charles W. 1982. *The Island Churches of the South Pacific*. Maryknoll: Orbis Books.

Fox, C. E. 1971. *Melanesian Prayer Book*. Honiara, Solomon Islands: Provincial Press.

Freud, S. 1938. *Basic Writings*. New York: Modern Library.

Freund, R., R. Hett, and K. Reko. 1970. "The Enga Concept of God." In *Exploring Enga Culture*. Paul W. Brennan, ed. Wapenamanda, PNG: New Guinea Lutheran Mission. Pp. 141-166.

Fugmann, Gernot. 1984. "Salvation in Melanesian Religions." In *An Introduction to Melanesian Religions*. Ennio Mantovani, ed. Point Series No.6. Goroka, PNG: Melanesian Institute. Pp. 279-295.

Garrett, John. 1982. *To Live Among the Stars*. Suva: Institute of Pacific Studies.

Gaquare, Joe. 1977. "Indigenisation as Incarnation – the Concept of a Melanesian Christ." In *Christ in Melanesia*. James Knight, ed. Goroka, PNG: Melanesian Institute. Pp. 146-153.

Geertz, Clifford. 1973. *The Interpretation of Culture*. New York: Basic Books.

348

Gilliland, Dean S. 1989. "Contextual Theology as Incarnational Mission." In *The Word Among Us – Contextualising Theology for Mission Today*. Dean S. Gilliland, ed. Dallas: Word. Pp. 9-31.

Glasse, R. M. 1965. "The Huli of the Southern Highlands." In *Gods, Ghosts, and Men in Melanesia*. P. Lawrence and M. J. Meggitt, eds. Melbourne: Oxford University Press. Pp. 27-49.

Glick, Leonard. 1973. "Witchcraft and Sorcery." *Encyclopedia of Papua New Guinea*.

Goldsmith, Martin. 1983. "Contextualisation of Theology." *Themelios* 9 (1):20-21.

Golson, J. 1982. "The Ipomean Revolution Revisited: Society and the Sweet Potato in the Upper Wahgi Valley." In *Inequality in New Guinea Highlands Societies*. A. Strathern, ed. Cambridge: Cambridge University Press. Pp. 109-136.

Gordon, Robert P. 1986. *I and II Samuel: A Commentary*. Grand Rapids: Zondervan.

Gouvea, F. Q. 1984. "The Communion of Saints." In *Evangelical Dictionary of Theology*. Walter A. Elwell, ed. Grand Rapids: Baker. Pp. 257-258.

Green, Michael. 1981. *I Believe in Satan's Downfall*. London: Hodder and Stoughton.

Grenz, Stanley J. and Roger E. Olsen. 1996. *Who Needs Theology? An Invitation to the Study of God*. Downers Grove: InterVarsity Press.

Grudem, Wayne. 1994. *Systematic Theology*. Grand Rapids: Zondervan.

Habel, Norman C. 1979. *Powers, Plumes and Piglets*. Adelaide: Australian Association for the Study of Religions.

Hayward, Douglas J. 1983. *The Dani: Before and After Conversion*. MA thesis. Pasadena: Fuller Theological Seminary.

—. 1997. *Vernacular Christianity Among the Mulia Dani*. Lanham: University Press of America.

Harding, Barbara. 1968. "Towards a Poetics of Fiction: An Approach Through Narrative." *Novel* 2:5-14.

Healey, Joseph and Donald Sybertz. 1996. *Towards an African Narrative Theology*. Maryknoll: Orbis Books.

Henry, Rodney. 1986. *Filipino Spirit World*. Manila: OMF Literature.

Hendriksen, William. 1982. *More Than Conquerors*. Grand Rapids: Baker.

Hesselgrave, David J. and Edward Rommen. 1989. *Contextualisation: Meaning, Methods and Models*. Grand Rapids: Baker Book House.

Hesselgrave, David. 1997. "Christian Contextualisation and Biblical Theology." Paper delivered at the Evangelical Missiological Society, Midwest meeting. March 14-15 1997.

Hiebert, Paul G. 1987. "Critical Contextualisation." *International Bulletin of Missionary Research* 11 (3):104-111.

Hiebert, Paul G, R. Daniel Shaw and Tite Tienou. 1999. *Understanding Folk Religions*. Grand Rapids: Baker.

Hill, Harriett. 1996. "Witchcraft and the Gospel: Insights from Africa." *Missiology* 24 (3):323-344.

Hitchens, John. 1992. "Culture and the Bible: The Question of Contextualisation." *Melanesian Journal of Theology* 8 (2): 30-52.

Hodge, Charles. 1871. *Systematic Theology*. New York: Scribner Armstrong and Co.

International Bible Society. 1984. *Holy Bible, New International Version*. Zondervan Publishing House.

Horne, Shirley. 1973. *An Hour to the Stone Age*. Chicago: Moody Press.

Hoekema, Anthony. 1979. *The Bible and the Future*. Grand Rapids: Eerdmans.

Hovey, Kevin. 1986. *Before all Else Fails ... Read the Instructions*. Brisbane: Harvest Publications.

How, William W. 1966. "For All the Saints." In *The Book of Hymns*. Nashville: United Methodist Publishing House. P. 536.

Huber, Mary Taylor. 1988. *The Bishops' Progress: A Historical Ethnography of Catholic Missionary*. Washington: Smithsonian Institution.

Hughes, Jenny. 1985. *Chimbu Worlds: Experiences of Continuity and Change by a Papua New Guinea Highland People*. PhD dissertation. Melbourne: La Trobe University.

Hunter, George III. 2000. *The Celtic Way of Evangelism*. Nashville: Abingdon.

Imasogie, Osadolor. 1983. *Guidelines for Christian Theology in Africa*. Achimota, Ghana: Africa Christian Press.

Imbach, S. R. 1986. "Syncretism." In *Evangelical Dictionary of Theology*. Walter A. Elwell, ed. Grand Rapids: Baker. Pp. 1062-1063.

Ingebritson, Joel. Ed. 1990. *Human Sexuality in Melanesian Cultures*. Point Series No. 14. Goroka, PNG: Melanesian Institute.

Ireneaus. 1995. "Irenaeus against Heresies." In *Ante-Nicene Fathers*. Vol. I. Alexander Roberts and James Donaldson, eds. Peabody: Hendrickson. Pp. 315-567.

Irvine, Doreen. 1973. *From Witchcraft to Christ*. London: Concordia.

Jackson, Graham. 1975. *The Kopon: Life and Death on the Fringes of the New Guinea Highlands*. PhD dissertation. Auckland: Auckland University.

Jackson, Thomas. Ed. 1980. *The Works of John Wesley*. Third Edition. Grand Rapids: Baker.

Jensen, Adolf E. 1963. *Myth and Cult Among Primitive Peoples*. Chicago: University of Chicago Press.

Jentsch, T. and R. Doetsch. 1986. *Keman, eine Seidlung im Hochland von Papua Neuguinea*. Berlin: Deitrich Reimer Verlag.

John of Damascus. 1995. "Exposition on the Orthodox Faith." In *Nicene and Post-Nicene Fathers*. Second Series, Volume 9. Philip Schaff and Henry Wace, eds. Peabody: Hendrickson. Pp. 1-102.

Johnstone, Patrick. 1986. *Operation World*. Bromley, Kent: STL Productions.

Kallas, James. 1966. *The Satanward View: A Study in Pauline Theology*. Philadelphia: Westminster.

Kambao, Lawrence. 1989. "The Discovery of Weapo Yahweh in Enga Laiapu." *Catalyst* 19 (4):385-397.

Kearney, Michael. 1984. *World View*. Novato: Chandler and Sharp.

Kelly, J. N. D. 1986. *The Oxford Dictionary of Popes*. Oxford: Oxford University Press.

Keysser, Christian. 1980. *A People Reborn*. Pasadena: William Carey Library.

Kiki, Albert M. 1968. *Ten Thousand Years in a Lifetime: A New Guinea Autobiography*. Melbourne: Cheshire.

Knight, James. Ed. 1977. *Christ in Melanesia*. Goroka, PNG: Melanesian Institute.

Knight, J. 1979. "Interpreting the Pig-Kill Festival." In *Powers, Plumes and Piglets*. Norman Habel, ed. Adelaide: Australian Association for the Study of Religion. Pp. 173-193.

——. 1982. "Melanesia." In *Mission in Dialogue*. M. Motte and J. Lang, eds. Maryknoll: Orbis Books. Pp. 392-412.

Kolandi, Mark. 1979. "The Traditional Treatment of Illness in the Kiripia Area." In *Powers, Plumes and Piglets*. Norman Habel, ed. Adelaide: Australian Association for the Study of Religions. Pp. 91-96.

Kraft, Charles. 1981. *Christianity in Culture*. Maryknoll: Orbis Books.

—. 1989. *Christianity With Power: Your Worldview and Your Experience of the Supernatural*. Ann Arbor: Servant, Vine Books.

—. 1990. "Deliverance from Demons." Unpublished manuscript. Pasadena: Fuller Theological Seminary.

Kui, Peter. 1999. "My Experience With the Spirits." Unpublished paper. Mt Hagen, PNG: Melanesian Nazarene Bible College.

Lane, Anthony N. S. 1996. *The Unseen World: Christian Reflections on Angels, Demons, and the Heavenly Realm*. Carlisle: Paternoster.

Lausanne Committee for World Evangelism. 1978. *The Willowbank Report: Report of a Consultation on Gospel and Culture*. Wheaton: Lausanne Occasional Papers.

Lawrence, P. 1967. "Politics and 'True Knowledge' ... When God is Managing Director?" *New Guinea* 2.1: 34-49.

Lawrence, P. and M. J. Meggitt, eds. 1965. *Gods, Ghosts and Men in Melanesia*. Melbourne: Oxford University Press.

Lewis, Gordon R. 1975. "Criteria For the Discerning of Spirits." In *Demon Possession*. John W. Montgomery, ed. Minneapolis: Bethany Fellowship. Pp. 346-363.

Lewis, I. M. 1971. *Ecstatic Religion*. Harmondsworth: Penguin.

Lodahl, Michael. 1994. *The Story of God: Wesleyan Theology and Biblical Narrative*. Kansas City: Beacon Hill Press.

Love, William D. 1883. *Christ Preaching to the Spirits in Prison*. Boston: Congregational Sunday School and Publishing Society.

Luzbetak, Louis J. 1954. "The Socio-Religious Significance of a New Guinea Pig Festival." *Anthropological Quarterly* 27:59-80; 102-128.

—. 1956. "Worship of the Dead in the Middle Wahgi." *Anthropos* 51: 81-96.

MacCulloch, J. A. 1930. *The Harrowing of Hell*. Edinburgh: T&T Clark.

MacDonald, Mary. 1982. "Sorcery and Society." *Catalyst* 12:168-181.

—. 1984a. "Symbolism and Myth." In *An Introduction to Melanesian Religions*. Ennio Mantovani, ed. Point Series No.6. Goroka, PNG: Melanesian Institute. Pp. 123-146.

—. 1984b. "Magic, Medicine and Sorcery." In *An Introduction to Melanesian Religions*. Ennio Mantovani, ed. Point Series No.6. Goroka, PNG: Melanesian Institute. Pp. 195-212.

Maeliau, Michael. 1987. "Searching for a Melanesian Way of Worship." In *The Gospel is Not Western*. G. W. Trompf, ed. Maryknoll: Orbis Books. Pp. 119-127.

Mair, Miller. 1988. "Psychology as Storytelling." *International Journal of Personal Construct Psychology* 1(2):125-138.

Malinowski, Bronislaw. 1948. *Magic, Science and Religion and Other Essays*. Glencoe: Free Press.

—. 1961. *The Dynamics of Culture Change*. New Haven: Yale University Press.

Mantovani, Ennio. 1984a. "Traditional Religions and Christianity." In *An Introduction to Melanesian Religions*. Ennio Mantovani, ed. Point Series No.6. Goroka, PNG: Melanesian Institute. Pp. 1-22.

—. 1984b. "What is Religion?" In *An Introduction to Melanesian Religions*. Ennio Mantovani, ed. Point Series No.6. Goroka, PNG: Melanesian Institute. Pp. 23-47.

—. 1984c. "Comparative Analysis of Cultures and Religions" In *An Introduction to Melanesian Religions*. Ennio Mantovani, ed. Point Series No.6. Goroka, PNG: Melanesian Institute. Pp. 49-86.

—. 1984d. "Celebrations of Cosmic Renewal." In *An Introduction to Melanesian Religions*. Ennio Mantovani, ed. Point Series No.6. Goroka, PNG: Melanesian Institute. Pp. 147-168.

—. 1984e. "Ritual in Melanesia." In *An Introduction to Melanesian Religions*. Ennio Mantovani, ed. Point Series No.6. Goroka, PNG: Melanesian Institute. Pp. 169-194.

—. Ed. 1984. *An Introduction to Melanesian Religions*. Point Series No.6. Goroka, PNG: Melanesian Institute.

—. 1997. "Is Magic Excluded from Dialogue? Missiological Reflections on Magic." *Catalyst* 27:134-146.

—. 1998. "Challenges of the Bible to Christian Life in PNG Today." *Catalyst* 28:102-116.

—. 1987. *Marriage in Melanesia: A Theological Perspective*. Point Series No.11. Goroka, PNG: Melanesian Institute.

—. 1992. *Marriage in Melanesia: An Anthropological Perspective*. Point Series No.17. Goroka, PNG: Melanesian Institute.

Mbiti, John S. 1969. *African Religions and Philosophy*. Oxford: Heineman.

—. 1976. "Theological Impotence and the Universality of the Church." In *Mission Trends No 3: Third World Theologies*. Gerald Anderson, ed. Grand Rapids: Eerdmans Publishing. Pp. 6-18.

McAll, Kenneth. 1982. *Healing the Family Tree*. London: Sheldon Press.

McGavran, Donald A. 1980. "Foreword." In *A People Reborn*. Christian Kessler. Pasadena: William Carey Library. Pp. viii-xxiii.

McGregor, Don. 1976. "Basic Papua New Guinea Assumptions." *Catalyst* 6:175-213.

355

—. 1982. *The Fish and the Cross*. Goroka, PNG: Melanesian Institute.

McIlwain, Trevor with Nancy Everson. 1991. *Firm Foundations*. Sanford: New Tribes Mission.

Meggitt, Mervyn J. 1965. "The Mae Enga of the Western Highlands." In *Women, Gods, Ghosts and Men in Melanesia*. P. Lawrence and M. J. Meggitt, eds. Melbourne: Oxford University Press. Pp. 105-131.

—. 1977. *Blood is Their Argument*. Palo Alto: Mayfield Publishing.

Michaelson, Joanna. 1982. *The Beautiful Side of Evil*. Eugene: Harvest House.

Miller, Elmer S. 1973. "The Christian Missionary: Agent of Secularisation." *Missiology* 1 (1): 99-107.

Mitton, Michael and Russ Parker. 1991. *Requiem Healing: A Christian Understanding of the Dead*. London: Darton, Longman and Todd.

Montgomery, John Warwick ed. 1976. *Demon Possession*. Minneapolis: Bethany Fellowship.

Morris, Leon. 1971. *The Gospel According to John*. The New International Commentary on the New Testament. Grand Rapids: Eerdmans.

Muck, Terry C. 2001. "Why Study Religion? What is Religion?" *Introduction to World Religions MW 708*. Wilmore: Asbury Theological Seminary.

Narokobi, Bernard. 1977. "What is Religious Experience for a Melanesian?" In *Christ in Melanesia*. James Knight, ed. Goroka, PNG: Melanesian Institute. Pp. 7-20.

—. 1983. *The Melanesian Way*. Port Moresby, PNG.

—. 1985. "A Truly Noble Death." In *Living Theology in Melanesia: A Reader*. John D'Arcy May, ed. Point Series No.8. Goroka, PNG: Melanesian Institute. Pp. 54-66.

National Statistical Office. 2002. *Papua New Guinea 2000 Census: Final Figures*. Port Moresby: National Statistical Office.

Nicholls, Bruce. 1975. "Theological Education and Evangelisation." In *Let the Earth Hear His Voice*. J. D. Douglas, ed. Minneapolis: World Wide Press. Pp. 634-645.

—. 1979. *Contextualisation: A Theology of Gospel and Culture*. Downers Grove: InterVarsity Press.

—. 1995. "Contextualisation and Syncretism Debate." In *Biblical Theology in Asia*. Ken Gnakanan, ed. Bangalore: Theological Book Trust. Pp. 19-38.

Nilles, John. 1969. *The Kuman-English Dictionary*. Chimbu, PNG: Catholic Mission.

—. 1977. "Simbu Ancestors and Christian Worship." *Catalyst* 7:163-198.

Numanu, Simeon. 1983. "Spirits in Melanesia and the Spirit in Christianity." In *Religious Movements in Melanesia Today (2)*. Wendy Flannery, ed. Point Series No.3. Goroka, PNG: Melanesian Institute. Pp. 92-116.

Oden, Thomas C. 1992. *The Word of Life. Systematic Theology: Volume II*. New York: Harper Collins.

O'Hanlon, Michael. 1995. *Reading the Skin: Adornment, Display and Society Among the Wahgi*. London: Trustees of the British Museum

Osadolor, Imasogie. 1983. *Guidelines for Christian Theology In Africa*. Achimota, Ghana: Africa Christian Press.

Outler, Albert C. 1985. "The Wesleyan Quadrilateral – In John Wesley." *Wesleyan Theological Journal* 20: 17-18.

Packer, James I. 1967. *Guidelines: Evangelical Anglicans Face the Future*. London: Church Pastoral Aid Society.

Page, Sydney H.T. 1995. *Powers of Evil: A Biblical Study of Satan and Demons*. Grand Rapids: Baker

Papua New Guinea Yearbook 2005. 2004. Brian Gomez, ed. Port Moresby: the National and Cassowary Books.

Patterson, Mary. 1974. "Sorcery and Witchcraft in Melanesia." *Oceania* 45:132-160, 212-234.

Paulsen, Kathryn. 1970. *The Complete Book of Magic and Witchcraft*. New York: New American Library.

Pech, Rufus. 1979. *Myth, Dream and Drama*. Master's thesis. Ohio: Columbus Lutheran Seminary.

Penelhum, Terence. 1997. "Christianity." In *Life After Death in World Religions*. Harold Coward, ed. Maryknoll: Orbis Books. Pp. 31-47.

Peterson, Robert L. 1976. *Trail of the Serpent*. New Canaan: Keats Publishing.

Philpott, Kent. 1973. *A Manual of Demonology and the Occult*. Grand Rapids: Zondervan.

Pokawin, Polonhou. 1987. "Interaction between Indigenous and Christian Traditions." In *The Gospel is Not Western*. G.W. Trompf, ed. Maryknoll: Orbis Books. Pp. 23-31.

Ramsey, Evelyn M. 1975. *Middle Wahgi Dictionary*. Mt Hagen, PNG: Church of the Nazarene.

Rappaport, Roy. 1968. *Pigs for the Ancestors*. New Haven: Yale University Press.

Reay, Marie. 1959. *The Kuma*. Melbourne: Melbourne University Press.

—. 1987. "Foundations of Highlands Warfare." In *Sorcerer and Witch in Melanesia*. Michele Stephen, ed. New Brunswick: Rutgers University Press. Pp. 83-120.

Read, Terry. 2000. "Bring the Plant, Not the Soil." *Holiness Today* 2 (8):36-37.

Richardson, Don. 1976. *Peace Child*. Glendale: Regal.

—. 1981. *Eternity In Their Hearts*. Glendale: Regal.

Riebe, Inge. 1987. "Kalam Witchcraft: A Historical Perspective." In *Sorcerer and Witch in Melanesia*. Michele Stephen, ed. New Brunswick: Rutgers University Press. Pp. 211-245.

Robbins, Russell Hope. 1959. *Encyclopedia of Witchcraft and Demonology*. New York: Crown.

Rowsome, Marilyn. 1982. *Mid-Wahgi Religious Beliefs and Implications for Ministry*. Unpublished paper. Banz, PNG: Christian Leaders Training College.

—. 1993. "Spiritual Powers in Paul's Writings." *Melanesian Journal of Theology* 9 (2):36-62.

Rusoto, Moses. 1980. "Traditional Western Mae Enga Religion." *Oral History* 8 (1):7-9.

Schaefer, Alfons. 1981. "Christianised Ritual Pig Killing." *Catalyst* 11(4): 213-223.

Schendal, Daryl A. 1978. *The Edge of Nowhere*. Kansas City: Nazarene Publishing House.

Schreiter, Robert J. 1985. *Constructing Local Theologies*. Maryknoll: Orbis Books.

—. 1997. *The New Catholicity: Theology Between the Global and the Local*. Maryknoll: Orbis Books

Schwarz, Brian. 1984. "Cargo Movements and Holy Spirit Movements." In *An Introduction to Melanesian Religions*. Ennio Mantovani, ed. Point Series No.6. Goroka, PNG: Melanesian Institute. Pp. 231-278.

—. 1985. "Contextualisation and the Church in Melanesia." In *An Introduction to Ministry in Melanesia*. Brian Schwarz, ed. Point Series No.7. Goroka, PNG: Melanesian Institute. Pp. 104-120.

Sherry, Frank. 1994. *Pacific Passions: The European Struggle for Power in the Great Ocean in the Age of Exploration.* New York: William Morrow.

Silas, Br. 1993. "Myth and Countermyth in the Siane." *Melanesian Journal of Theology* 9 (2): 63-72.

Sinclair, James. 1981. *Kiap.* Sydney: Pacific Publications.

Smalley, William. 1967. "Cultural Implications of an Indigenous Church." In *Readings in Missionary Anthropology.* William A. Smalley, ed. Tarrytown: Practical Anthropology. Pp. 147-156.

Snow, Philip and Stephanie Waine. 1979. *The People From the Horizon: An Illustrated History of the Europeans Among the South Sea Islanders.* London: McLaren.

Snyder, Howard. 1989. *Signs of the Spirit.* Grand Rapids: Academie Books.

—. 1995. *EarthCurrents: The Struggle for the World's Soul.* Nashville, Abingdon.

Spence, Lewis. 1960. *An Encyclopedia of Occultism.* New Hyde Park: University Books.

Steadman, Lyle. 1975. "Cannibal Witches in the Hewa." *Oceania* 46(2):114-121.

Steffen, Tom A. 1996. *Reconnecting God's Story to Ministry.* La Habra: Centre for Organisational and Ministry Development.

—. 1998. "Foundational Roles of Symbol and Narrative in the (re)Construction of Reality and Relationships." *Missiology* 26:477-494.

Steinbauer, Freidrich. 1971. *Melanesian Cargo Cults.* London: George Prior Publishers.

Stephen, Michele. 1987a. "Master of Souls: The Mekeo Sorcerer." In *Sorcerer and Witch in Melanesia.* Michele Stephen, ed. New Brunswick: Rutgers University Press. Pp. 41-80.

—. 1987b. "Contrasting Images of Power." In *Sorcerer and Witch in Melanesia*. Michele Stephen, ed. New Brunswick: Rutgers University Press. Pp. 249-304.

—. Ed. 1987. *Sorcerer and Witch in Melanesia*. New Brunswick: Rutgers University Press.

—. 1989. "Constructing Sacred Worlds and Autonomous Imagining in New Guinea." In *The Religious Imagination in New Guinea*. Michele Stephen and Gilbert Herdt, eds. New Brunswick: Rutgers University Press. Pp. 211-236.

Stephen, Michele and Gilbert Herdt. Eds. 1989. *The Religious Imagination in New Guinea*. New Brunswick: Rutgers University Press.

Stott, John. 1975. *The Lausanne Covenant: An Exposition and Commentary*. Minneapolis: World Wide Publications.

—. 1986. *The Cross of Christ*. Downers Grove: InterVarsity Press.

Strelan, John G. 1977. *Search For Salvation*. Adelaide: Lutheran Publishing House.

Sundkler, Bengt. 1960. *The Christian Ministry in Africa*. London: SCM Press.

Swadling, Pam. 1981. *Papua New Guinea's Prehistory: An Introduction*. Port Moresby: National Museum and Art Gallery.

Swain, Tony and Garry Trompf. 1995. *The Religions of Oceania*. London: Routledge.

Syvret, Ellen. 1999. *It All Began With a Vision*. Mt Hagen, PNG: Victory Books.

Taber, Charles. 1978a. "The Limits of Indigenisation in Theology." *Missiology* 6 (1): 53-79.

—. 1978b. "Is There More Than One Way to Do Theology?" *Gospel in Context* 1:4-10.

Telford, John ed.. 1931. *The Letters of Rev. John Wesley*. 8 vols. London: Epworth.

Tertullian. 1995. "Apology 47." In *Ante-Nicene Fathers*. Vol. 3. Alexander Robertson and James Donaldson, eds. Peabody: Hendrickson. Pp. 17-60.

Thielieke, Helmut. 1974. *The Evangelical Faith*. Vols. 1-3. Grand Rapids: Eerdmans.

Thorsen, Donald A. D. 1990. *The Wesleyan Quadrilateral*. Grand Rapids: Zondervan.

Tippett, Alan R. 1967. *Solomon Islands Christianity: A Study of Growth and Obstruction*. New York: Friendship Press.

—. 1971. *People Movements in Southern Polynesia*. Chicago: Moody Press.

—. 1973. *Verdict Theology in Missionary Theory*. South Pasadena: William Carey Library.

—. 1976. "Spirit Possession as it Relates to Culture and Religion." In *Demon Possession*. John Warwick Montgomery, ed. Minneapolis: Bethany Fellowship. Pp. 143-174.

—. 1977. *The Deep Sea Canoe*. Pasadena: William Carey Library.

Trompf, G. W. 1979. "Man Facing Death and After-life in Melanesia." In *Powers, Plumes and Piglets*. Norman Habel, ed. Adelaide: Australian Association for the Study of Religions. Pp. 121-136.

—. Ed. 1987. *The Gospel is Not Western*. Maryknoll: Orbis Books.

—. 1991. *Melanesian Religions*. Cambridge: Cambridge University Press.

—. 1994. *Payback*. Cambridge: Cambridge University Press.

Tudor, Judy. 1974. *Papua New Guinea Handbook*. Seventh edition. Sydney: Pacific Publications.

Tuwere, Sevati. 1987. "Thinking Theology Aloud in Fiji." In *The Gospel is Not Western*. G.W. Trompf, ed. Maryknoll: Orbis Books. Pp. 148-154.

Unger, Merrill. 1952. *Biblical Demonology*. Wheaton: Scripture Press.

Vincent, David. 1993. "Documentation on the Churches in PNG." *Catalyst* 23 (1): 39-56.

Von Alleman, Daniel. 1975. "The Birth of Theology." *International Review of Mission* 64 (253): 37-55.

Vos, Geehardus. 1930. *The Pauline Eschatology*. Princeton: Princeton University Press.

Wagner, M. 1970. "The Enga Concept of Fear." In *Exploring Enga Culture*. Paul W. Brennan, ed. Wapenamanda, PNG: New Guinea Lutheran Mission. Pp. 245-318.

Wagner, Roy. 1972. *Habu: The Innovation of Meaning in Daribi Religion*. Chicago: University of Chicago Press.

Wagner, H. and H. Reiner. 1986. *The Lutheran Church in Papua New Guinea: The First Hundred Years. 1896-1996*. Adelaide, Australia: Lutheran Church.

Wallace, Anthony F. C. 1956. "Revitalisation Movements." *American Anthropologist* 58:264-281.

Walls, Andrew. 1982. "The Gospel as the Prisoner and Liberator of Culture." *Missionalia* 10 (3): 93-105.

Warner, Timothy M. 1991. *Spiritual Warfare: Victory Over the Powers of This Dark World*. Wheaton: Crossway Books.

Weissman, Polly and Akii Tumu. 1998. *Historical Vines: Enga Networks of Exchange, Ritual and Warfare in Papua New Guinea*. Washington: Smithsonian Institution.

Wesley, Charles. 1966. "Happy the Souls to Jesus Joined." In *The Book of Hymns*. Nashville: United Methodist Publishing House. P. 536.

Wesley, John. 1978. "Preface to Sermons on Several Occasions." In *Works of John Wesley*. Third edition. Grand Rapids: Baker.

White, John. 1988. *When the Spirit Comes With Power*. London: Hodder and Stoughton.

White, R.E.O. 1986. "Resurrection of the Dead." In *Evangelical Dictionary of Theology*. Walter A. Elwell, ed. Grand Rapids: Baker. Pp. 941-944.

Whiteman, Darrell. 1983. *Melanesians and Missionaries*. Pasadena: William Carey Library.

—. 1984a. "Melanesian Religions: An Overview." In *An Introduction to Melanesian Religions*. Ennio Mantovani, ed. Point Series No. 6. Goroka, PNG: Melanesian Institute. Pp. 87-122.

—. 1984b. "The Cultural Dynamics of Religious Movements." In *Religious Movements in Melanesia Today (3)*. Wendy Flannery, ed. Point Series No. 4. Goroka, PNG: Melanesian Institute. Pp. 52-79.

—. 1997. "Contextualisation: The Theory, the Gap, the Challenge." *International Bulletin of Missionary Research* 21 (1):2-7.

Wiley, H.O. 1940. *Christian Theology*. Kansas City: Beacon Hill Press.

Wink, Walter. 1984. *Naming the Powers*. Philadelphia: Fortress Press.

Winter, Ralph. 1994. "Editorial Comment." *Missions Frontier Bulletin* 16 (1-2): 4-6, 51.

Zahniser, A.H. Mathias. 1997. *Symbol and Ceremony*. Monrovia: MARC.

Zocca, Franco. 1995. "'Winds of Change' Also in PNG?" *Catalyst* 25 (2):174-187.

—. 2004. "Religious Affiliation in Papua New Guinea According to the 2000 Census." *Catalyst* 34 (1):40-56.